THE WHOSEDAY BOOK A MILLENNIUM JOURNAL

THE WHOSEDAY BOOK 2000AD

THE WHOSEDAY BOOK
(a millennium journal)

First published in the
Republic of Ireland in 1999 by
The Irish Hospice Foundation,
9 Fitzwilliam Place,
Dublin 2, Ireland.

Designed by DesignWorks
Typeset by Keystrokes
Printed by Modus Media International
ISBN 0 9534880 0 4

MM

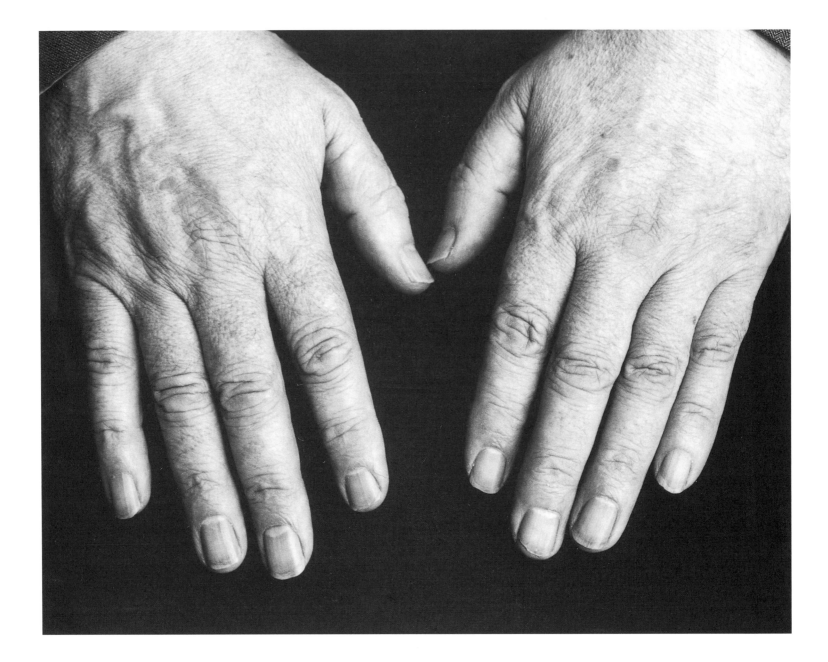

Introduction

HOSPICE. The dictionary defines it as a house of rest, a home, and traces its origin to the Latin *hospitium* meaning hospitality or lodging, which in turn relates it to *hospes*, the word for a host. And by one of those happy double–takes which are part of every language, *hospes* was also the Latin word for a guest.

As usual, the language was coming out ahead. Long before the great religious orders of the Middle Ages opened their own hospices for the traveller and the sufferer, the double meaning of the Latin word was telling people that those in need of sanctuary and those with sanctuary to offer should be bound together in a single mutual venture. As a concept, as a working institution, the hospice acknowledges this deep human need for care and depends upon the human capacity to provide it. It is as if T.S. Eliot's line, 'The whole earth is our hospital,' had come marvellously to life.

The Irish Hospice Foundation thrives upon the commitment of everyone involved with it. Their efforts show that 'the survival of the fittest' is not the only factor at work in the evolution of our species. Something nobler is in evidence here, something evolving from an equal and opposite and far more radiant vision of mutual protection. The writers and artists contributing to *The Whoseday Book* want to see that vision realised and generously supported. They want to remind us of that threshold of possibility where what is sympathetic in our nature recognises and embraces what is dependent, and to remind us further that this is a threshold where the two halves of the word *farewell* can separate and see themselves again for what they really are, not a parting salute but an encouragement to meet what comes with spirit and force: to fare well.

Seamus Heaney
Patron

MCMXCIX MM MMI

Foreword

As we approach the new millennium many initiatives will be launched to record the year 2000. What more appropriate method of marking the first year of the next millennium than a journal in which people will record their memories for posterity.

Not only is this journal a very apt millennium diary but it is a most innovative and unique fund–raising project on behalf of the Irish Hospice Foundation. The Foundation undertakes excellent work as a support organisation for the development and improvement of hospice service in Ireland.

When the Foundation's Chairman, Marie Donnelly, first approached AIB Group to outline its ambitious plans we were delighted to become fund–raising partners in such a worthwhile cause. The bank's support will be used specifically to resource education and training programmes for professionals working in the area of grief and loss. It will also be used to guide vital research into palliative medicine. We would like to take this opportunity to wish the Foundation every success with its comprehensive fund–raising project.

The very fact that Nobel Laureate Seamus Heaney is the Patron of the book speaks for itself and makes it a very special publication. Each date in the book presents a reflective moment through words or images. The contributors come from varied backgrounds and their work represents a fantastic anthology of Irish cultural life.

Enjoy the masterpiece that is *The Whoseday Book*.

Lochlann Quinn
AIB *Group*

The Irish Hospice Foundation

SLOWLY, as we thought about this project, what we decided we wanted to do was create a beautiful object for the millennium. We asked writers and artists to send us words and images which meant something to them, that seemed to them to distil the essence of their work, words and images which they would like to be there long after they've gone. *The Whoseday Book* is a showcase for what Irish writers and artists can do at the end of the twentieth century.

One of the extraordinary things which has happened in the compilation of this book is that many of the contributors have written us a letter as well about the work of the hospice; the letters are full of appreciation and encouragement, the writers and artists know about our work, how important it is, and how much it has meant to people. I believe that the hospice movement is having a real effect on the quality of people's lives in Ireland now, and working on this book has been heartening and helpful for us.

Hospice, or palliative care, is a special kind of care, which provides symptom relief and support for people in the final phase of terminal illness. Hospice treats the person rather than the disease and emphasises quality rather than length of life. Hospice considers the entire family.

This unique volume is published as part of the Irish Hospice Foundation's fund–raising campaign to help extend hospice facilities for adults and children requiring ongoing palliative care. The cover price will go directly to the cause of hospice care. Hospice care is expensive: access and availability should be determined by need and need alone, and should be available all over Ireland and in every hospital. We welcome the involvement of AIB Group as our Millennium fund–raising partner in this aim.

Very special thanks to Seamus Heaney, who immediately and enthusiastically took on the role of Patron, and to all our friends and contributors, without whom there would be no *Whoseday* Book.

Marie Donnelly
Chairman, The Irish Hospice Foundation

Hiroshi Sugimoto: *Irish Sea, Isle of Man II 1990* Courtesy: Sonnabend Gallery, New York

2000AD

DAVID EVANS, aka The Edge, was born abroad (in Barking, Essex) in 1961 to Welsh parents. He came to Dublin aged one and a half and decided to stay. He started playing guitar, and became part of a group called Feedback, which became The Hype, which became U2 all in the space of a few hectic teenage years. Then things got really interesting, U2 going on to become a household name, travelling the world, doing concerts, writing songs, releasing albums, etc., etc. He has four daughters, Hollie, Arran, Blue and Sìan, and lives with his lover, Morleigh Steinberg, in Dublin.

The Edge

- Learn french.
- Pay your TV licence.
- Talk to the neighbours.
- Read some Shakespeare.
- Cut your toenails.
- Stop being so nice.
- Stop buying shoes you never wear.
- Go to Vietnam.
- Teach the orangemen how to Jig.
- ~~Forgive Barry Egan.~~
- Say goodbye to the past.
- Get down on your knees.
- Think again.

JOHN BANVILLE was born in Wexford in 1945. In 1970 he published his first collection of stories, *Long Lankin*. Since then he has published ten novels and his work has been translated into many languages. Banville has been concerned in his work with the tensions between order and chaos, history and artifice, the creative impulse and ideas of evil. His novel *The Book of Evidence* was shortlisted for the Booker Prize in 1989.

John Banville

I have never really got used to being on this earth. Sometimes I think our presence here is due to a cosmic blunder, that we were meant for another planet altogether, with other arrangements, and other laws, and other, grimmer skies. I try to imagine it, our true place, off on the far side of the galaxy, whirling and whirling. And the ones who were meant for here, are they out there, baffled and homesick, like us? No, they would have become extinct by now. How could they survive, these gentle earthlings, in a world that was made to contain us?

John Banville

from The Book of Evidence

DOROTHY CROSS. Artist. Born in Cork in
1956. Works in Dublin.

Dorothy Cross

A Snake, on a Raft, in the Sea Connemara, 1997

GABRIEL BYRNE was born in Dublin in 1950. As an actor he has starred in many films, including *Defence of the Realm*, *Miller's Crossing*, *The Assassin*, *A Dangerous Woman*, *Into the West*, *The Usual Suspects*, *The Man in the Iron Mask* and *Smilla's Feeling for Snow*.

He was executive producer of *In the Name of the Father*, nominated for seven Oscars, and the award-winning *Into the West*. He published a collection of autobiographical essays, *Pictures in My Head*, in 1994.

Gabriel Byrne

I have reined in my horse at the Apollo in Walkinstown and galloped up Bunting Road dar–darring at any doggone gun–slingin' critter who crossed my path. Have watched with envy the linking lovers pass under the street lights on their way to the forbidden evening shows. The cocksure hair–oiled boys in their gougers' shoes and Elvis suits and their mots click–clicking in slingbacks always just a step behind, leaving that sinful smell of perfumes in the air for a glorious second. Sat behind them in the balcony, watched and listened in the dark to the sounds of their kissing and tapped them on the shoulders to ask them for a light. Until I got myself a mot of my own, a frail, dark–haired, convent girl, who loved Fabian, Sal Mineo, Ricky Nelson and me in that order. And I hung up my gunbelt forever, and my whinnying horse was heard no more in the streets of Walkinstown.

From 'Reel Memories', Pictures in My Head

KEVIN VOLANS, born in South Africa, has lived in Ireland since 1986 and is now an Irish citizen. During the 1970s he was a pupil and later teaching assistant of Karlheinz Stockhausen in Cologne. In 1980 he embarked on a series of pieces aimed at reconciling African and Western aesthetics which quickly established him as a distinctive voice in new music. His work is regularly performed, broadcast and choreographed worldwide by such organisations as the Vienna State Opera and the BBC Proms. Fourteen discs featuring his music have been released, including recordings which topped the world music and classical charts in the United States.

Kevin Volans

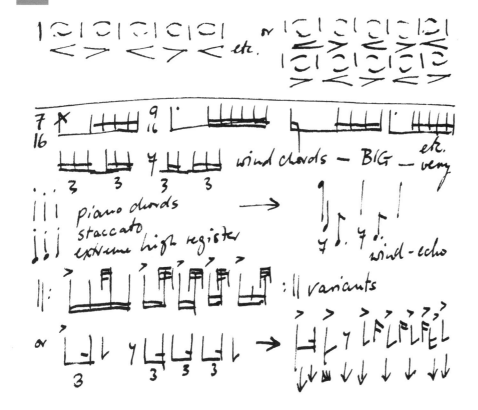

NOEL PEARSON, born in Dublin in 1942, has been a theatre and film producer for twenty years. Among his film credits are the Academy Award winner *My Left Foot, The Field, Frankie Starlight* and *Dancing at Lughnasa*. His Broadway productions include *Translations, Someone Who'll Watch Over Me, Wonderful Tennessee, Dancing at Lughnasa* and *An Inspector Calls*; the last two won Tony Awards in 1991 and 1993 respectively. Noel Pearson is a former chairman and artistic director of the Abbey Theatre, Dublin.

Noel Pearson

On the first day of principal photography on a feature film, when the actors, director, assistant directors, photographers, electricians, set and costume designers, carpenters, props, extras and trainees are gathered, the air of expectation is palpable. It is like the first day of school; some people you know and some you don't and by the end of a shoot there are some people you don't want to know. All this effort, energy and imagination, in a collective attempt to turn money into light. When it works it is a minor miracle. That's why we keep trying.

CONOR HORGAN was born in London in 1962. He has spent time as a waiter, illustrator, pizza chef, puppeteer, actor and geo–electrical surveyor. He has been a photographer since 1984, with work commissioned by *Vogue*, *GQ* and *Image*. For the last five years he has also worked as a TV commercials and pop video director. He has won many awards, including the Fashion 'Oscar' for Photographer of the Year in 1989 and 1991, the IRMA for best pop video in 1996 and several ICAD awards.

Conor Horgan

The picture is of a tin with a self–portrait by Joe Horgan, my late grandfather, scratched into the lid.

ELAINE CROWLEY was born in Dublin and left school at fourteen to become an apprentice tailor. She worked at several occupations before turning to writing, articles first, then novels. She now lives in Wales. Her books include *Dreams of Other Days*, *A Man Made to Measure*, *Waves upon the Shore*, *The Petunia-Coloured Coat*, *The Ways of Women* and *A Family Cursed*. She has also published two books of memoirs, *Cowslips and Chainies* and *Technical Virgins*.

Elaine Crowley

St Stephen's Day in the Hospice 1941

My father was dying. All the patients were. They wore sage–green bedjackets. Unbecoming to those jaundiced by cancer. Tuberculosis flushed my father's cheeks; sage–green suited him.

Paper chains decorated the ward. Visitors kissed and hugged their terminally ill relatives and friends. Laughed and gossiped with them. The atmosphere was holy and festive.

A nun brought in a gramophone. The record was 'We Parted on the Shore'. She coaxed visitors to dance. I was fifteen and couldn't put a foot under me. My aunt and father insisted I should try. In her arms I got the rhythm and waltzed. Patients smiled, some clapped and lilted the melody.

When the dancing finished my father squeezed my hand. 'You'll make a great dancer. You can teach me when I come home,' he said.

He died on 8 January 1942.

MICHAEL COLEMAN was born in Dublin in 1951. Through the 1970s and 1980s he exhibited regularly with the Oliver Dowling Gallery in Dublin. During this time his work was monochrome colour field painting. In recent years there has been a move towards the three-dimensional. Slashed, punctured and layered folds of painted canvas are tacked on to adjoining stretchers to form diptychs, triptychs and multi–panelled works. He has exhibited in London, New York, Vienna and Munich. During the 1980s Coleman lived in Vienna. He now lives in Dublin and is a member of Temple Bar Gallery & Studios.

Michael Coleman

Phone Messages

Tom MacIntyre was born in Cavan in 1931 and educated at University College, Dublin before teaching English at Clongowes Wood College, followed by posts in the United States. A book of short stories, *Dance the Dance*, and a novel, *The Charollais*, were both published in 1969 and his first play, *Eye-Winker, Tom Tinker*, was produced three years later at Dublin's Peacock Theatre. His best-known work is a series of plays, including *The Great Hunger* (1983), *The Bearded Lady* (1984), *Rise Up Lovely Sweeney* (1985) and *Dance for Your Daddy* (1987), all of them characterised by surreal imagery and a fragmented approach to language.

Tom MacIntyre

Ag Dréapadóireacht

Uisce an dhath
na cré ag rith tharam,
báisteach fhliursteach
tamall beag ó shin,
báisteach atá ar m'aithne,
an chruinne ché, is romhat
clo sruthán ar dhath na cré.

Tom MacIntyre

11.01.2000

January/Eanáir

TUESDAY / MÁIRT

EDNA O'BRIEN was born on a farm in Tuamgraney, County Clare in 1932 and was educated at the Convent of Mercy in Loughrea, County Galway and at the Pharmaceutical College in Dublin. She practised pharmacy briefly before becoming a writer. She moved to London and published her first novel, *The Country Girls*, in 1960. A dramatic personality, she wanted her work to 'in some way celebrate life and do justice to my emotions'. Her books include *Girls in Their Married Bliss*, *August is a Wicked Month*, *A Pagan Place* and *Time and Tide*.

Edna O'Brien

History is everywhere. It seeps into the soil, the subsoil. Like rain, or hail, or snow, or blood. A house remembers. An outhouse remembers. A people ruminate. The tale differs with the teller.

It's like no place else in the world. Wild. Wildness. Things find me. I study them. Chards caked with clay. Dark things. Bright things. Stones. Stones with a density and with a transparency. I hear messages. In the wind and in the passing of the wind. Music, not always rousing, not always sad, sonorous at times. Then it dies down. A silence. I say to it, Have you gone, have you gone. I hear stories. It could be myself telling them to myself or it could be these murmurs that come of the earth. The earth so old and haunted, so hungry and replete. It talks. Things past and things yet to be. Battles, more battles, bloodshed, soft mornings, the saunter of beasts and their young. What I want is for all the battles to have been fought and done with. That's what I pray for when I pray. At times the grass is like a person breathing, a gentle breath, it hushes things. In the evening the light is a blue black, a holy light, like a mantle over the fields. Blue would seem to be the nature of the place though the grass is green, different greens, wet green, satin green, yellowish green, and so forth. There was a witch in these parts that had a dark–blue bottle which she kept cures in. She was up early, the way I am up. She gathered dew. Those that were against her had accidents or sudden deaths. Their horses slipped or their ponies shied on the hill that ran down from her house. She had five husbands. Outlived them all. I feel her around. Maybe it is that the dead do not die but rather inhabit the place. Young men who gave their lives, waiting to rise up. A girl loves a sweetheart and a sweetheart loves her back, but he loves the land more, he is hostage to it...

From *House of Splendid Isolation*

JENNIFER JOHNSTON, the writer, was born in Dublin in 1930 to the playwright Denis Johnston and actress and theatre director Shelah Richards. Being the child of famous parents is sometimes a blessing and sometimes a curse since you carry the burden of their fame with you as well as the burden of their expectations. Filled with anxiety about death and immortality, she began to write in her mid–thirties and eleven novels and several plays later she is still at it; ever hopeful, which is really the only way to be.

Jennifer Johnston

When I was a child I had friends who lived on the corner of Rochestown Avenue and the Cabinteely Road in a pale house that had stood there for about two hundred years, surrounded by fields with cows and creaking trees and a garden that was charming and a paradise of disorder. Under a grassy mound not far from the house was an ice–house as old, it seemed, as time. It was black and cold and frightening and still, in those wartime days, in use. The house has been gone a long time now, and roads of houses and neat gardens have taken the place of the cows and the creaking trees. I wonder sometimes what has become of the ice–house. Do any of the new residents know of its existence?

MARTYN TURNER was born in Essex, England in 1948. He has been contributing political cartoons to *The Irish Times* since 1971 and has published twelve collections. In 1995 he won Commentator of the Year at the Irish Media Awards. In 1998 he was given an honorary doctorate by the University of Ulster. He would probably retire about now if he could afford it.

Martyn Turner

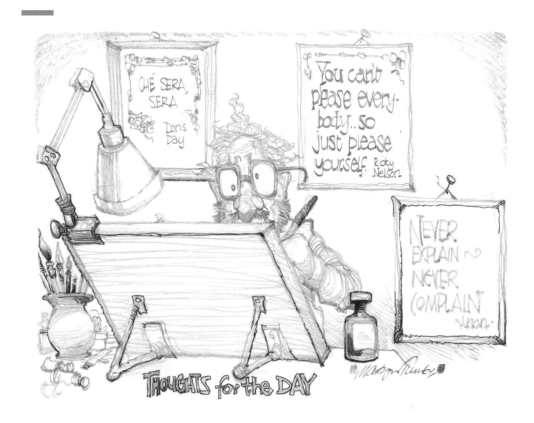

PETER HARBISON, born suitably in Dublin's Hatch Street, worked for almost thirty years with Bord Fáilte, as linguist, archaeologist and editor of *Ireland of the Welcomes*. Now honorary academic editor of the Royal Irish Academy, he has nearly 5,000 published pages to his credit and over a dozen books, covering the Stone Age to the Georgian period. Recently, the National Library sponsored his second volume on the eighteenth-century artist Beranger. He lectures on both sides of the Atlantic and in it – on cruises.

Peter Harbison

My youth was spent pondering prehistoric archaeology, and my middle age spread on the medieval period. Now, the older I get, the more I savour the delights of the eighteenth century — Haydn, Mozart et al., and the topographical drawings of Beranger and the artists associated with the Hibernian Antiquarian Society. There be treasures yet to be published, money and health permitting!

Peter Harbison

FELIM EGAN was born in Strabane, County Tyrone in 1952. He studied at the Slade School of Fine Art, London. In 1979 he received the Rome Scholarship and in 1986 was elected to Aosdána. He received the premier UNESCO prize for the arts in Paris in 1993 and the 1997 gold award at Cagnes–sur–Mer. He has had numerous one–person exhibitions in Ireland, Britain, Germany and the USA and has represented Ireland on many occasions, including the Biennale de Paris in 1980 and the Bienal de São Paulo, Brazil in 1985.

Felim Egan

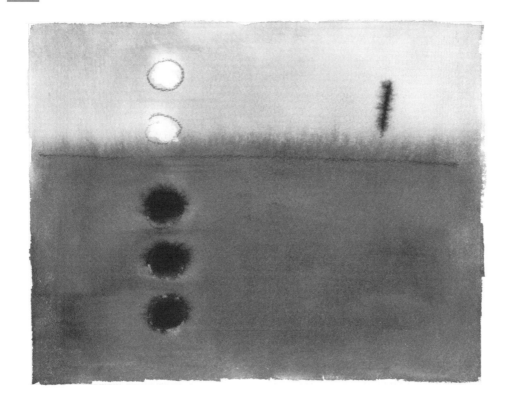

Sandymount Strand 1998

SHANE CONNAUGHTON was born in County Cavan and brought up in a police station along the Fermanagh border. He trained as an actor at the Bristol Old Vic before becoming a writer. He co-wrote the Academy Award–winning film *My Left Foot* with Jim Sheridan. His film *The Playboys* was made in his native County Cavan and his novel *The Run of the Country* was also filmed. He wrote *A Border Station*, a novel, and *A Border Diary*, an autobiographical book. He now lives in London.

Shane Connaughton

STONEFACE

They lie to hand
Grey eggs nestling on grass
Sexless, dead still.
Spang –
Into the bucket
Then into the ditch
The snooker ball clacks of them.

Next morning
New ones are to hand.
Humped, heaved to the surface
Or sucked by the moon.
The sea. Periods. Stones.

They sit tight on the grass
As if placed. To drive you mad.
The big ones need pick–axing.
Flint–eyed, foul–tempered brutes

They hate being disturbed.
Look at those dark wombs
Full of phosphorescent wrigglers
Creatures more stone than flesh.

He also bequeathed briars...

A second before he died
He stared at Padre Pio on the wall.
Old stonefaces. Chiselled bones.
Briar eyes.
Those too he left me.

I stay well clear of mirrors.

MICKY DONNELLY was born in Belfast in 1952. He studied at the University of Ulster from 1976 to 1981 and received his BA and MA in fine art. He was a founder member of *Circa* art magazine and also of the Artists' Collective of Northern Ireland and has written extensively on art. Winner of awards and prizes throughout Ireland, he has had numerous exhibitions here and abroad, and his works have been included in many international shows.

Micky Donnelly

MARY O'DONNELL was born in Monaghan. A former drama critic, she has a special interest in arts criticism and combines writing with the teaching of creative writing. Her publications include the acclaimed novel *The Light-Makers* (1992), *Virgin and the Boy*, a story of the Irish rock scene, and *Strong Pagans* (1991), a collection of stories. Her poetry collections include *Reading the Sunflowers in September* (1990), *Spiderwoman's Third Avenue Rhapsody* (1994) and *Unlegendary Heroes* (1999).

Mary O'Donnell

MY FATHER WAVING

In the New Year, we drove away.
I glanced back at the house on the hill.
It was shrinking, shrinking,
encased in ice, fragments of Christmas
in winking fairy-lights.
My father waved with both arms,
like Don Quixote's windmill.

On the brink of motherhood,
I saw lives swept almost to oblivion,
scuttled on reefs of the present;
then a processional, those quiet generations
moved through evening ice the colour of Asia,
described the entrances and exits –
parents of parents
like Russian dolls re-entering my body,
telling what was never told anyone,
announcing it now to my unborn girl.

The unstill past entered, forgotten
ghostlings and wanderers fussed
and made ready for the future –
one step ahead, bridging dawns,
afternoons between birthdays and Christmas.
The vision displaced the crammed wells
of fear, fed my courage.
In the New Year, we drove away.
The child turned beneath my ribs,
the parents of parents waved.

From *Unlegendary Heroes*

TOM HAYDEN has been active in American politics since the movements of the 1960s. He was behind successful legislation to include the Great Hunger in the California school curriculum and is the editor of *Irish Hunger*, a book of essays by Irish and Irish-American writers.

Tom Hayden

Belfast Girl Let us pray and work for a new century as hopeful as her eyes.

MICHAEL D. HIGGINS was born in Limerick in 1941 and educated at University College, Galway, Indiana University and Manchester University. An author, poet and politician, he served as the first Minister for Arts, Culture and the Gaeltacht (1993–7). His first book of poems, *The Betrayal*, was published in 1990, followed by *The Season of Fire* in 1993. He has contributed widely to political and philosophical journals and has made two television documentaries. He was the first recipient of the Seán MacBride Peace Prize in 1992. His home is in Galway.

Michael D. Higgins

LONE DINER ON KOH SAMET
(THAILAND, KOH SAMET, '98)

He sits alone at tables
An exception
A Fantasy loner
Eating fried rice
Among the accompanied
The beautiful
Validated.

In the slow evenings
of the New year
Even the older man
Alone
Holds on
In the humid warmth
To the overflow
Of back–pack intimacies.

As to the future
Flotsam
Late night children
Indulged
In the hearing of parents and the Sea
Make their own stories.

The Stories
The Children
The full moon on Koh Samet
Give an artificial strength
Of understanding.
Watching the tide go out
Waiting for its return
Firing finite thoughts
At infinity
And the high tide
In Koh Samet.

He weeps for things lost
And moments left empty
Of love.
The years slip away

In the swell
Their return
More than one tide away.
Gives only an assurance
Of question without answer
Endless.
And all around the sounds of
laughter
needing no answers.

For the moment
Under
The Full Moon on Koh Samet.

DEREK HILL, the artist, was born in Southampton, England in 1916 and educated at Marlborough. After travelling and working all over Europe, he bought a house, St Columb's, in County Donegal in 1954 and lived there until 1981, when he generously gave the house and its contents to the Irish nation. A gifted landscape and portrait artist, he helped found the Tory Island school of naive painters on the small island off the Donegal coast. In January 1999 he was awarded honorary citizenship of Ireland.

Derek Hill

Dawn on Tory

JOHN MACKENNA was born in Castledermot, County Kildare in 1952. He was educated at St Clement's College, Limerick and University College, Dublin. He worked as a teacher before becoming a producer with RTÉ radio. His books include: *The Occasional Optimist* (poems), *The Lost Village* (social history), the short-story collections *The Fallen* and *A Year of Our Lives*, and the novels *Clare*, *The Last Fine Summer* and *A Haunted Heart*. He is a winner of the Hennessy, C. Day-Lewis and *Irish Times* fiction awards.

John MacKenna

HAIKU SEQUENCE

i

The tractor roars and
slows, turning in a spray of
swirling paper gulls.

ii

In this room it is
silent. Outside, an orange
sliced in smoke, the moon.

iii

The 'phone continues
silent, whispering: 'the past
is an old story'.

iv

Jug of yellow flags,
sheet soaked in sweat and seed. Rich,
languid memories.

v

Wind on the corner,
teenage coats flap about each
other. Love, oh love.

In memory of Roberta Corr

MICK CULLEN was born in County Wicklow in 1946 and studied at the National College of Art & Design, Dublin and the Central School of Art in London. Since 1976 he has had numerous one-person exhibitions in Ireland and abroad and his works have been included in some of the most prestigious thematic group exhibitions representing contemporary Irish art at home and internationally. From 1969 he has been living and working for long periods of time in England, Spain, Morocco, the United States, Germany and France. He has won many awards and in 1985, owing to his contribution to cultural life in Ireland, he was elected a member of Aosdána. His works are in the collections of the Irish Museum of Modern Art, the Ulster Museum, the Hugh Lane Municipal Gallery of Modern Art, the Arts Council of Ireland, the Arts Council of Northern Ireland, the Irish Contemporary Art Society, Bank of Ireland, Allied Irish Banks, Trinity College, Dublin, Derry City Council, and in numerous private collections.

Mick Cullen

Emerald Tiger in Black and White with Fish

EILÉAN NÍ CHUILLEANÁIN was born in Cork in 1942. She has published several collections of poetry, including *Acts and Monuments* (1972), *The Second Voyage* (1977), *The Magdalene Sermon* (1989) and *The Brazen Serpent* (1994). A senior lecturer in English at Trinity College, Dublin, in 1975 she founded, along with Pearse Hutchinson, Macdara Woods and Leland Bardwell, *Cyphers* literary magazine. The recipient of the *Irish Times* Literary Award in 1966, she was also winner of the Patrick Kavanagh Award in 1973.

Eiléan Ní Chuilleanáin

somtimes a window maketh some remember

Somtimes a chimney telleth them of many late drinkinges and

sitting up by the fire.

At the time of rebellion in Northfolke, there was a Priest...

seeing the place...

Now Lorde God what a thing is this. It comes to my

remembraunce now, that about fowerteene yeares past, I was

merrie here upon this bancke, with an other Priest, and wallowing

me downe upon the grasse, I said these words: *Haec requies mea* _{This rest my}

for ever and ever here I will dwell because I chose it
in – *saeculum saeculi, hic habitabo quoniam elegi eam.*

SHAY CLEARY was born in Cork in 1951 and educated at University College, Dublin. He began practising as an architect in Dublin in 1977. Completed projects include the Irish Museum of Modern Art RHK, Arthouse in Temple Bar, and the redevelopment of Beggars Bush Barracks. Current projects include the new Project Arts Centre, Temple Bar and the Donegal Town Civic Offices. His practice has received numerous awards. In 1991 it was part of Group 91, which won the competition for the redevelopment of the Temple Bar area of Dublin.

Shay Cleary

DERMOT HEALY was born in County Westmeath in 1947. He has published two novels, *Fighting with Shadows* and *A Goat's Song*, and the poetry collections *The Ballyconnell Colours*, and *What the Hammer.*

He is the recipient of two Hennessy Awards for his short stories, of which a collection, *Banished Misfortune*, was published in 1982. He has directed and acted in a number of plays and wrote the screenplay for the

Cathal Black film *Our Boys*. He is the editor of a community arts magazine, *Force 10*, and a member of Aosdána. His memoir, *The Bend for Home*, was published in 1996.

Dermot Healy

JOE DONLON

I stand in the doorway
like Joe Donlon before me,

hunched–up huge
in the candlelight on the stones,

looking at the broad black theatre
of the inland night:

only two blooms in my garden –
the moon–white pool of flood water

in the bog, and the quiet race
from the bog to the beach.

The dog lands a stick at my feet.
Throw it! Throw it! he says.

I throw it as far as I can
and he disappears

towards the sound
of its fall in the grass.

A long time he's searching out there
in the dark.

Then he lands it again at my feet
without a sound, without a bark.

We seem then to flounder,
the dog and the house and myself,

towards what I cannot name,
We move a little across the street,

down darkness,
by sheds, through grief,

in this strange place
where the vastness closes in,

as it must have, on certain nights,
round Joe Donlon.

LELIA DOOLAN was born in Cork, the fifth of six children of Patrick Doolan and Lelia (Lil) Molony, both of County Clare. She has worked in theatre, television, film and journalism – for the Abbey Theatre, RTÉ, Bord Scannán na hÉireann/The Irish Film Board, *The Irish Press* and other national newspapers and journals. She has lived and worked in Dublin, Belfast and Mayo. Some years ago she settled in south Galway, where she now freelances as a writer, teacher, student, homeopath and gardener.

Lelia Doolan

On Sunday 27 January 1918, father – then a junior officer in the British Civil Service – wrote in his diary at 19, North Road, Bishopston, Bristol:

Glorious day and night. Heard Mrs Pankhurst speak this afternoon at David Thomas Hall. Was struck by her charming personality. Still good looking – with a quiet, patient, steady kind of expression – and with feeling and tenderness. Her voice is soft and musical and she speaks well – simply and clearly. We must have victory before peace, she said – Count Hertling's speech left no alternative. That is the first necessity.

Regarding the new women's votes, and the Women's Party, her policy is a constructive one. No party entanglements – no I.L.P. programmes. And not the destructive methods of the Russian state builders. The present average income of £102 per head could be doubled and working hours reduced to 6. More leisure would follow. Then great schemes of "domestic" reform – better opportunities for every child – health, housing and education.

I have faith in the Women's Party under her leadership.

28.01.2000

January/Eanáir

TONY O'MALLEY, born in Callan, County Kilkenny in 1913, began painting in 1945 when he was confined to hospital during an illness. He continued to paint in his spare time while working as a bank official but devoted his full attention to painting after leaving his job in 1958. He settled in Cornwall in 1960 but returned to County Kilkenny thirty years later. In 1973 he married Canadian-born artist Jane Harris. A member of Aosdána, he was elected to the position of Saoi in 1993. His work can be found in public and private collections throughout Ireland and the rest of Europe and the United States.

Tony O'Malley

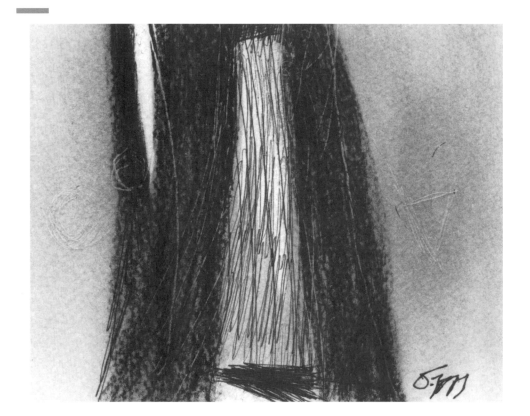

OLIVIA O'LEARY, born in Borris, County Carlow, is a freelance writer and broadcaster who has presented current affairs programmes in Ireland and Britain – BBC's *Newsnight*, Yorkshire Television's *First Tuesday*, Thames Television's *This Week*, and RTÉ's *Today Tonight*, *Questions and Answers* and *Prime Time*. She has written about politics for both *The Sunday Tribune* and *The Irish Times*. Her recent television work included a documentary on John Hume and she has co-written the authorised biography of former Irish president Mary Robinson. She is married with one daughter.

Olivia O'Leary

Shoes

Bread of ages caked my mother's
                                    shoes
The daisy snowfall built a baker's
                                    crust,
A permafrost of floury mornings.
"I'll do the first batch, Pat"
                              she'd say
And in my sleep I'd hear the creak
On the stairs, the back door latch,
Her step across the yard.
Hours later, when she woke us,
                            she smelt
Of Creation, fresh sliced and warm
From the oven. My eyes opened to
A new drift of snow on her laces.
"Good morning" sang my mother
                                    who
Had just made the world.
"This is a lovely day."

Olivia O'Leary,
January '97.

First published *Spirituality*, Spring 1997

CONOR FALLON was born in Dublin in 1939, the third of the six sons of the poet Padraic Fallon. Brought up in Wexford, he is self–taught, starting to paint while a student at Trinity College, Dublin and turning gradually to sculpture, under the guidance of Denis Mitchell in Cornwall, where he lived for seven years. He is married to the painter and composer Nancy Wynne–Jones, and now lives and works in County Wicklow.

Conor Fallon

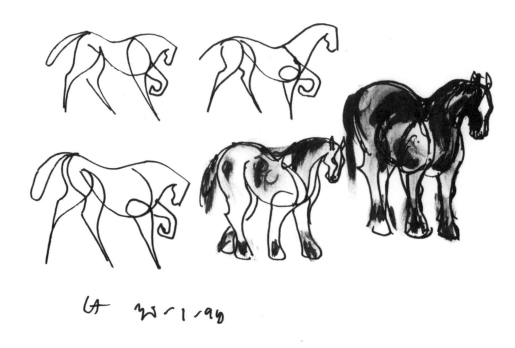

This drawing is dated on my birthday – I draw most days – and the hairier horses are tinkers' horses, standing at my gate.

PATRICK IRELAND, aka Brian O'Doherty, was born in Ballaghaderreen, County Roscommon and educated at University College, Dublin and Harvard University. He has lived in New York since 1961 and works as an artist. He has exhibited in over forty one-person shows in Europe and the United States and in numerous group exhibitions, among them Rosc, Documenta and the Venice Biennale. He is represented in such museum collections as the Metropolitan Museum of Art, the National Museum of American Art and the Hugh Lane Municipal Gallery of Modern Art. As Brian O'Doherty, his books include *Inside the White Cube* and *The Strange Case of Mlle. P.*

Patrick Ireland

FOR THE ART HISTORIAN BARBARA NOVAK
ON OUR SILVER WEDDING ANNIVERSARY

The pleasures of the retrospective view
Attractive though they are are not for me
– or you – since we always must renew
the habit of re-learning how to see.

To hold the object in the naked eye,
Implode its past and future into now –
Now looking at each other as we ply
The consequences of the ancient vow

we know each other fully and are yet
unknown. As time contracts, we multiply,
New planets round a common sun. We bet
The past upon the future's alchemy.

What does not tarnish underground and cold?
We have turned time to silver. Now to gold.

SINÉAD O'CONNOR was born in Dublin in 1966, and made her live debut at the age of fourteen when she was asked to sing at a wedding. In 1990 her version of 'Nothing Compares 2 U', written by Prince, went to number one in seventeen countries. She has released four albums, as well as a number of singles and EPs, and in 1997 marked a decade in the music business with the release of *So Far…The Best of Sinéad O'Connor*. She has also acted in film, appearing as the Virgin Mary in *The Butcher Boy*, directed by Neil Jordan.

Sinéad O'Connor

I have chosen St Brigid's day in honour of God the Mother, the Spirit of Compassion. As represented by Brigid who brought Music to soothe the world. I realise this doesn't look like Brigid! But it is a representation of feminine creativity. And Peace. In honour of the Goddess.

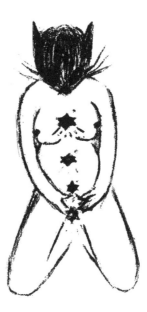

PETER MAYBURY was born in Dublin in 1969. Graduating from Dun Laoghaire College of Art & Design and St Martin's School of Art in London, he set up a design studio in Dublin with clients including the Douglas Hyde Gallery (awarded ICAD gold) and the Dublin French Film Festival (ICAD bronze). He lectures at Dun Laoghaire Institute and produces limited-edition books and prints, photography, music and video projects. In 1998 he exhibited at 90 Degrés gallery in Bordeaux and was selected for ID magazine's international ID Forty. His work has appeared in *Blueprint: Print* and *Émigré* magazines.

Peter Maybury

COLM TÓIBÍN was born in Enniscorthy, County Wexford in 1955. He is the author of four novels: *The South* (1990), *The Heather Blazing* (1992), *The Story of the Night* (1996) and *The Blackwater Lightship* (1999). His travel books include *Bad Blood: A Walk Along the Irish Border* (1987) and *Homage to Barcelona* (1990). His books have been translated into fourteen languages. In 1995 he was awarded the E.M. Forster Prize by the American Academy of Arts and Letters.

Colm Tóibín

Three or four times like this the break came. There was a way. Any mark on the canvas would be a way. A random stroke, meaning nothing, pointing towards nothing. Any colour, any shape. There must be no doubts. Thus in the small hours paintings came into being.

The valley as though painted from beneath, as though it were a map. The curve in the Slaney sneaking across the painting in every colour to re–create the water, the sky in the water and the river bed underneath. And then there was the land around, the way it had been tilled, the farmed ground. And the house her father built during the Troubles. And everywhere the sun pouring down its light on the world.

From *The South*

SEÁN SCULLY was born in Dublin in 1945. His family moved to London in 1949 and he studied art at Croydon College of Art & Design and Harvard University. He now lives and works in New York. His work combines the two main streams of the twentieth century, expressionism and abstraction.

Seán Scully

Lone Lewis Shack

CATHAL Ó SEARCAIGH, a full-time poet in the Irish language, lives on a small hill farm at the foot of Mount Errigal in County Donegal. He has held various posts as writer-in-residence in universities throughout Ireland, north and south.

Selections of his work have already been published in German, Italian, French, Catalan, Breton, Danish and Hindi. He is the author of many volumes of verse, the most representative being *Homecoming/An Bealach'na Bhaile, Na Buachaillí Bána* and

Out in the Open. Affectionately known as Gúrú na gCnoc, he spends Christmas snugly sheltered between a Yak and a Yeti in the Nepal Himalayas. He is a member of Aosdána.

Cathal Ó Searcaigh

Pilleadh An Deoraí:

Teach tréigthe Roimhe Anocht.
Ar an tairseach, faoi lom na gealaí, nocht,
Scáile an tseanchrainn a chuir sé blianta ó shoin.

Exile's Return:

He's back tonight to a deserted house.
On the doorstep, under a brilliant moon, a stark
shadow: the tree he planted years ago is an old tree.

translated by Seamus Heaney

DEIRDRE PURCELL was born in Dublin and educated in County Mayo. Her first career was acting, beginning at the Abbey Theatre and later moving to Chicago as the first European Theatre Artist-in-Residence at Loyola University. Back in Dublin, she worked as a TV journalist for RTÉ and graduated to chief features writer with *The Sunday Tribune*. From 1989 she became a full-time successful fiction writer and she is adapting her sixth novel, *Love Like Hate Adore*, for the cinema and working on a four-part original sequel to the TV adaptation of her third novel, *Falling for a Dancer*.

Deirdre Purcell

I suppose I'd better go out to get her. I'm dreading it, especially after the last time when she made a show of me in front of the entire rush–hour population of Church Street. Dublin's grinding to a halt, you know. Millennium my eye. It'll be sooner than the millennium we'll have gridlock. Bring it on, I say. Bring on the gridlock. Then they'll have to do something about it.

And at least that'll be one thing they can't blame the Lanigans for.

As you may or may not have heard, there are parties in this city who spit on the name Lanigan. Well don't blame me, I only married into this family.

So who's Esme. Right. Esme's the last of Mick's aunties. She came to live with us in 1983, 16 long, long years ago. She'd nowhere else to go after her sister died. So Mick took her in and she's been here since. Into each life some rain must fall.

From *Entertaining Ambrose*

MARTIN HAYES was born in Maghera, County Clare and was raised in the local tradition of the old players whose music 'made the hair stand up on the back of your neck or made you want to laugh and cry all at the same time'. He ranks among the most elegant fiddlers to emerge from Ireland. His father, P.J. Hayes, has led the renowned Tulla Céilí Band for over fifty years. He and his musical partner, guitarist Dennis Cahill, perform in concerts all over the world.

Martin Hayes

The music I play exists as part of an ongoing tradition, starting for me with my father and neighbouring musicians and extending all the way back to a mythological past where only the soul and the imagination can freely wander. Apart from the tunes, technique and style I learned, the most important insight I had access to from the old musicians was knowledge and experience of an intangible yearning in their souls, a yearning which they sought to satisfy in music. When they play you know them, and through them you know the music. The past is forever present with them, they are the carriers of soul, they open a window to that mythological past. Many of these players are unknown, humble, shy and non-virtuosic. In order to experience their magic you have to first become a non-judgmental open receiver, a listener/participator in the conversation so that the depth of their souls can be revealed to you. They are not performers, or entertainers; they are something more.

The great secret of all creative geniuses is that they possess that power to appropriate the beauty, the wealth, the grandeur, and the sublimity contained within their own souls, which are parts of Omnipotence, and to communicate those riches to others.

PUCCINI

Thanks to all the musicians who have opened their hearts and shown me the meaning and power of music.

Bob Geldof was born in Dublin in 1952 and reluctantly educated at Blackrock College. He left Ireland to work in Canada as a rock journalist and returned home in 1975, when he formed the successful rock band The Boomtown Rats. At the end of 1984 he was so shaken by famine pictures from Ethiopia that he began a charity record campaign that culminated in 'Live Aid' on 13 June 1985, when simultaneous concerts in London and Philadelphia raised £48 million. He was awarded an honorary KBE in 1986.

Bob Geldof

Beasts rear up in horror
Mute
Their tongues cut out
To keep the neighbours happy
Clawing with their steel–shod feet
Right there behind my ear
They drool all night
Their spume from tired
Flanks and lips
Flies about my dreams
I wake up
Bruised by
Mad black horses
Panicked to exhaustion
By the cruel
Rigmarole of sleep
Somewhere in my bowels they lie
In snorting and uneasy rest
Their stinking breath
Hissing from my every pore

I wake up
Drooling on my pillow
My tired flanks and lips
Covered in the spume
And froth of unrelenting
Fear.

Will this do?
Bob Geldof

PHILIP CASEY was born to Irish parents in London in 1950 and grew up in County Wexford. He has published three poetry collections, including *The Year of the Knife* and *Poems 1980–1990*. His one-act play *Cardinal* was performed in Hamburg in 1990. His first novel, *The Fabulists*, was published in 1994, and won the inaugural Kerry Ingredients Book of the Year Award at Listowel Writers' Week, 1995. His novel *The Water Star* was published in 1999. He is a member of Aosdána and lives in Dublin.

Philip Casey

DIALOGUE IN FADING LIGHT

The moon sits in the chilled zenith.
Emptied of everything but your grace,
night long, I stare at its mask of light.

I recall ice dripping into a drain.
The drain is deep and the sound faint;
the measure of the drip is ominous.

Our sun is many times the size of the earth,
and red giants like Betelgeuse dwarf the sun,
and for all I know Betelgeuse is a mote
in the scale of creation. Yet we belong.

The eye craves rhythm and colour.
There's no healing or ease
in a vista where nothing coheres.

You renewed me by losing yourself
to our deepening dialogue in fading light.
To stardust we shall return.

A pink moon rose as we parted,
its presence over the rooftops a focus,
a celestial light through the dust of pollution,
composing all that had been in isolation.

EIMEAR O'CONNOR was born in Dublin in 1965. She became a full-time visual artist in 1988. She has exhibited widely in Ireland, Denmark and the United States and her work is in public and private collections in those countries and in Germany and France. She has designed book and album covers, television and theatre sets, costumes and posters and is a board member of the Association of Artists in Ireland. In recent years she has become interested in multimedia, as illustrated by the piece shown here, which is plaster on board with an accompanying poem.

Eimear O'Connor

FRACTURED

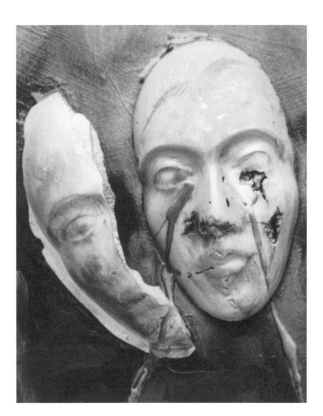

Behind the mask
The façade, the face
The soul takes flight from thee
Cracked open from the
pain of life
Fractured,
yes...
But free...
A tribute to my mother.

FRANCIS STUART was born in Australia of Antrim stock in April 1902. After the death of his father later that year, he returned to Antrim with his mother, and was brought up there and in County Meath, moving to Dublin in 1918. His first book of poetry, *We Have Kept the Faith* (1923), received an award from W.B. Yeats's Academy of Irish Letters. He published his first novel, *Women and God*, in 1931. The novels *Redemption*, *The Pillar of Cloud* and *Black List, Section H* have recently been reissued.

Francis Stuart

ADVERTISEMENT

Taking myself apart in the potting shed
At a bleak hour of a late winter morning,
Among the folded deck chairs and seed catalogues,
I was reminded of the Evening Poppy
That lends (the word in the brochure)
A touch of colour to an elegant dinner table,
While in me I was discovering layers of greyness.

GENE LAMBERT, the son and namesake of Ireland's most famous puppeteer, grew up in Finglas, Dublin. At the age of twelve, hoping to meet the artist L.S. Lowry, he took a boat to England and spent a year living with a group of travellers before returning home. After school, he attended the National College of Art & Design and then set up an etching school with a group of friends. Following a serious accident in the early 1980s which left him physically disabled, he organised an exhibition of his own photographs called *Work from a Dark Room*, which travelled throughout Ireland, and he became involved in the Clashganna Trust in Borris, County Carlow. He co–edited, with Theo Dorgan, *The Great Book of Ireland/Leabhar Mór na hÉireann* (1991).

Gene Lambert

Who's a Big Boy Then?

NELL MCCAFFERTY was born in Derry city in 1944 and educated at Queen's University, Belfast. After college, she travelled extensively in Europe and the Middle East and worked on a kibbutz in Israel. She returned to Derry in 1968, where she joined the Derry Labour Party, the Civil Rights Movement and the dole. She moved to Dublin and joined *The Irish Times* in 1970. A collection of her journalism, *The Best of Nell*, was a best–seller in 1983; and in 1985 she published *A Woman to Blame*, about the 'Kerry babies' case.

Nell McCafferty

THERE'LL BE ANOTHER DAY

Bloody Sunday was carried out with one objective. The British Army decided coldly and deliberately to shoot the risen people off the streets. We were shot with our backs turned, in some cases with our hands in the air as we went to rescue the wounded. We were killed on the barricades, in the courtyards...and a few people died God knows where. The vultures picked them up first. But the siege goes on. The 808 acres of Bogside, Brandywell and Creggan remain free. Forty of the forty–two entrances to Free Derry remain barricaded.

Sunday, Bloody Sunday, was a fine day and a foul day. It was a fine thing to swing down Southway, thousands of us, singing, to pick up thousands more of our comrades at the Brandywell. And then to swell through the Bogside where it all began four years ago. Do you remember?...

We asked them to ban the Unionist Corporation and they said no, and then they banned it. We demanded houses and they said no, and then they built them. We demanded that Craig should go and they said no and then he went. We told the RUC to leave the Bogside and they said no – running all the way to barracks.

And when Sam Devenney died, paying the price of it all, we thought it more than we could bear, but we did. Death was strange to us then. Death is no stranger now but the price is higher and no easier to bear. No–one who died yesterday was a stranger to us.

What impossible things did we demand this time? That our internees be freed, that we walk in our own streets, that the Stormont cesspool be cleaned up. For the least of these and the best of these demands, thirteen men were murdered last week. Let it be said of them with pride they died on their feet and not on their knees. Let it not be said of us they died in vain.

Stay free, brothers and sisters. There'll be another day.

Published in *The Starry Plough*, newspaper of the Official Republican Movement, the week after Bloody Sunday

CECILY BRENNAN, a visual artist, was born in Athenry, County Galway in 1955. She studied painting at the National College of Art & Design in Dublin. Her work since then has ranged through a wide variety of media: drawing, printmaking, painting and, most recently, three-dimensional pieces in wax. She has represented Ireland internationally on a number of occasions and has exhibited widely both in Ireland and abroad. Her work is included in all the major public and private collections in Ireland. She is a member of Aosdána.

Cecily Brennan

Bandaged Heart

KATHY PRENDERGAST, born in Dublin in 1958, studied at the National College of Art & Design in Dublin, where an exhibit at her diploma show was purchased by the Hugh Lane Municipal Gallery of Modern Art. One of the works in that show, *Sea Bed*, featured a female body made of plaster and painted in cartographers' greens and blues; map-making and sexual identity have remained central concerns for her. Completing a master's degree in sculpture at London's Royal College of Art, she won two GPA Emerging Artist awards during the 1980s before being presented with the Year 2000 prize for the Best Young Artist at the 1995 Venice Biennale.

Kathy Prendergast

Prayer Gloves

Colum McCann was born in Dublin. He is the author of two novels, *Songdogs* and *This Side of Brightness*. He has also written a short-story collection, *Fishing the Sloe-Black River*. He has won the Rooney Prize, the Hennessy Award for Irish Fiction, and the Pushcart Prize in the US. He currently lives in New York with his wife, Allison, and their two children.

Colum McCann

New York 1916

They arrive at dawn in their geography of hats. A dark field of figures, stalks in motion, bending toward the docklands.

Scattered at first in the streets of Brooklyn – they have come by trolley and ferry and elevated train – they begin to gather together in a wave. Hard men, diligent in the smoking of cigarettes, they stamp yesterday's mud from their boots as they walk. A trail of muck is left in the snow. Ice puddles are cracked by the weight of their feet. The cold inveigles itself into their bodies. Some of the men have big moustaches that move like prairie grasses above their lips. Others are young and raw from razors. All of them have faces hollowed by the gravity of their work; they smoke furiously, with the knowledge of those who might be dead in just a few hours. Hunching down into their overcoats, they can perhaps still smell last night on their bodies – they might have been drunk or they might have been making love or they might have been both at once. Later they will laugh at these stories of drink and love, but for now they are silent. It is far too cold to do anything but walk and smoke. They move toward the East River and cluster near the tunnel entrance, stamping their boots on the cobblestones for warmth.

And when the long whistle calls the sandhogs to work, they take a last pull on their cigarettes. The red tops of the butts flare and are dropped to the ground, one by one, as if swarms of fireflies are laying themselves down to rest.

From *This Side of Brightness*

PATRICK MCCABE, born in Clones, County Monaghan in 1955, received a Hennessy Award in 1979 for his first published short story. He has since published a children's story, *The Adventures of Shay Mouse*, and five adult novels, *Music on Clinton Street*, *Carn*, *The Butcher Boy* (adapted for stage as *Frank Pig Says Hello*), *The Dead School* and *Breakfast on Pluto*. *The Butcher Boy* won the Irish Times/ Aer Lingus Literature Prize and was filmed by Neil Jordan, who co–wrote the screenplay with the author. Patrick McCabe lives in Sligo with his wife and two daughters.

Patrick McCabe

PACKO: You know where Loco County is, Vance? (*Taps temple*) Right in here.

MOSS: I don't care if I have a heart attack. It makes no odds now.

PACKO: You don't care about heart attacks, Moss.

MOSS: That's right, Packo. Damn the bit do I care! I couldn't give a fecking damn now and that's the truth! (*Clutches chest*) Agh!

PACKO: Della, quick! Mr Brady's having a heart attack!

DELLA: (*Still upset, makes no response*)

PACKO: (*Massaging his chest*) Here. Show me. Where does it hurt?

MOSS: Hee hee.

PACKO: Hell if old Moss ain't going loco now too.

MOSS: Loco! Oh now God bless us! Don't be talking!

PACKO: The muscles on you, Moss!

MOSS: I haven't much now, Packo. But when I was a young fellow I can tell you – oh now! (*Pause*) Mary doesn't bother much with muscles or that these times. Not since our wee girl died. We used to go up to Clancy's too. (*Breaks down*)

PACKO: Oo Moss – did you now? Drop the hand, did you!

DELLA: Leave him alone, Packo! Just leave him alone!

MOSS: Her hair was like bog cotton in the breeze. That's true. It was way back in the old days but. They're all dead now them days. There's nothing now only legs. Just the legs now.

DELLA: Cut it out, Packo. It's not funny anymore.

ROD TUACH, born in Dublin in 1945, has photographed for the theatre, magazines and books. He has exhibited in Ireland, Holland and Belgium and taken part in group shows in America, Canada, Russia and recently Slovenia. A member of Aosdána, he lives in County Wicklow.

Rod Tuach

JUNE LEVINE was born in Dublin in 1931. A journalist and broadcaster, she was a founder member of the Irish Women's Liberation Movement. She is the author of three books: *Sisters*, a personal history of the IWLM; *Lyn*, a story of prostitution, co–authored with Lyn Madden; and *A Season of Weddings*, a novel set in India, where she spends time every year. She is a contributor to the current *Irish Women's Field Day Anthology* and is now teaching meditation and writing a new novel.

June Levine

The Germans had come for Jews. Mrs Molloy was right: 'If you people think you're safe in Kimmage, you have another think comin'. The Jerries will find ye, sure as apples.'

Mammy and Daddy were arguing. She didn't want him to go out with the ARP, but he went. And Nella crept from the landing back across the icy linoleum to her bed.

All the Germans had to do was ask Jimmy Molloy's mother. Or Mrs Moriarty. And Mrs Reed? 'They live in number eighty–five,' they'd say, 'and they crucified Jesus.'

'Close that curtain and put off the bloody light, Missus,' shouted the ARP man. 'D'you want to bring them on top of you?' Then everything shook with a terrible noise. Nella covered her head and scurried into her secret prayer: 'Hail Mary, full of Grace...now and at the hour of our death...'

From a novel in progress

JOHN KELLY was born in 1932 and studied at the National College of Art & Design in Dublin. A figurative artist, he was the director of the Graphic Studio in Dublin for over ten years and was a founder of the Black Church Print Studio. He has had many solo exhibitions in Dublin and among his awards is the Douglas Hyde Gold Medal for 1992. He was elected a member of the Royal Hibernian Academy in 1991 and a member of Aosdána in 1996.

John Kelly

MARY MAHER was born in Chicago and has lived in Ireland since 1965, when she joined the staff of *The Irish Times*. She was the first woman's editor of the newspaper and a founding member of the Irish Women's Liberation Movement. Her first novel, *The Devil's Card*, was published in 1992 and in 1997 she co-edited *If Only*, a collection of short stories by Irish women writers, with the late Kate Cruise O'Brien.

Mary Maher

What happened, Matt said, was that her daughter found out she was getting these calls from a man in Ireland and wondered did she have a fellow or what. 'So finally the mother just crumbled and told her about me, the whole story. Then I went over. I brought everything, Aran sweaters, perfume, plenty of duty free, you name it. People always ask "what was the very first thing you said when you met her, what did you say?" But the thing is she lived way up a hill in this housing estate, I had to climb and climb and I could see her there, this big woman standing at the door with her arms folded. So when I got to the top I said "the air up here must be good, you're looking well." She burst into tears then, this tough old bird. My mother.'

From a work in progress

ANITA GROENER, born in the Netherlands, has been living and working in Ireland since 1982. She is included in many private and public collections in Ireland and elsewhere. In 1995 a monograph on her work was published. She is represented by the Rubicon Gallery in Dublin.

Anita Groener

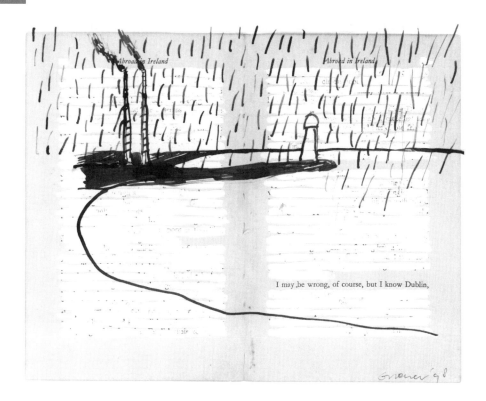

JOHN ARDEN, playwright and novelist, was born in Barnsley, England in 1930. He has lived in Galway (city and county) for over thirty years. Plays include *Live Like Pigs*, *Serjeant Musgrave's Dance*, *The Workhouse Donkey*, and many in collaboration with Margaretta D'Arcy, for example: *The Island of the Mighty*, *The Business of Good Government*, *The Little Gray Home in the West*, *The Non–Stop Connolly Show*, *Vandaleur's Folly*, *Whose is the Kingdom?* Novels include *Silence Among the Weapons*, *Books of Bale*, *Jack Juggler and the Emperor's Whore*.

John Arden

—

A playwright has some thoughts about the nature of his craft...

My little people in a row
Sit on the stage and watch the show.
The show they watch is rows and rows
Of people watching them. Who knows
Which is more alive than which?
If you fidget, if you twitch,
Blow your nose or nod your head,
Little people (sprung from who can say whose seed?)
Can frame an antic gesture just as good.

Laugh and leap or shake with terror,
Little people are your mirror.
What you do or what you did
From little people can't be hid:
They will know it and reflect
In strut and jerk your every act –
Your thoughts expressed in dark of night
They body forth in broad daylight.
Who is to say what stories these shall show you?
You tell 'em who you are and they will know you –

(Sit and watch them) – little people,
Snarling smiling murmuring men and women –
And you will know yourselves again
And yet again and then again
Again, I can't stop saying it, yet again.

RICHARD GORMAN, a painter and printmaker, was born in Dublin in 1946. Having graduated from Trinity College, Dublin in 1969, he worked in business until 1977, when he entered Dun Laoghaire College of Art & Design. Since that time he has painted, exhibiting both in Ireland (at the Kerlin Gallery) and abroad. In 1986 he won the gold award at Cagnes-sur-Mer and in 1996 he received a Pollock-Krasner Award. He divides his time between Dublin and Milan.

Richard Gorman

25.02.2000

February/Feabhra

BILLY DRAKE was born in Dublin, where he now lives and works. His main area of concern is the human figure – rendered primarily in pen and ink. He has also experimented with etching and other media. His work is held in public and private collections in Ireland, Germany, Holland, Belgium, Japan and the USA.

Billy Drake

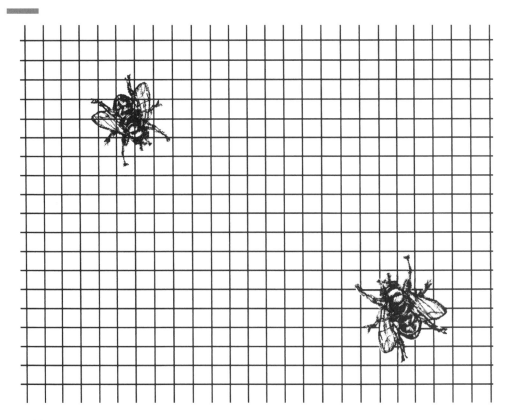

Website

MICHAEL HARTNETT was born in Croom, County Limerick in 1941. In the 1970s he lectured in creative writing at Thomond College, Limerick. In 1975 he decided to write poetry only in Irish. This he did until 1985, when he began writing again in English. He received the American Ireland Fund Literary Award in 1990. A member of Aosdána, he lives in Dublin.

Michael Hartnett

We felt very deeply for each other
and, strange to tell,
we got on very well.

We often played at 'Husband and Wife'
and, strange to tell,
we did not bicker, we did not fight;
our jokes we happily shared,
we kissed, we embraced.

And, in the end, with young delight,
we played 'Hide and Seek' in wood and lane.

We became so good at going ahide
that we never found each other again.

From *Heinrich Heine*

KATY HAYES was born in Dublin in 1965. She worked as a theatre director for many years, concentrating on the promotion of women's writing, and was a founder member of Glasshouse Productions. She is now a full-time writer. She has published a collection of short stories, *Forecourt*, and a novel, *Curtains*, and written a play, *Playgirl*. Her short stories have been widely anthologised and broadcast on RTÉ and the BBC. She is married to critic Tony Roche and lives in Dublin.

Katy Hayes

MICHEAL O'SIADHAIL is a poet. Among his collections are Hail! Madam Jazz: New and Selected Poems (1992), A Fragile City and Our Double Time (1998) and Poems 1975–1995 (1999). He reads and broadcasts his poetry often in Ireland, Britain, Europe and North America. Awarded an Irish–American Cultural Institute prize for poetry in 1981 and the Marten Toonder Award for Literature in 1998, he has lectured at Trinity College, Dublin and was a professor at the Dublin Institute for Advanced Studies. He has served on the Arts Council and is a former editor of Poetry Ireland Review. He is a member of Aosdána.

Micheal O'Siadhail

OUT OF THE BLUE

Nothing can explain this adventure – let's say a quirk
Of fortune steered us together – we made our covenants,
Began this odyssey of ours, by hunch and guesswork,
A blind date where foolish love consented in advance.
No my beloved, neither knew what lay behind the frontiers.
You told me once you hesitated: *A needle can waver,*
Then fix on its pole; I am still after many years
Baffled that the needle's gift dipped in my favour.
Should I dare to be so lucky? Is this a dream?
Suddenly in the commonplace that first amazement seizes
Me all over again – a freak twist to the theme,
Subtle jazz of the new familiar, trip of surprises.
Gratuitous, beyond our fathom, both binding and freeing,
This love re–invades us, shifts the boundaries of our being.

THOMAS KINSELLA was born in Dublin in 1928 and studied at University College, Dublin. His first collection, Poems (1956), was issued as a wedding gift to his wife, Eleanor Walsh. He was writer-in-residence and Professor of English at Southern Illinois University and Professor of English at Temple University. His collections include Another September (1958), Downstream (1962), Nightwalker (1969), Blood & Family (1988) and The Pen Shop (1997). He also edited The New Oxford Book of Irish Verse. He translated many old Irish texts, including The Táin (1969), and founded Peppercanister in Dublin in 1972 for the publication of first editions. He lives in County Wicklow.

Thomas Kinsella

The times were bad
and we were in bad hands.
There was nothing to be done,
only record.

FERGAL KEANE was born in London in 1961 to Irish parents. He is BBC News Special Correspondent and in 1997 was awarded the OBE for his journalism. Among the awards he has won are Royal Television Society Journalist of the Year, a BAFTA for television reporting and the George Orwell Prize for political writing. He has written *The Bondage of Fear*, *Season of Blood* and *Letter to Daniel*.

Fergal Keane

FIRSTBORN

A critic writes of me: 'I wish he'd stop wittering on about his newborn son. He's trying to make it sound as if he invented fatherhood.' But what would he know, my darling, who has never heard you laughing in your sleep?

CIARÁN Ó GAORA was born in Dublin
in 1967. He is creative director of
DesignWorks, Dublin.

Ciarán Ó Gaora

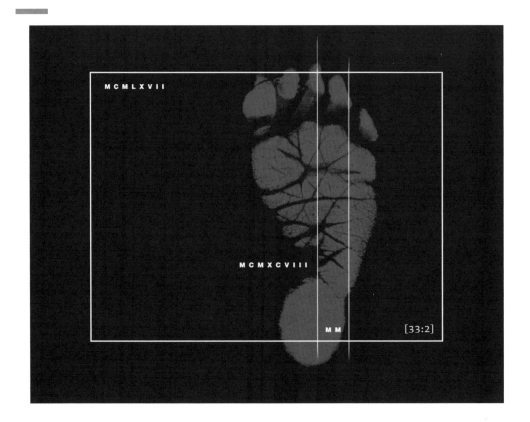

AIDAN HIGGINS was born in County
Kildare in 1927 and educated at Clongowes
Wood College. He lived for periods in South
Africa, London, Berlin and Andalucia. In
1984 he returned to Ireland as a recipient of
Aosdána. He won the James Tait Black

Memorial Prize in 1966 for his novel
Langrishe, Go Down. His writings include
Asylum & Other Stories, *Images of Africa*,
Balcony of Europe, *Bornholm Night-Ferry* and
Dog Days. He is married with three sons.

Aidan Higgins

THE FIRST-BORN

JOHANNESBURG 58

VIVIENNE ROCHE is a sculptor based in Cork. Her work is in many public and private collections in Ireland, Sweden, England, France, Germany and the United States. Recent public commissions include *The Sea Garden* at Ringaskiddy, *Plumb–Line* in Dublin Castle, and *Inclination*, NMRC at University College, Cork. A former member of the Arts Council (1993–8), she is a founder director of the National Sculpture Factory and a member of Aosdána.

Vivienne Roche

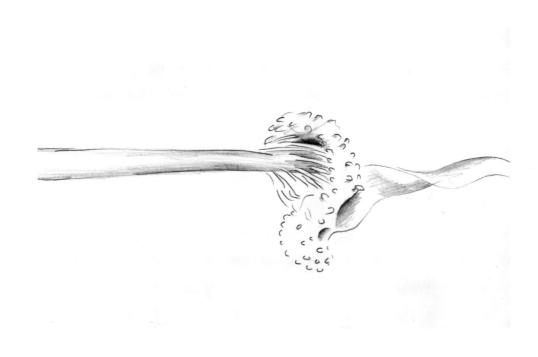

CLARE BOYLAN was born in Dublin in 1948 and has worked as a journalist on newspapers and magazines, TV and radio. In 1974 she was awarded a Benson & Hedges Award for outstanding journalism. She has published four collections of short stories *A Nail on the Head* (1983), *Concerning Virgins* (1989), *That Bad Woman* (1995), and *Another Family Christmas* (1997). Her novels include *Holy Pictures* (1983), *Last Resorts* (1984) and *Home Rule* (1992).

Clare Boylan

Irish Spring Song

It's March, and through a drift of snow
I hear the matins of a crow:
'Who made an igloo of my nest,
Grant unto me a thermal vest.'
To which the Mighty One retorts,
'Praise me for your feathered shorts!'

On the ground, beneath a silt
Of tasteless sorbet, bluebells wilt.

Written for my friend Pauline Bewick, during an unseasonally snowy spring lunch

PAUL MULDOON, who was born in
Northern Ireland in 1951, is the author of
eight collections of poetry, most recently
Hay (1998). His New Selected Poems 1968–1994
won the 1997 Irish Times Prize for Poetry. The
Field Day Anthology of Irish Writing (1991)
describes Muldoon as 'a fastidious
miniaturist who uses words with a kind of
quiet awe'. He teaches at Princeton
University.

Paul Muldoon

THE DROWNED BLACKBIRD

O beautiful daughter of Conn O'Neill,
you've slept long after your great loss.
Don't let your noble kinsmen hear
    you wail
for your one precious thing amid all
    the dross.

The music of that lively, lightsome bird
has gone from you, my bright seagull,
    all gone.
But there's a silver lining to every cloud.
Leave off your hand–claps and ullagones.

From your hand–claps and howls
of grief, hold off, my little chickabiddy;
O beautiful daughter of Conn O'Neill,
on a common bird don't waste your pity.

My pretty one that sprang from Ulster's
    high kings,
compose yourself, lest you go out of your
    mind
for the sake of a bird, albeit the sweetest
    that sings.
It's washed white now, see, in a bucket
    of lime.

After Séamas Dall Mac Cuarta 1647–1733

HUGO HAMILTON was born in Dublin in 1953 of Irish/German parentage. His writing has always reflected the duality of his upbringing, with novels set in Germany, such as *The Last Shot* (1990) and *The Love Test* (1995), and more recently novels set in Dublin, *Headbanger* (1997) and *Sad Bastard* (1998). He lives and works in Dublin.

Hugo Hamilton

He seemed to be talking to the potato all along. Come on, take your jacket off, like a good lad. You're far too hot. He patiently undressed it, juggling the hot core around on a tripod of his fingers until he had finished and dropped it neatly on to the plate, right beside the cabbage. Then he plunged the knife into the centre and the yellow–white landfalls of flesh fell apart. Steam bursting up from the scalding interior. Butter melting into a golden pool.

From *Sad Bastard*

TONY O'SHEA was born on Valentia Island, County Kerry and educated at University College, Dublin. He has been a professional photojournalist since 1981 and his work appears in national and international magazines and newspapers. In 1990 he collaborated with Colm Tóibín on the book *Dubliners*. He works as a contract photographer with *The Sunday Business Post* and is engaged on personal photographic projects.

Tony O'Shea

Draghunt, Whitechurch, County Cork

JOHN MCGAHERN, the writer, was born in 1934 in Dublin and brought up in various parts of the west of Ireland. The spare artistry of his first novel, *The Barracks* (1963), won him the AE Memorial Award. Other novels include *The Dark, The Pornographer* and *Amongst Women*, which was shortlisted for the Booker Prize in 1990. His *Collected Stories* were published in 1992. He received the GPA award the same year and Le Prix Étranger Écureuil in 1994. He lives in County Leitrim.

John McGahern

It is very quiet here. Nothing much ever happens. We have learned to tell the cries of the birds and the animals, the wing-beats of the swans crossing the house, the noises of the different motors that batter about on the roads. Not many people like this quiet. There's a constant craving for word of every sound and sighting and any small happening. Then, when something violent and shocking happens, nobody will speak at all after the first shock wave passes into belief. Eyes usually wild for every scrap of news and any idle word will turn away or search the ground.

From *The Love of the World*

JOHN WATERS was born in County Roscommon in 1955. Despite the efforts of local schools, he remained uneducated in any acceptable sense. He occupied a range of positions after leaving school, including railway clerk, showband roadie, petrol pump attendant and mailcar driver. As a journalist, editor and columnist, he has specialised in raising unpopular issues of public importance, including the repression of Famine memory and the denial of rights to fathers. His books include *Jiving at the Crossroads* (1991), *Race of Angels* (1994), *Every Day Like Sunday* (1995) and *An Intelligent Person's Guide to Modern Ireland* (1997). His plays include *Long Black Coat* (1994), *Holy Secrets* (1996), *Easter Dues* and *Adverse Possession* (1998).

John Waters

RAIDIÓ RÓISÍN

I called it Raidió Róisín, the baby monitor I used to place near your cot, to check on you while you slept. It reminded me of your grandfather, who died seven years before you arrived. I wished I had had one back then, to check on him in the night, to ascertain whether he was still breathing, rather than crouching at the bedroom door with my ear to the keyhole, listening for sounds of life. I wished I had had one on the morning he died, so I could have reached his side in time to say goodbye. Once, while living in our apartment in Colville Terrace, Londing Town, I discovered that there was another baby on the other channel, to whose breathing I had been listening for an hour by mistake. But the first sigh was a bum note that sent me scrambling for the tuner. For a moment I fretted that you might have been awake and calling me. But the moment passed, for in truth I did not need the monitor. Always I would wake two minutes before you stirred, and lie there waiting. There was a time in my life when this might have seemed a massive inconvenience. But whenever it happened, I'd find myself longing for your cry, so I could see your face again.

PAUL SEAWRIGHT, artist, was born in Belfast in 1965. His large photographic works mine the political and social complexities of Northern Irish culture. He has made works that deal with sectarian murder, the Orange Order, policing in Northern Ireland and, more recently, metaphoric landscapes from the periphery of Protestant and Catholic communities in Belfast. His work has been exhibited in many galleries internationally and in 1997 he was awarded the IMMA/Glen Dimplex Art Prize. He lives and works in Newport, Wales, where he is head of research at the University of Wales, College Newport.

Paul Seawright

Bonfire Site, Belfast 1997

EAMON GRENNAN was born in Dublin in 1941. He was educated by the Cistercians in Roscrea before taking a degree in English and Italian at University College, Dublin. He went to America as a graduate student and received a doctorate in English from Harvard in 1972. Collections of his poems have been published in Ireland and the United States, as have his translations from the Italian poet Leopardi. He teaches in Vassar College, Poughkeepsie, New York, dividing his time between there and Ireland.

Eamon Grennan

SHED

You wouldn't know it had been there at all, ever,
the small woodshed by the side of the garage
that a falling storm–struck bough demolished
some seasons back, the space and remains now
overcome by weeds, chokecherry, wild rose brambles.
But, at the verge of where it stood, a peach tree
I'd never seen a sign of before has pushed
its skinny trunk and sparse–leaved branches up
above that clutter into the thoroughfare of light
and given us, this fall, a small basketful
of sweet fruit the raccoons love too and sit at midnight
savouring, spitting the stones down where the shed
used to stand – those bony seeds ringing along
the metal ghost of the roof, springing into the dark.

From *So It Goes*

ALAN ABOUD was born in Dublin in 1966 and educated at Belvedere College, Dublin and St Martin's School of Art in London. Influenced by record sleeve imagery, notably Ireland's Steve Averill and England's Malcolm Garrett, he embarked on a career in graphic design. In 1990 he established ABOUD–SODANO with Sandro Sodano, specialising in fashion advertising and photography. The company has shaped the advertising image of designer Paul Smith and won awards for its work for the AIDS charity, the Terrence Higgins Trust. Since 1993 Aboud's work has been mainly for New York and Tokyo clients. He lives in London.

Alan Aboud

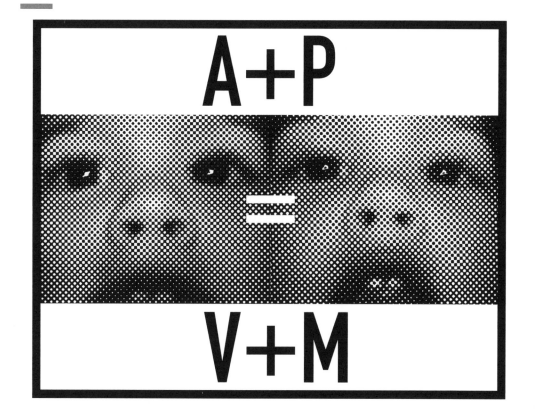

GLENN PATTERSON, novelist, was born in 1961 in Belfast. His first novel, *Burning Your Own*, was published in 1988 and won the Rooney Prize for Irish Literature. Both this book and its successor, *Fat Lad* (1992), focus on the Northern Irish Troubles, while in *Black Night at Big Thunder Mountain* (1995) the action moves to mainland Europe. After being writer in the community for Lisburn and Craigavon 1989–91, he moved to the north of England but subsequently returned to Ireland, acting as writer-in-residence first at University College, Cork and subsequently at Queen's University, Belfast.

Glenn Patterson

She wanted to get to the heart of the matter, to be able to point and say, there, that's where it all started to go wrong.

When we moved over to this side of town.

When we came back from Dublin.

The day and hour we met.

Before we met.

Before we were even born.

Before our parents were born.

Before our parents' parents were born.

Before our parents' parents' parents were born.

But it was like trying to hold a pattern in a kaleidoscope, one tiny chip slipped and the whole configuration changed. There was always at least one more factor to be taken into account and the heart of the matter, she came to see, was that there was no heart of the matter; or else (which amounted to the same thing) many millions of hearts.

From *Fat Lad*

LYNNE PARKER was born in Belfast, educated at Trinity College, Dublin and is artistic director of Rough Magic Theatre Company. She has directed for Charabanc, Druid, the Abbey and the Gate in Dublin and in the UK for the Bush, the Almeida, the Old Vic and the West Yorkshire Playhouse. Work for Rough Magic includes *Top Girls* by Caryl Churchill, *Digging for Fire* and *Love and a Bottle* by Declan Hughes, and *Pentecost* by Stewart Parker. Her work received a Bank of Ireland/*Arts Show* Award, the 1990 *Time Out* Award and the 1995 Dublin Theatre Festival Award for Best Irish Production.

Lynne Parker

(Lily begins to sing)

LILY: Oh God our help in ages past...

MARIAN: Don't fight me, Lily...

LILY: *(Continuing to sing over Marian's lines)* Our hope for years to come...

MARIAN: I need you, we have got to make this work, you and me...

LILY: *(Singing on regardless)* Our shelter from the stormy blast, And our eternal home!

MARIAN: You think you're haunting me don't you? But you see it's me that's actually haunting you. I'm not going to go away. There's no curse or hymn that can exorcise me. So you might as well just give me your blessing and make your peace with me, Lily.

LILY: You'll have no peace in this house.

Photo: Eleanor Methven and Carol Scanlan in Lynne Parker's production of *Pentecost* by Stewart Parker for Rough Magic, Dublin Theatre Festival 1995. Photo credit: Amelia Stein.

MARGARETTA D'ARCY, born in 1934, is a playwright, grandmother and member of Aosdána. She lives in Galway. She has written thirty-odd plays, often in collaboration with John Arden. Some titles: *The Little Gray Home in the West, The Non-Stop Connolly Show, Vandaleur's Folly, Whose is the Kingdom?* Prose works: *Tell Them Everything, Awkward Corners, Galway's Pirate Women, A Global Trawl.* She is a founder member of Women in Media & Entertainment and Radio Pirate-Woman (the world's only autonomous women's radio station). She has been to gaol several times in England and the north of Ireland as a human rights/civil liberties activist.

Margaretta D'Arcy

WRITTEN FROM GREENHAM COMMON WOMEN'S PEACE CAMP, ENGLAND, 16 MARCH 1998

An unprecedented, privileged day: I have attended the first hours of the trial of two intrepid women, Sarah Hipperson, a grandmother, and Peggy Walford, a great-grandmother, both over 70; both of them at last with a chance to fulfil their years of lifelong struggle, to hear nuclear armaments outlawed by a national court of justice. Charged with criminal damage at Burghfield Atomic Weapons Establishment, they assert they committed a lesser crime in order to prevent a greater; with the help of expert witnesses, they will argue the validity of the 1996 ruling of the Hague International Court that 'the threat and use of nuclear weapons would generally be contrary to the rules of international law', being neither for peace nor defence but only for genocide. This, for the first time ever, to be decided by a jury of ordinary people...

MESSRS DAVID MACDERMOTT (born 1952) and PETER MACGOUGH (born 1958) have been working together as collaborative artists for the last eighteen years, initially in New York and latterly in Dublin. Dressing as turn-of-the-century dandies and depicting the world through the eyes of such, they create works in a diversity of media. But by living among the accoutrements of that bygone era, they also create time capsule domiciles, thus blurring the distinction between their art and their lives. Their exhibiting careers have encompassed both solo and group shows around the world, including three Whitney Biennials, a retrospective and, more recently, an IMMA/Glen Dimplex nomination and installation in 1998.

Messrs MacDermott & MacGough

MacDermott - MacGough

TOM PAULIN was born in Leeds in 1949, grew up in Belfast and was educated at the Universities of Hull and Oxford. He has published five volumes of poetry – the latest of which is *Walking a Line* (1994) – as well as his *Selected Poems 1972–1990*, two major anthologies, versions of a Greek drama, and several critical works, including a study of Thomas Hardy. Well known for his appearances on the BBC's *Late Review*, he is also the G.M. Young Lecturer in English Literature at Hertford College, Oxford. A section of *The Day–Star of Liberty* was given as the T.S. Eliot Lectures at the University of Kent in 1996.

Tom Paulin

At the turn of the stairs in an Elizabethan manor-house near the centre of Maidstone, there is a darkened, damaged self-portrait of the young William Hazlitt. To paint it, the apprentice artist used a brown bituminous pigment, which produced an instant Rembrandt-like effect, and helped create the chiaroscuro he was seeking. Unfortunately, this type of paint never dries completely, though eventually it produces a broken surface that looks like crocodile skin. In his cream, almost clamping neckcloth, the young Hazlitt stares at us with dark eyes, a little patch of sunlight on his right forehead. The cracks make him look strangely damaged – there is something raw, unformed, even dangerous, in his direct, but somehow vulnerably shrouded gaze. This is Hazlitt as he describes himself at the age of nineteen – 'dumb, inarticulate, helpless, like a worm by the wayside', and perhaps he was thinking of this early portrait when he went on to say that his soul has remained 'in its original bondage, dark, obscure, with longings infinite and unsatisfied'. He is presenting himself as an eternal caterpillar or chrysalis. This is a portrait of the artist as a young prisoner – that bandaging neckcloth makes him look oddly convalescent. Above it, the studious, brooding, gummily young face appears to be disappearing into the night.

JAMES PLUNKETT was born in Dublin in 1920 and educated at the Christian Brothers' School in Synge Street. He has worked as a clerk, as a critic and as a writer and was especially associated with *The Bell* under Sean O'Faolain and Peadar O'Donnell. As a secretary in the Workers' Union of Ireland he worked with the Irish trade union leader James Larkin. Soon after, he became assistant head of drama with Radio Éireann and later head of features in RTÉ. His books include *The Trusting and the Maimed*, *Strumpet City*, *The Gems She Wore*, *Farewell Companions* and *The Circus Animals*.

James Plunkett

A MEMORY

Had I a grey donkey
And a low green cart
And the peace of that old man
And his kingship of heart.

With a sack for my cloak
And that hat for a crown
One foot on the shaft
And one hanging down.

I would smoke my clay pipe
And chew a wise thought
And find in reflection
The far thing I sought.

Contented to follow
That little white road
In sunshine to Dingle
So light as to load.

A memory of a walking tour in Kerry long, long ago and the old man who saluted me as he passed me by on his donkey and cart

ROBERT BALLAGH was born in Dublin in 1943. He was an architectural student, an engineering draughtsman, a musician and a postman before taking up painting in 1967. He has executed many important commissions, from portraits, murals, posters and graphic designs to stage designs, limited prints and book covers. He has also designed more than sixty stamps for An Post and the current banknotes for the Central Bank of Ireland. His publications include *Dublin, A Photographic Essay* and *Ballagh on Stage*, featuring his work in the theatre. He is a member of Aosdána.

Robert Ballagh

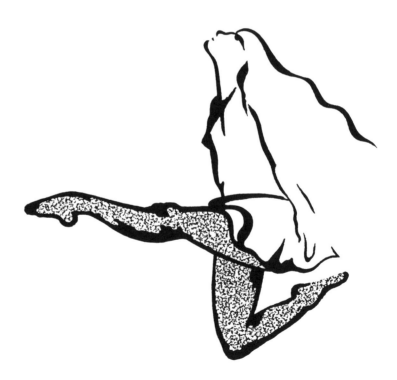

Irish Dancer

BARRIE COOKE was born in England in 1931. He was educated at Harvard, Skowhegan and Kokoschka's School of Seeing in Salzburg. He settled in Ireland in 1954, first in County Clare and then in County Kilkenny. In 1992 he moved to County Sligo. Barrie Cooke has exhibited widely. His solo exhibitions in Dublin have been at the Hendriks Gallery and latterly at the Kerlin Gallery. Three retrospective exhibitions were compiled of his work: in the Douglas Hyde Gallery in 1986, in the Haags Gemeentemuseum, curated by Rudi Fuchs, in 1992, and in the LAC in Perpignan in 1995.

Barrie Cooke

Mermaid and Salmon   Barrie Cooke

DESMOND HOGAN has published five novels, *The Ikon Maker*, *The Leaves on Grey*, *A Curious Street*, *A New Shirt* and *A Farewell to Prague*, and four books of stories, *The Diamonds at the Bottom of the Sea*, *Children* of *Lir*, *The Mourning Thief* and *Lebanon Lodge*; the last two were published in the United States as one volume entitled *A Link with the River*.

Desmond Hogan

We are performing W.B. Yeats's *The Cat and the Moon* on Dollymount Strand late on a summer's afternoon for children from the Dublin slums. A piebald horse grazes nearby on a mound of grass. Some of the little girls wear daisy-chains. I am the lame man, on the blind man's back, both of us going to the saint for a cure. The big, broad-shouldered girl with grey hair is the blind man. Suddenly a little black-haired boy, in a blue cardigan with black cord bas-relief running over the front of it and patent shoes, with skin like dented crockery, breaks from the crowd and starts shouting at the saint, 'Please saint, cure me. My Daddy says I've got a girl's voice and beats me up all the time. Please saint, give me a man's voice.'

From *A Farewell to Prague*

DECLAN HUGHES was born in Dublin in 1963. He is writer-in-residence with Rough Magic Theatre Company. His plays include *I Can't Get Started, Love and a Bottle, Digging for Fire, New Morning, Halloween Night* and *Twenty Grand*. He won the Stewart Parker Award and the BBC TV Drama Award for *I Can't Get Started* in 1991. *Digging for Fire* and *Love and a Bottle* won a *Time Out* Award in 1992. His work for television and film includes *Career Opportunities* and *Joe My Friend*.

Declan Hughes

DANNY: And what happens when you don't have a sense of place? When I arrived in New York for the first time, and as the cab swung past that graveyard and around the corner and I got my first glimpse of the Manhattan skyline, I felt like I was coming home. The landscape was alive in my dreams, the streets were memories from a thousand movies, the city was mine.

RORY: Well you have a sense of place, Danny. It just happens to be somebody else's place.

DANNY: No it doesn't, it's as much Ireland as Dublin is; millions of Irish went out and invented it, invented it as much, probably more than any ever invented this poxy post–colonial backwater.

BREDA: So what's the problem? You don't like it here, fine, you don't live here; you feel at home there, great, you live there. What's the big deal?

DANNY: The big deal, the big deal is, that there is as much here as here is…and I don't believe the here you're describing exists here. To me, here is more like…there.

(Pause)

EMILY: Danny, are you on drugs?

From *Digging for Fire*

ANNE HAVERTY grew up in Holycross and Thurles, County Tipperary. After attending Trinity College, Dublin and the Sorbonne, she worked as a journalist, chiefly for The Irish Times and The Times Literary Supplement. She co-directed the Channel 4/RTÉ documentary The Whole World in His Hands. She has published a biography of Constance Markievicz and a history of Brown Thomas. Her novel One Day as a Tiger won the Rooney Prize in 1997.

Anne Haverty

FROM A TRAIN 1

Two young men in a tilled field
And a horse's ghost with them.

FROM A TRAIN 2

at the close of stubborn light
the secret and obstinate mirror
nested in birches
of an anticipative pond

NIGEL ROLFE, who was born on the Isle of Wight in 1950, lives and works in Dublin. Best known in the fields of performance, video and sound, in recent years he has exhibited works with photography. He has had two retrospectives: *Archive* at the Irish Museum of Modern Art in 1994 and *Nigel Rolfe Videos 1983–1996* at the Musée d'Art Moderne de la Ville de Paris. He is currently course tutor in fine art at the Royal College of Art in London.

Nigel Rolfe

Dust in Face 1989

JOHN F. DEANE was born on Achill Island in 1943 and now lives in Dublin, where he runs The Dedalus Press. In 1979 he founded Poetry Ireland, the national poetry society, and its journal, *Poetry Ireland Review*. He has published several collections of poetry, the most recent being *Christ, with Urban Fox* (1997). In 1996 he was elected secretary general of the European Academy of Poetry. He was awarded the O'Shaughnessy Prize for Poetry in 1998 from the Centre for Irish Studies, St Paul, Minnesota.

John F. Deane

Milord the Hare

The mist was smothering the grasses
like an army of spirits drugged in sleep

and there he was, big-fellow the hare,
as if he had grown, mushroom-silently, overnight;

I envied him his out-there-ness otherness,
his world surviving, original and young;

moved mincingly at first like a man-servant
with high-piled tray, then disappeared

at speed into some downstairs basement;
takes now post-prandial moments of composure

in the good air, land lord and local hero,
important as a parish priest and busybody,

surefooted in a world at odds with everything,
a watcher, like me, on the battlements of himself.

John F. Deane

BRIAN NOLAN, a graphic designer, was born in Dublin in 1966 and graduated in visual communications from the College of Marketing and Design in 1989. He has worked in all aspects of the business from cultural to corporate and has received nine awards from the Institute of Creative Advertising and Design and three international awards. He lives in Dublin, where he is a partner in Dynamo Design Consultants.

Brian Nolan

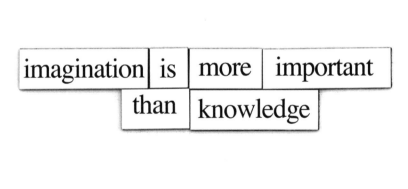

Albert Einstein

NUALA O'FAOLAIN was born in Dublin and educated at University College, Dublin. She has worked as an academic and television producer and for the past decade has written a column for *The Irish Times*. Her autobiography, *Are You Somebody?*, was published in 1996 and became a best–seller on both sides of the Atlantic.

Nuala O'Faolain

Being born was something done to me, but my own life began – I began for myself – when I first made out the meaning of a sentence. I remember everything about it. I was puzzling at a line when all of a sudden the meaning of one word I understood hopped across to join the meaning of the next word I understood, until there were enough words that meant something to make sense of the sentence. I was overcome with delight. I was still small – not yet four. I ran across the field and up the road to the shop. 'I can read! I can read!' I shouted up at the woman who ran the shop.

From *Are You Somebody?*

BERNARD MAC LAVERTY was born in Belfast in 1942 and lived there until 1975, when he moved to Scotland. He has been a laboratory technician, a mature student, a teacher and writer-in-residence at the University of Aberdeen. After living in Edinburgh and the Isle of Islay, he is now in Glasgow. A member of Aosdána, he has published four collections of short stories: *Secrets* (1977), *A Time to Dance* (1982), *The Great Profundo* (1987) and *Walking the Dog* (1994), and three novels: *Lamb* (1980), *Cal* (1983) and *Grace Notes* (1997). He has also written versions of his fiction for other media – radio plays, television plays and screenplays.

Bernard Mac Laverty

THE SKILL

Your man had such
an Inferiority Complex
he gave Masterclasses in it.

ANTOINE Ó FLATHARTA's stage plays include *Gaeilgeoirí, Imeachtaí na Saoirse, Blood Guilty, An Solas Dearg* and *Silverlands*. His work has been produced by the Abbey, Druid, Team Theatre, the Traverse Theatre in Edinburgh, the Cleveland Playhouse and the Ensemble Studio Theatre in New York. He has had radio plays broadcast by RTÉ, BBC and WDR. Work for television includes *Raic, Grásta i Meiriceá* and *An Bonnán Buí*. His plays have been published by Cló Iar–Chonnachta and New Island Books. A children's book, *The Prairie Train*, has been published by Random House.

Antoine Ó Flatharta

'Cuireann an ghealach cumha orm agus níl fhios agam cén fáth'
Melancholia a tugtar air sin dúirt mise
An fhoghlaim a thoil agus a shaothraigh tú dom
'Níl fhios agam faoi sin' dúirt tusa
'Sílim go b'é an chaoi a gcuireann an ghealach mo mháthair i gcuimhne dom'

BRIAN BOURKE was born in Dublin in 1936 and studied for a time at the National College of Art & Design. In 1953 he moved to London where he attended St Martin's School of Art and Goldsmiths College. Distrustful of formal teaching, he returned to Ireland in 1959 to become a full-time figurative painter and sculptor, often working directly from life.

Brian Bourke

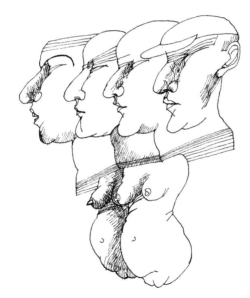

Family portrait.   Brian Bourke

MARY FITZGERALD was born in Dublin in 1956. She studied at the National College of Art & Design in Dublin, the Osaka University of Foreign Languages, Japan and Tama University of Fine Art, Tokyo. She has had many solo shows at the Oliver Dowling Gallery and the Green on Red Gallery in Dublin and exhibited in many parts of the world, including New York, Boston, Brazil, Japan, Brussels and Paris. She lives in Dublin.

Mary FitzGerald

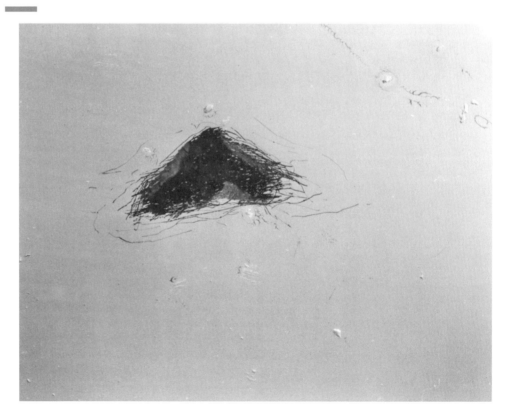

Refuge

MAEVE INGOLDSBY was born in Dublin in 1947, married Bernard McDonagh in 1970 and shortly afterwards gave up her career as a national teacher to be educated by six children. She turned from domestic bliss to writing pantomimes and satirical reviews as Gaeilge. She contributed to the popular radio programme *Only Slaggin'*. Television work includes *Glenroe* and *Fair City*. She wrote her first play for Team in 1990 and since then has written nine plays and one opera for young people and several pantomimes for the Gaiety Theatre. Since 1995 Maeve has been writer-in-residence with Barnstorm (Kilkenny Theatre Arts).

Maeve Ingoldsby

MOTHER'S DAY

3 a.m. –
Never again!
Thirteen hours
Hard labour.
What next time?
Barbed wire down the bloody bed next time!
Don't tell me not to push!
Tell that bruising bullying bundle...of perfection.

3 a.m. – Not again!
Thirteen minutes sleep.
Must be colicky
Insecure
Sickening for something
Demanding
Spoilt rotten
Or maybe just scared in the dark!

3 a.m. – Late again!
Mugged
Drugged.

Dead in a ditch
Drowned in the sea
Drunk on the doorstep!
He'll fall off the window–sill!

Pace the floor
Check the door
Check the clock
Walk the block
No sign
No key
No consideration
What's he doing out at this hour?
Don't ask.
Coffee!
Can't take any more
Pace the floor
Was that the door?
Thank God he's safe!
I'll kill him!

JACK HIGGINS was born in 1929 as Harry Patterson. He lived in Belfast until the age of twelve. He left school at fifteen for such diverse occupations as circus roustabout, truck driver, clerk and university lecturer. *The Eagle has Landed* turned him into an international best-selling thriller writer and his books have since sold over 250 million copies. His novels include *The Violent Enemy*, *A Prayer for the Dying*, *Night of the Fox*, *Angel of Death*, *Drink with the Devil* and *The President's Daughter*. He is a Fellow of the Royal Society of Arts and an expert scuba-diver and marksman. He lives on Jersey in the Channel Islands.

Jack Higgins

BAD POEM BY JACK HIGGINS

Only an Irishman would be writing this on a coffee table in a smart restaurant. I'm honoured to be asked to contribute to the Whoseday venture.

Unlike the Jack Higgins image my readers have I also write bad poetry. At least that's what I call it. Heaney it isn't.

For my novel and film of 'Night of the Fox', I made this a joke. The hero wrote bad poetry so I gave him one of my efforts. I trust it will meet your needs. Here we go.

> The station is ominous at midnight. Hope is a dead
> letter. Time to change trains/or something better. The
> local train now, long since departed. No way of getting
> back to where you started.

In the movie, Sir John Mills started reading it and George Peppard, as the hero, walked in on him and finished it.

There's irony for you. I get letters all the time from all over the world — the book was hugely translated and from readers asking where the poem can be found? They can't imagine Jack Higgins, thriller writer, writing poetry and me with a doctorate!!

SEBASTIAN BARRY was born in Dublin in 1955. He has been a full-time writer since 1977 and has published many books, most recently a novel, *The Whereabouts of Eneas McNulty*. His work for the theatre includes *The Steward of Christendom*, which won many awards, including the Ireland Funds' Literary Award, Lloyds Private Banking Playwright of the Year 1995 and the Christopher Ewart–Biggs Literary Prize. He lives in Wicklow with his wife, Alison, and three children, Merlin, Coral and Tobias.

Sebastian Barry

The Steward of Christendom

"And I would call that the mercy of fathers, when the love that lies in them deeply like the glittering face of a well is betrayed by an emergency, and the child sees at last that he is loved, loved and needed and not to be lived without, and greatly."

SAM McAUGHTRY was born in a loyalist area of north Belfast in 1923. He served in the RAF from 1940 to 1946. His first book, *The Sinking of the Kenbane Head*, was published in 1976. He became familiar to listeners in the Republic of Ireland through his RTÉ radio broadcasts on *Sunday Miscellany* and wrote a column for *The Irish Times* from 1981 to 1987. He has published eight books, including short stories, autobiographies, travel and one novel. He entered Seanad Éireann by way of a by-election in February 1996. He was awarded an honorary doctorate from the National University of Ireland in 1998.

Sam McAughtry

GRAMMA

She was small; her grey hair was pulled back in a bun; her rimless glasses had wool on the bridge, to protect her nose; the bottoms of her eyes were red crescents, and her throat wobbled when she moved her head.

She was a tough old bird: in the 1941 blitz on Belfast a 250–kilo bomb brought the house down around her. She was dug out, dusty, and foul-tempered, and brought to our house nearby. Mother handed her a cup of tea: 'Have you anything else?' Gramma asked. We knew what she meant: 'Try this,' said Mother, handing her a glass of brandy.

She was eighty–three; her face was grimy and she was covered in dust. She examined the brandy: 'I hope you haven't watered it,' she said; then Gramma sank it in one, and that was the blitz dealt with…

From *The Sinking of the Kenbane Head*

MAL STEVENSON was born in Dublin in 1953. He has worked as an art director in advertising all his life, although sometimes it seems longer. During his career he has persuaded people to part with money for drink, travel, cars, petrol, clothes and cosmetics; inveigled them into using banks, building societies, airlines, public transport systems and their heads. The best advice he has ever received is, 'If you're going to lie, do it in Helvetica Bold' – although, of course, it's a typeface he would never, ever use. He is married with two children, neither of whom exhibits any desire to follow in his footsteps, thank God.

Mal Stevenson

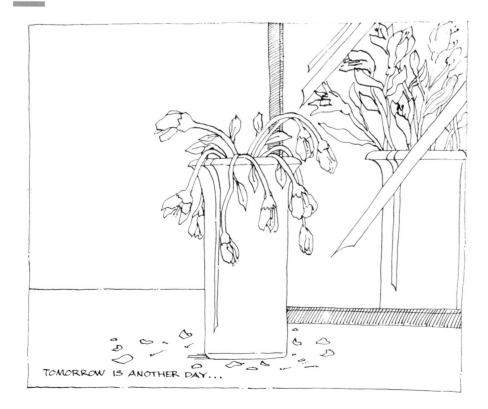

TOMORROW IS ANOTHER DAY...

CHRISTY NOLAN very nearly died of asphyxiation at his birth in 1965 but survived with severe brain damage. Cut off in his own silent world by a mute and paralysed body, he began to write, encouraged by his mother. *Dam–Burst of Dreams* was published in 1981, followed in 1987 by *Under the Eye of the Clock*, which won the Whitbread Book of the Year Award. *Torchlight and Laser Beams* (1988) is a dramatisation of his writings. He has just completed a new novel, *Banyan Tree*.

Christy Nolan

HAEMATIN

Let's look at bleeding–man's wounded,
Lift off each divergent skin,
No longer note birth's life–looks,
Rather, identify characterizing haematin.

Age fourteen years, 2 September 1980

SIMON REILLY was born in Dublin in 1960 and is an artist. After taking a foundation course at Dublin's College of Marketing and Design, he studied for a fine arts BA at the University of Ulster in Belfast. Since graduating, he has exhibited regularly, not just in Ireland but in Italy, Greece, Germany and the UK. His work, expressionistic and tending towards the monumental, is held in many public and private collections. He is currently living in New York.

Simon Reilly

Untitled, oil on canvas, 1988

PEARSE HUTCHINSON was born in Glasgow in 1927 and educated at University College, Dublin. He won the Butler Award for Gaelic Writing in 1969 and was Gregory Fellow in Poetry at the University of Leeds 1971–3. He learned Catalan and Galician in Barcelona and his first book was a volume of translations from the Catalan of Josep Carner, *Poems* (1962). In 1963 Dolmen Press published his first poetry collection, *Tongue without Hands*. Other works include *Faoistin Bhacach* (1968), *The Frost is All Over* (1975) and *The Soul that Kissed the Body* (1990).

Pearse Hutchinson

LEGEND

The Russian word for beautiful
is the Russian word for red.
The Chinese word for silk
is the Chinese word for love.

Beautiful red silk love.

Silk isn't always red –
is love always beautiful?
When you are with me,
yes.

MARTINA GALVIN was born in Dublin in 1964. She studied fine art at the National College of Art & Design, Dublin and the Cardiff Institute of Higher Education. Her work consists mainly of installations, site-specific pieces and sculptural objects, and is concerned with landscape, light and transparency. She shows regularly in Ireland and abroad.

Martina Galvin

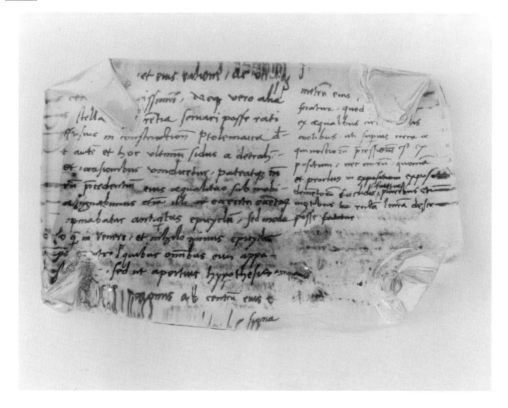

Mercury

MICHAEL WARREN, sculptor, was born in County Wexford in 1950. He completed his studies in Italy at the Brera Academy, Milan. He has made many large-scale outdoor sculptures for sites throughout Europe, America, the West Indies and in the Middle and Far East. His work has received numerous international and national awards. He lives and works at his home and studio outside Gorey, County Wexford. His most recent work, while retaining its philosophic and contemplative character, is clearly moving towards a more immediate, gestural form of expression.

Michael Warren

His Mark

PAUL BRADY, singer/songwriter, was born in 1947 in Strabane, County Tyrone. Leaving University College, Dublin (1967), he joined the folk group The Johnstons and later (1975) Planxty. In 1980 he moved away from folk music, writing and recording the album *Hard Station*. Since then he has written and recorded many popular songs ('Crazy Dreams', 'Nobody Knows', 'The Island', 'Helpless Heart'), periodically revisiting his folk roots with songs like 'The Homes of Donegal'. His songs have been sung in many languages and by many artists from Tina Turner, Cher and Phil Collins to Ireland's Maura O'Connell, Mary Black and Dolores Keane. He now lives in Dublin, where he continues his work as a songwriter, performer and recording artist.

Paul Brady

Shutters on the windows
Chains upon the door
Sleepless nights spent waiting for an answer
Dreams of heaven falling
Panic in the town
Lonely men with fingers on the future

Days of beauty calling
Vanish through a haze
Lost inside some spiral with no ending
Still you bring me loving
Free me with a touch
Lead me out to greet the calm descending

When all is said and done
You are the only one

Follow on,
For the open road is waiting
Like the song,
We will welcome what tomorrow has to bring
Be it fair or stormy weather
Take my hand
And we'll walk the road together
I won't mind
If it turns out that we never find the end
All I ask is that you want me for a friend

13.04.2000

April/Aibreán

THURSDAY / DÉARDAOIN

LOUIS LE BROCQUY was born in Dublin in 1916. In 1938 he abandoned his laboratory work and left Ireland to become a painter. Self–taught, he studied directly in European museums. Returning to Ireland, he co–founded the Irish Exhibition of Living Art in 1943. In 1946 he moved to London, exhibiting widely in the USA and Europe. He won a major international prize at the Venice Biennale of 1956. Two years later he married the painter Anne Madden, and he has since worked in France and Ireland. Exhibitions of le Brocquy's work have been held by museums in Ireland, the UK, the USA, Australia, Spain, Estonia, Japan, Belgium and France, where he was elected *Chevalier de la Légion d'Honneur* and *Officier des Arts et des Lettres*.

Louis le Brocquy

BIRTH DAY OF SAMUEL BECKETT

14.04.2000
April/Aibreán
FRIDAY / AOINE

MARIE HEANEY was born on the shores of Lough Neagh in Ardboe, County Tyrone, the second in a family of six girls and one boy. She trained as a teacher in Belfast where she met her husband, Seamus. After leaving the North in the early seventies, she and her husband moved to County Wicklow with their three children and later settled in Dublin. She has worked as a teacher and journalist and has written for radio and television.

Marie Heaney

The three kings who ruled Ireland at the time were brothers and when Ith arrived at their fort at Aileach they were quarrelling among themselves as to who had seized the greatest part of their father's wealth and lands. Ith was amazed that such a disagreement should take place in a land where there was plenty for all.

'Settle your differences,' he told them. 'There is no need for brothers to quarrel over such things. You should treat each other fairly. Your father has been generous to you and the land you have inherited is beautiful. It has fertile soil and the waters teem with fish. You have grain and honey and salmon to eat. The weather is comfortable. You don't suffer from too much heat or too much cold. This lovely island can give you everything you need.'

From *Over Nine Waves*

RITA ANN HIGGINS was born in Ballybrit, County Galway in 1955. She first began writing in 1982 and has since published five volumes of poetry, including *Goddess on the Mervue Bus*, *Witch in the Bushes* and *Sunny Side Plucked*, which won a Poetry Society Recommendation. In recent years she has held prison workshops in Portlaoise, Limerick, Cork and Loughan House. Her poetry has been anthologised and dramatised and taught at Yale University. She received the Peadar O'Donnell Award in 1989.

Rita Ann Higgins

OUR MOTHERS DIE ON DAYS LIKE THIS

When there isn't a puff
and the walk from the bus stop
to the front door
isn't worth the longed for
out of the question cup of sweet tea
she can never have
because doctor–do–little–or–nothing
told her to her face
it was the sugar or the clay
the choice was hers.

The choice was no choice
he knew it, she knew it.

When the heavy bill on the hall floor
with the final notice prompted her
once and for all she must turn out the lights
her Angelus bell rang and rang.

MICHAEL KANE, born in 1935, came to the forefront of the Irish art world in the mid–1960s. For many years, he has been a vigorous and polemical presence in the art world and has been a primary advocate of the idea that painting can act as a lightning conductor of meaning in human experience. His work is strong, figurative and often uncompromising. His slaughtered landscapes are steeped in grotesque loneliness and often refer to an apocalyptic tension between the sexes. His imagery is infused with biblical and mythological references, played out on the skeletal but familiar Dublin stage.

Michael Kane

Two Figures

FERDIA MAC ANNA was born in Dublin in 1955. He has written two novels, *The Last of the High Kings* and *The Ship Inspector*, as well as a memoir, *Baldhead*. He is married with three children.

Ferdia Mac Anna

The Lord plucks neon from every city on earth
and showers it upon O'Connell Street.
He puts yellows in the Burger joints,
Milky–whites on the Movie Marquees
and pinks and golds inside the amusement arcades.

At O'Connell Bridge I pause
Foot off the pedal
As a young one leads across a sturdy black and white speckled horse
Freckled youngfella perched atop like a king.

From the horse's shaggy rear
hangs a red tail–light
Put there by the Lord
Just for gas.

Song from *Cartoon City*

JACQUELINE O'BRIEN was born in Perth, Australia. Educated at the Loreto Convent in Claremont, she graduated with an honours degree in economics from the University of Western Australia. Always interested in photography, she obtained a diploma in technical photography from Kevin Street College and has published four books. *Great Irish Houses and Castles* and *Dublin: A Grand Tour* were both co-authored with the Hon. Desmond Guinness, and *Ancient Ireland* with Peter Harbison. With Ivor Herbert, she co-authored and photographed *Vincent O'Brien's Great Horses*. Her photographic work has been widely exhibited and she lectures internationally. She is married to well-known racehorse trainer Vincent O'Brien, now retired.

Jacqueline O'Brien

BERNARD FARRELL, playwright, was born in Sandycove, County Dublin. He has written fifteen stage plays and also television drama for RTÉ and BBC. His plays include *I Do Not Like Thee, Doctor Fell* (1979), *Canaries* (1980), *Happy Birthday Dear Alice* (1994) and *Stella by Starlight* (1996). He is a member of Aosdána, a recipient of the Rooney Prize for Irish Literature and was Writer–in–Association with the Abbey Theatre where he has also served on the board. He lives in Greystones, County Wicklow.

Bernard Farrell

JOE: Yes, my name's Joe Fell...no, ju...just Joe.

RITA: Do you like cats?

JOE: Cats? They're alright. I had one once. It died.

RITA: Poor thing. My husband loved cats. We had twelve of them. We called them after the Twelve Apostles. Judas was our favourite. (*pause*) I miss him very much.

JOE: Wh...what happened to him?

RITA: He was savaged by dogs.

JOE: That often happens to cats.

RITA: No, no, Judas is still alive. It was my husband who was savaged by dogs.

From *I Do Not Like Thee, Doctor Fell*

CHRIS AGEE, a poet, was born in 1956 and studied literature at Harvard University. His first collection of poems, *In the New Hampshire Woods* (1992), was shortlisted for the Kingsley Tufts Poetry Prize in the United States. A second book, *The Sierra de Zacatecas*, was published in 1995, and his third, *First Light*, is forthcoming. Of his work, the poet Samuel Menashe has written: 'Agee's poems evoke the original world of the creation, not nature, seen in the light of that first day, which still reaches us.' A former editor of *Poetry Ireland Review*, he edited an acclaimed anthology, *Scar on the Stone: Contemporary Poetry from Bosnia*, which received a 1998 Poetry Book Society Recommendation. He lives in Belfast, where he teaches at the Open University.

Chris Agee

AT SIX

As we sped through Killybegs the radio brought
and now let us pause for the Angelus

But when the car turned uphill, towards a brow's blue cloak,
what I felt most were the bell–rests' crackling half–silences.

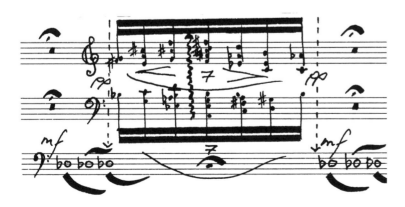

GEORGE J. MITCHELL was appointed to the United States Senate in 1980, and since 1989 he has been the Senate Majority Leader. He served as chairman of the peace negotiations in Northern Ireland. Under his leadership, a historic accord, ending decades of conflict, was agreed by the governments of Ireland and the United Kingdom and the political parties of Northern Ireland. In May 1998 the agreement was overwhelmingly endorsed in referendums by the voters of Ireland, north and south. Senator Mitchell's leadership in Northern Ireland earned him worldwide praise.

George Mitchell

SENATOR GEORGE MITCHELL ON THE GOOD FRIDAY AGREEMENT

I believe it will endure because it's fair and balanced. It stresses the need for mutual respect and tolerance between communities. It's based on the principle that the future of Northern Ireland should be decided by the people of Northern Ireland.

It's important to recognize that the agreement does not, by itself, guarantee a durable peace, political stability, or reconciliation. It makes them possible. But a lot of effort, in good faith, will be required for several years.

I'm hopeful about the future, because the clear and strong desire of the people is for their differences to be resolved by peaceful and democratic means.

They want peace. They want political stability. They want for their children a decent chance in life.

PATRICK HICKEY was born to unfashionably white–skinned parents in India. Educated in a so-called public school in England, he graduated in a thoroughly undistinguished manner from University College, Dublin. He got a scholarship which brought him to Urbino in Italy, where he learned the rudiments of etching and lithography; with the knowledge so gained he started the Graphic Studio in Dublin – which amazingly still flourishes and forms an important facet of the art scene in Ireland. He made over 400 etchings. Patrick Hickey taught and painted but most of the arts – music, modern poetry, history, maths (he gained three marks out of 300 in the 'Leaving') – remained a closed book. He died in October 1998.

Patrick Hickey

IRELAND – FOR TWO VOICES

Voice I
I love this land

Voice II
When you say this land
Do you mean the earth
The rocks, the trees, the farming and birth
Or is it
Composite
Of people's smiles and rages?

Do you include
With leaves and flowers and wetting rain
The interlude
Of Irish people's calm deceit
Their false promises and sweet
Assurance of the unassured?

Do you love too
The dirty streets and unswept mind
The ill–formed pride in being blind

To avarice and man's mean grind?
The profligate and pub–spent wealth
The contract gained by vinous stealth
The darkened teeth and hazard health
The soul's bland death?

Woes now intrude
The easy history of despair
Our progress stopped at lion's lair
Our language, culture, problems dead
The conscience salved by prayer, prayer?

Voice I
I love this land
For fault lies spread
On all who live alone by bread
And silence with their monied tread
The voice of love, and from their knees
Keep charity for charities.
The Irish are no worse than these.

ULICK O'CONNOR was born in Dublin in 1929. A biographer, poet and playwright, he is well known for his biography of Brendan Behan and for his biography of the Irish literary renaissance, *Celtic Dawn*. His play *Execution* broke attendance records at the Peacock Theatre in 1985 and was followed two years later by *A Trinity of Two*, a piece about Edward Carson and his fellow student Oscar Wilde. He has published three books of poetry, as well as an acclaimed translation of Baudelaire's *Les fleurs du mal*.

Ulick O'Connor

THE KISS

She said to me,
'Kiss me specially',
And with her lips on mine
Traced a design
To show the way
Bees on a drowsy day
Suck honey from fuchsia.
How could I be so sure
That the artificer who spun
The golden honeycomb
For her at Erice,
The goddess in exile,
Could ever have gleaned
What I found
When I leaned
To that command?

SÍLE DE VALERA has been a Dáil deputy for Clare since 1987 and in 1997 was appointed Minister for Arts, Heritage, Gaeltacht and the Islands. She was Fianna Fáil front bench spokesperson on Arts, Culture and Heritage 1995–7. Deputy 1977–81 for the then constituency of Dublin Mid-County, she was at that time the youngest member of the Dáil. She is a granddaughter of Eamon de Valera.

Síle de Valera

Grand Canal at Mespil Road (the location of the Department of Arts, Heritage, Gaeltacht and the Islands)

ENDA WYLEY was born in Dublin in 1966 and graduated from Carysfort College with first place in English literature before taking an MA in creative writing from Lancaster University in 1982. Her poems have appeared in various anthologies and magazines in Ireland, England, Australia and the United States. She has taught creative writing in many of the same countries. Her first book of poetry, *Eating Baby Jesus*, was published by Dedalus Press in 1994; the title poem was shortlisted for the British National Poetry Competition two years earlier. Her second book, *Socrates in the Garden*, appeared in 1998.

Enda Wyley

MOTHER

There is a room in my head, to which you often come,
orchid gifts wet with rain in one hand –
in the other, your love
wrapped up in a cut–out newspaper piece
you'd saved just for me
or maybe sealed tight in irregular pots
of home–made orange jam.

You come in and we quickly leave behind
the thorny rose–gardens of our grown–up fights.
I smooth out the creases in your gentle face
I know I've often caused –
while you, keeping me from the shabby coldness
of this outside world,
put the last stitch on my coat.

From *Socrates in the Garden*

MICHAEL FARRELL was born in Kells, County Meath in 1940. He studied in London at St Martin's School of Art and the Colchester College of Art. He has lived, worked and exhibited in Australia and the USA and has also had shows in various European countries. He now divides his time between Dublin and France. He exhibits regularly at the Taylor Galleries in Dublin. A mid–career retrospective of his work was held in the Douglas Hyde Gallery, Dublin in 1979.

Michael Farrell

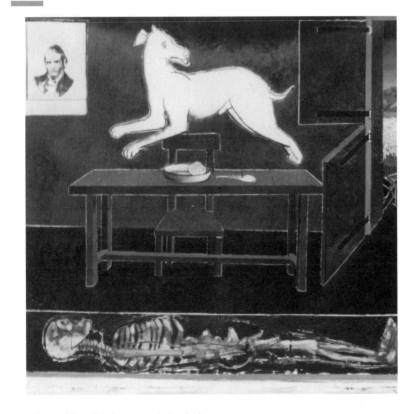

'The Wounded Wonder', The Potato Famine in Ireland 1846–52

JOHN E. MEAGHER was born in Dublin in 1947. Educated at the School of Architecture, College of Technology, Dublin 1966–71 and at Helsinki University of Technology, School of Architecture, Otaniemi, Finland 1971–2. MRIAI, AAI, FRIAI. Director/board member, Rosc 1975–83, Hugh Lane Municipal Gallery of Modern Art 1985–90, Dublin Graphic Studio 1989–92, Black Church Print Studio 1994, and Irish Museum of Modern Art 1989–95. He has travelled extensively in Europe, the USA, Australia and Mexico. Has worked in Dublin, Germany and the USA. Commenced practice with Shane de Blacam in Dublin in 1976. The practice has won numerous national and international competitions and awards and is widely published.

John Meagher

JULIA O'FAOLAIN was brought up in Ireland, took a degree in modern languages at University College, Dublin, then moved to Perugia, Italy and subsequently to France, Los Angeles and London, where she now lives. She has published six novels and three collections of short stories. Her husband is the historian Lauro Martines and her father and mother, Sean and Eileen, were both writers.

Julia O'Faolain

At dusk, Mr Lacy, the keeper, eager for his tea, rang a bell to chase dawdlers home. They were hard to flush out, because the park was dotted with gazebos, and if you hid in one you could always get out later by climbing the tall iron gates. There were places, too, where footholes had been gouged in the perimeter wall.

'I'll have yez summonsed!' Mr Lacy's peaked cap sliced through the dimness. Authority shone from his brass–buttons. 'I'll tell yeer Mammies.' There was a by–law – but what was a by–law? – forbidding anyone to linger in the locked, possibly perilous park.

Mysterious goings–on had been reported. A girl from Teresa Dunne's school had fainted when a man did some momentous thing, appearing to her out of a bush. The *gardaí* had come, but then the matter was hushed up and the girl cowed into discretion.

BARRY CASSIN has worked as a theatre director and actor for over fifty years. He broadcast a number of talk series on RTÉ, including reminiscences of touring days in the 1940s entitled *On the Road*.

Barry Cassin

CHANGED TIMES

A drama company I toured with in the forties turned to variety when times were bad. The piano was dusted off and anyone with a turn to offer, song, skit or recitation, was ordered to brush it up.

Our leading lady offered 'The Trimmings on the Rosary'. The homely verses reminded everyone of the family bowed in prayer, chairs for pews, backsides in the air, the man of the house leading the first decade, his missus the next and following them the children.

Following the Rosary came 'The Trimmings' – an Our Father for Mick who emigrated to the States, a Hail Mary for fine weather for the harvest, a Glory Be for the grace of a happy death.

Popular ballads rarely pass the test of literary excellence but they are matchless expressions of popular sentiment. 'The Trimmings' drew a reassuring picture of close–knit Irish family life cemented by religious belief, and when our actress finished she won rounds of heartfelt applause.

Times change. In a recent production we oldies had to teach the words of the Hail Mary to the young ones. They thought us quaint.

30.04.2000
April/Aibreán
SUNDAY / DOMHNACH

RONALD TALLON was born in Dublin in 1927 and educated at University College, Dublin. He is the senior partner in Scott Tallon Walker Architects. His major works include University Masterplanning, Telefís Éireann Buildings, the Carroll Factory, Dundalk, Bank of Ireland Headquarters, Dublin and the Science Building in Trinity College, Dublin. He was awarded a papal knighthood in 1980 and the triennial Gold Medal for Architecture from the Royal Institute of the Architects of Ireland.

Ronald Tallon

PADDY DEVLIN comes from the Lower Falls in Belfast. He worked in the trade union movement and became involved in radical politics. A member of Belfast City Council for sixteen years, he was also elected to Stormont and later held the post of Minister of Health and Social Services in the power-sharing executive in 1974. His autobiography, *Straight Left*, won the *Irish Times*/Aer Lingus Prize. He was awarded a CBE in the 1999 British New Year's honours list for his contribution to trade unionism.

Paddy Devlin

BILLY MCMULLEN – SHANKILL ROAD PROTESTANT, AND LABOUR LIBERAL

At the Poor Law elections in 1927, to the Board of Guardians, the Labour movement, breaking the Unionist stranglehold, elected two of its most notable and aggressive representatives, Jack Beattie and William McMullen. Both were trade union leaders, and fierce critics of the Poor Law system.

At their first meeting the Chairman refused Beattie the right of reply to a motion which Beattie had moved. Beattie, a blacksmith by trade, refused physically to let anyone else speak. He was backed up by McMullen, no less determined and formidable a figure. The meeting was quickly brought to an end. Police were present at each meeting afterwards...

Extract from *Yes, We Have No Bananas: Outdoor Relief in Belfast, 1920–30*

BRIAN MAGUIRE was born in Bray, County Wicklow in 1951. He began painting in 1980 and over the past two decades has shown his paintings extensively in Ireland, Holland and the USA. Working on long-term projects with different communities (including prisoners), he has developed social critical works using video and photography together with drawing and painting. Issues of class dominate his work, as do language, emotion, mood and expression. He is represented by the Kerlin Gallery, Dublin.

Brian Maguire

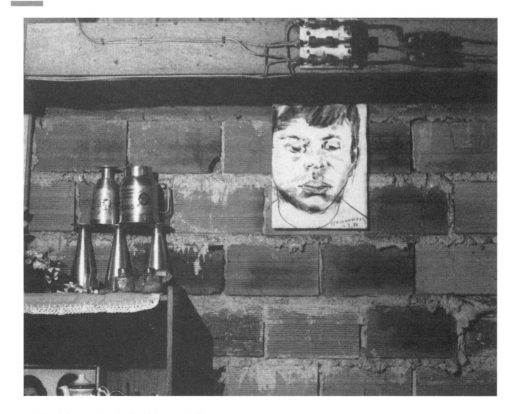

Ferdinand, from a project developed in São Paulo in 1998

NUALA NÍ DHOMHNAILL was born in England in 1952 to Irish–speaking parents, and grew up in the Dingle Gaeltacht and County Tipperary. She attended University College, Cork where she became involved with the 'INNTI' school of poets. She is the author of six volumes of poetry, including *Féar Suaithinseach* (1984), *Pharaoh's Daughter* (1990), *Feis* (1991) and *The Astrakhan Cloak* (1992). She is a member of Aosdána and the recipient of the 1988 O'Shaughnessy Award for Poetry and the 1991 American Ireland Fund Literary Award. She lives in Dublin.

Nuala Ní Dhomhnaill

ÉINÍN BÍDEACH

Léimeann éinín bídeach
ar chraobh uachtair an chrainn ghiúise
ar aghaidh na fuinneoige os mo chomhair.
Ní féidir liom a aithint
óna thoirt nó óna ghluaiseacht
an dreoilín é nó meantán
is tá léas na gréine am' dhalladh
ar a dhath.

Níl oiread na frí ann
ag luascadh ar an gcraobh uachtair.
Ní troimide é mo chroí
ag féachaint air i mbarr an chrainn ghiúise.

ENDA McDONAGH, born in May 1930, is a priest of the archdiocese of Tuam and was Professor of Moral Theology in Maynooth from 1958 to 1995. He has been a visiting professor and lecturer in universities in the UK, the USA, France, Belgium, Germany, Australia, Africa and Asia and has worked with HIV–AIDS education groups in Africa and Asia. He was President of the Association for North-South Relations from 1988 to 1991. A founder member of *CÉIDE: A Journal from the Margins* in 1997, he is consultant editor to *The Furrow*. He has published twenty books on theology and related subjects.

Enda McDonagh

THE RISKS OF CREATION

The chasm between the blank sheet and the completed paragraph hypnotises. Like Yeats's 'long–legged fly upon the stream [The] mind moves upon silence.' Still no life, no word. The frustration and the achievement in the waiting, punctuated by the occasional fresh, impatient cast – to no bite, to no where. Paragraph, poem and prayer are cast upon the waters in vain. The waiting becomes ominous, despairing, 'My word, my word, why have you forsaken me?' As if the writer were the first, not the parent, not the God. Until the torrent is loosed. Creation and procreation. World and word. Cherub and child. And then the new fears and the new frustrations. Will it be alright? Who will recognise it, review it, care for it? Can one really let it go just to become itself?

The risks of God and mother and artist. And the certainty of failure too. Overcome only in new creation, recurring – yet at risk. Frustrated, perhaps crucified and finally prevailing. Even the lowliest in the Creator's image has to share the risks, and trust in the Spirit hovering over the waters in her disguise of 'long–legged fly upon the stream'.

DILLIE KEANE was born in Portsmouth, the daughter of Dr Francis Keane of Ballina, County Mayo and Miriam Slattery of Tralee, County Kerry. She is a songwriter, cabaret performer, actress, sometime scribbler of short journalistic pieces and professional blonde *d'un certain âge*. She founded the cabaret act Fascinating Aida in 1983 and hasn't been able to quit since. Her favourite hobbies include gardening, tapestry, carousing and being an aunt.

Dillie Keane

SEW ON A SEQUIN, it's sure to cheer you up;
SEW ON A SEQUIN when you've drained life's bitter cup;
Sequins will brighten up the oldest shabby dress;
Sequins are guaranteed to bring you happiness.
Oh a sequin is such a little thing,
But sure as hell, you know that it'll bring
You through when you've got writer's block;
Yes, it's easier to smile
As you face each fearful trial
When you've got a bit of heaven on your frock.

From the Fascinating Aida song 'Sew on a Sequin'

BERNADETTE GREEVY was born in Dublin. She has performed on all five continents in a career that has encompassed all aspects of musical expression, from oratorio to opera and from recital to the great orchestral repertoire. She holds honorary doctorates of music from the National University of Ireland and Trinity College, Dublin, and in 1996 was appointed the first artist–in–residence at the Dublin Institute of Technology and Faculty of Applied Arts. Her annual masterclasses at the IMMA at the Royal Hospital in Kilmainham are an important feature of Dublin cultural life.

Bernadette Greevy

Picture me, a young singer in cold–war Prague, on my way to rehearse in St Vitus's Cathedral with a driver who mistook me for a tourist and was giving me the grand tour. Eventually I got through to him by waving my music score and a picture of the cathedral and he dropped me outside the building. I could hear the choir rehearsing as I raced around finding every door bolted and barred. Suddenly I saw a little monk who beckoned to me to follow him, which I did without fear, only intense relief that I was at last inside the cathedral, albeit down in the ancient crypt. My rescuer never spoke but used graceful sign language pointing out various treasures to me. He seemed to sense my anxiety because he then led me to an ascending stone staircase, and I emerged through a kind of trapdoor in the middle of the nave. When I described my adventure to the Czech concert authorities, they scoffed at my story and stated categorically there were no monks whatever working at this cathedral in any capacity. Thus ends my story of a gentle ghost who helped me in Prague and for whom I still pray after all these years.

NANCY WYNNE–JONES was born in Wales in 1922. She studied in London with Peter Lenyon in St Ives, Cornwall. From 1962 she exhibited successfully with the New Vision Centre in London, and with various galleries in Italy and Germany. She married the sculptor Conor Fallon in 1966, moved to Kinsale, County Cork in 1972 and to Ballinaclash, County Wicklow in 1987. Primarily a landscape painter, in 1994 she was awarded a fellowship by the Ballinglen Arts Foundation to work for a period in Mayo. She exhibits with Taylor Galleries, Dublin, is an honorary RHA and a member of Aosdána.

Nancy Wynne–Jones

VINCENT WOODS, playwright and poet, was born in County Leitrim in 1960. His work for theatre includes *At the Black Pig's Dyke* and *Song of the Yellow Bittern*, as well as a number of plays for children. He has been writer-in-residence with Mayo County Council and now lives in County Sligo.

Vincent Woods

Bruce Chatwin

We dream ourselves:
   Antique eggs,
Blue porcelain, a doctor
   with a silver syringe

We dream our tracks:
   Green deserts,
Trees of sand, a child
   waving a red Kalashnikov

We dream our dreams:
   Jade houses,
Black horizons, a woman
   cradling a lizard

We dream our past:
   Tibetan butterflies,
Chinese greatcoats, a lover
   vowing white ebony

We dream our knowledge:
   Dictionaries,
A Taoist scholar, a crocus
   painting an orchid

We dream our deaths:
   Silk hands,
Bright flames, a river
   of peach petals floating

From *The Colour of Language*

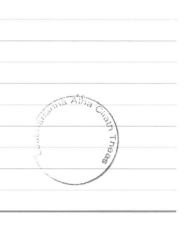

WILLIAM TREVOR, short-story writer and
novelist, was born in Mitchelstown,
County Cork and educated at St Columba's
College and Trinity College, Dublin.

William Trevor

The fathers of the bride and bridegroom, Mr Atty and Mr Cornish, were talking about greyhounds, keeping close to the bar. They shared a feeling of unease, caused by being in the lounge-bar of Swanton's, with women present, on a Saturday morning. 'Bring us two more big ones,' Mr Cornish requested of Kevin, a youth behind the bar, hoping that this addition to his consumption of whiskey would relax matters. They wore white carnations in the button-holes of their suits, and stiff white collars which were reddening their necks. Unknown to one another, they shared the same thought: a wish that the bride and groom would soon decide to bring the occasion to an end by going to prepare themselves for their journey to Cork on the half-one bus. Mr Atty and Mr Cornish, bald-headed men of fifty-three and fifty-five, had it in mind to spend the remainder of the day in Swanton's lounge-bar, celebrating in their particular way the union of their children.

From *Teresa's Wedding*

BONO (born Paul David Hewson in Dublin 1960) received his nom de guerre, aged fourteen, from his lifelong friend, the painter Guggi. As the millennium closes, he considers his pop group U2, featuring The Edge (guitar), Adam Clayton (bass) and Larry Mullen Jnr (drums), to be 'the best little combo on the planet'. In certain quarters his name is pronounced Beau–no, which is a no–no; the lead singer consoles himself with the Latin cadence Bonn–o and lives between Dublin and France with his two daughters, Jordan and Eve, and the love of his life, Ali, whom he began courting the same month he joined U2...November 1976.

Bono

SHOWTIME

Before you come out, it's like you're underwater, then the low hum, the seeping din of the outside world is drowned out by the rhythm of your own pulse, which increases its tempo until your head is a jungle and your heart is at a rave, where all you hear is the bass drum...blackness but you're just around a corner from an arc of lights so bright you should wear a welder's hood...the big entrance...you'll be out in a second, a minute, an hour...you feel sick, your eyes are screwed up but it's a push, a rush you will try for the rest of your life to recreate. The screams are what you're about...not so much freedom, more like...I'm here, I'm alive, who organised this event? Well, the tenth of May is my birth day...and on my birthday, I think of my mother.

GAVIN FRIDAY was born in Dublin in 1959. He survived a Christian Brothers' education to become a singer, composer and painter. His debut exhibition of paintings, *I Didn't Come Up the Liffey in a Bubble*, was in 1988. He was a founder member of the avant-garde punk group The Virgin Prunes, and since 1988 has composed and performed with Maurice Seezer. His film scores include *In the Name of the Father* and *The Boxer*.

Gavin Friday

GERARD MANNIX FLYNN was born and reared in Dublin. His first play, *The Liberty Suit*, co-written with Peter Sheridan, was performed in the Olympia (1977) and in the Royal Court in London (1978). A novel, *Nothing to Say*, followed in 1984. Since then he has written and performed a one-man piece, *Talking to the Wall*, which took a Fringe First award in Edinburgh in 1997. He is currently working on the second part of the play and on other projects.

Gerard Mannix Flynn

When my father made his exit from my mother's vagina after ejaculation, I, me, was on my way. For nine months I eclipsed in my watery cave, evolving non–stop, growing cell by cell, forming in unity within the walls of my universe. I lay suspended, secure. Every moment was new, for the first time, the very first time. The faint sound of something in the far–off distance, yet ever so near. Bum–bum, bum–bum. Signals, coded messages, my first friend. The heart. Strong, pumping, never–fading, calling me out to play. It was time, that time had come. I turned ever so gracefully in my mother's womb. Head first, nose down, I began my descent, my disconnecting began. Nature's labour locked us both in unity and combat with life's turbulent forces. 'No smoking please.' 'Fasten your safety belts.' 'Your life vests are under your seats.' 'We are coming in to land. Arrival time any moment now.'

From *Talking to the Wall*

PERRY OGDEN began taking photographs in 1979 for his school magazine. His subjects included Andy Warhol and Diana Vreeland. Three years later he turned professional, with studios in London and New York. In 1984 a photo assignment brought him to Ireland, where he now lives. He has directed television commercials and documentaries, designed theatre shows (notably Mannix Flynn's *Talking to the Wall*), and shot fashion spreads and portrait editorials. His book *Pony Kids* documents Dublin's urban horse-owners. He has a daughter, Violet.

Perry Ogden

SEAMUS HEANEY was born in County Derry in 1939 and educated at St Columb's College, Derry and Queen's University, Belfast. His first book of poems, *Death of a Naturalist*, was published in 1966. He has published nine volumes of poetry since then. His translations include *Sweeney Astray* and, from the Polish, with Stanislaw Baranczak, Jan Kechanowski's *Laments*. In 1989 he became Professor of Poetry at Oxford and in 1995 he was awarded the Nobel Prize for Literature.

Seamus Heaney

HYGEIA

At Epidaurus I pulled and posted grass
To one going in to chemotherapy
And one who had come through. I didn't want
To leave the place or link up with the others.
It was mid–day, mid–May, pre–tourist sunlight
In the precincts of the temple of Asclepius

Where pilgrims saw the healing god in dreams.
I wanted nothing more than to lie down
Under the hogweed, under the seeded grass
And to be visited in the very eye of the day
By Hygeia, his daughter, her name still clarifying
The haven of light she was, the undarkening door.

Liz McManus is a politician and an award-winning writer of fiction. She qualified as an architect from University College, Dublin. In 1992 she was elected to Dáil Éireann as a member of the Democratic Left party. In 1997 she was its spokesperson on Justice, Health and Arts & Culture and in 1999 she was appointed the Labour Party's spokesperson on Health. She has written extensively as a journalist. In 1981 she won the *Irish Press/Hennessy* Award for New Irish Writing and she went on to win the Irish PEN Award and Listowel Short Story Award. Her first novel, *Acts of Subversion*, was published in 1991. She is married with four children.

Liz McManus

Once you become a subversive you are never alone. From that moment on, a surveillance apparatus billows in your wake. No matter what you do or where you go, you carry an impression of men watching. You make allowances for the telephoto lens, the hidden tape recorder, the telephone tap. Just in case.

Sometimes you suspect that they have tunnelled an entry into your brain and are on the inside, taking everything down in triplicate.

From *Acts of Subversion*

BARBARA CULLEN, a painter, was born in Dublin in 1954. She studied fine art at the National College of Art & Design as a mature student, qualifying with a first-class honours degree in fine art painting in 1990. She has exhibited in Dublin, Waterford, Belfast and Quebec. In 1997 she worked as an artist-in-residence in NTDI, Navan on the 'Art Reach 2' programme for people with disabilities, initiated by Rehab. Barbara worked on a project in St Brendan's Hospital with Professor Ivor Browne which led to a series of paintings based on Dante's *Divine Comedy, Purgatory, Vol. II,* which will be on permanent exhibition in Madras, India. She lives and works in Dublin.

Barbara Cullen

Leaving 1998 – for Harry, who died at the Hospice on 17 May 1998

SEÁN SHANAHAN is an artist who was born in Dublin in 1960 and now lives and works in Sartirana, near Milan. He attended both the Heatherley School of Fine Art and the Croydon College of Art & Design in London and has exhibited in either solo or group shows every year since 1982. His stripped–back and abstract pictures, usually oil paint on MDF or on sheets of steel, have been seen in Milan, Amsterdam, Atlanta, Paris, Cologne and Dublin, where he is represented by the Kerlin Gallery.

Seán Shanahan

——

'...Now one feels blithe as a swimmer calmly
borne by celestial waters,
And then, as a diver into a secret world,
lost in subterranean currents.

Hence

Arduously sought expressions, hitherto evasive, hidden,
will be like stray fishes out of the ocean
bottom to emerge on the angler's hook;
...'

Lu Chi

From *Meditation Before Writing*

JOHN ENNIS was born in County
Westmeath in 1944. Having studied at
University College, Cork, University
College, Dublin and Maynooth, he is now
head of the School of Humanities at the
Waterford Institute of Technology. His first
collection, *Night on Hibernia*, won the
Patrick Kavanagh Award. A winner at the
Listowel Writers' Week Open Poetry
Competition ten times, in 1996 he was
presented with the Irish–American
Cultural Institute Award. His *Selected Poems*
appeared in 1996.

John Ennis

And each May, beneath greening canopies, there's that other firmament,
I remember my first astonishment at bluebells and their blue aura –

How they filled with an inviolable cadence the noonday woodside,
How the bees dared long, for the nectar, into their low gloom,
How it was sacrilege to march, or doubt, across that young tide,
How their short translucence sang out with voices for our time.

From 'Against the Wood'

JOHN O'DONOHUE was born in the Burren in County Clare. He was awarded a Ph.D. in philosophical theology from the University of Tübingen in 1990. His book on the philosophy of Hegel, *Person als Vermittlung*, was published in Germany in 1993 and his book of poems *Echoes of Memory* was published in 1994 and reprinted in 1997. His international bestseller *Anam-Čara: Spiritual Wisdom from the Celtic World* was published in 1997. His new bestseller *Eternal Echoes: Exploring our Hunger to Belong* was published in 1998. He is writing a post-doctoral thesis on the philosophy and mysticism of Meister Eckhart. He lives in the Conamara Gaeltacht.

John O'Donohue

THE OCEAN WIND

Through its mouth at Gleann Corráin, the rising
ocean can see into Fermoyle valley
that never moves from the absence opened
by the cut of its glacier parent.
With wind the ocean bends each lone blackthorn
to a dark sickle facing the mountain.

The wind would like to breathe its crystal breath
into the mind of the mountain's darkness
and riddle the certainty of its stone;
it lashes the cliffs with doubt, its sand lips
deepen the question each crevice opens
and sows hoards of fern seed in the scailps.

There is no satisfaction for the wind.
To blow through doors and windows of ruins
only reminds it how empty it is.
Above Caherbeanna's ruined village
the wind waits all year for the Garraí Clé
to fill with its tribe of golden corn.

Weary from the ghost geometry of the fog
and heaping itself blindly against walls,
the wind unfolds its heart in yellow dance,
only now in circles, spirals and waves
of corn can the wind see itself, swift
as the glance of moonlight on breaking tide.

POLLY DEVLIN was born in 1941 in County Tyrone. In 1964 she won the *Vogue* magazine talent contest and became a journalist. She has written widely for newspapers and magazines, including *The Sunday Times* and *Image* magazine, about her own life and her family. In 1983 she published a vivid memoir of her childhood, *All of Us There*. A collection of her articles for *Image* was published in 1998.

Polly Devlin

DAISY

After you'd gone I found the black initialled album,
The name, the place, the year, gilded onto the cover,
Meticulous and perfect, a cipher for a lover.

In other albums down the years I've done the same.
As if by carving in the time and setting out the names
I'd nail life down. My own spring flower; this book's a frame.

Life's widening up for you, mine's narrowing down.
I open up your book and trace where you have been.
Trajectories beyond me, familiar sight unseen.

You never know how much I love you;
I never know myself until you go
And open up your album where I look, you show.

MARY BECKETT was born in Belfast in 1926. While teaching in the Ardoyne, she wrote stories which were read on BBC radio or published in *The Bell*. When she married and moved to Dublin, she stopped writing until her children were reared. She is the author of two collections of stories, *A Belfast Woman* and *A Literary Woman*, and a novel about Belfast, *Give Them Stones*. She has also published children's stories: *Orla was Six, Orla at School, A Family Tree* and *Hannah, or Pink Balloons*.

Mary Beckett

The man said 'Do you know Belfast has the most beautiful sunsets in the whole world? And do you know why? It's because of all the smoke and dirt and dust and pollution. And it seems to me,' he said, 'it seems to me that if the dirt and dust and smoke and pollution of Belfast can make a sky like that, then there's hope for all of us.' He nodded and winked and touched his hat and went off and I went in and sat down at the table. And thinking of it I started to laugh, for it's true. There is hope for all of us. Well, anyway, if you don't die you live through it, day in, day out.

From *A Belfast Woman*

PATRICK GRAHAM was born in 1943. He has exhibited in Ireland and internationally since 1966 and is represented in major public and private collections at home and abroad. He is a member of Aosdána.

Patrick Graham

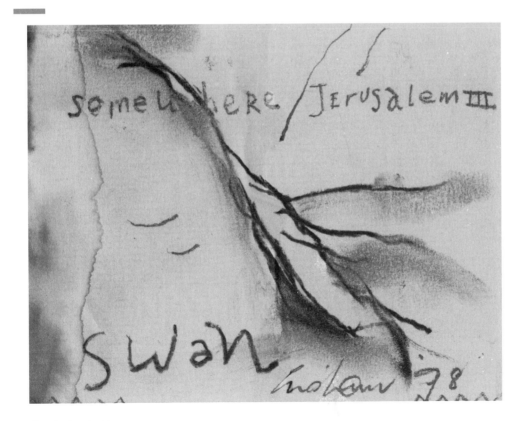

Somewhere Jerusalem (3)

THOMAS MCCARTHY was born in
Cappoquin, County Waterford in 1954, and
educated at University College, Cork and
the University of Iowa. He won the Patrick
Kavanagh Award in 1977, and the Annual
Literary Award of the American–Irish
Foundation in 1984. He has published five
collections of poetry, including *The Lost
Province* (1977), and two novels. His latest
book is a collection of essays, *Gardens of
Remembrance* (1998). A former editor of
Poetry Ireland Review, he is currently editor
of *The Cork Review*.

Thomas McCarthy

Mr Nathaniel Murphy Considers

His Wife

For me your coolness is flamboyant as Scarlatti.
The sinfonia is yours
When you pass before me in a sedan chair
On your way to Bolster's Bookshop.
Your voice, when it reaches me
Across the two hundred and eighty four
   travertine
Columns, is piano and forte, loud and soft:
Loud only with the effects of Orfeo,
Soft only with the depth of a loved word.
On the first day I followed your voice
Over the North Gate Bridge.
That noon I became more than a butter
   merchant.
The hour waved farewell to your madrigal.

I was made whole by your glide past,
Such gestures and strength. In you the Baroque
Of our city became bearable.
Dogs may bark at the lepers in Tivoli Wood,
Labourers shout from Mr Beale's garden;
But you slot into the sedan of each tasselled year.
Your birthday, again. Years Horatian and good.

PATRICK HALL, the painter, was born in County Tipperary and lived abroad until 1974. He moved to Dublin until 1997 and now lives in County Sligo. His work can be seen in the Irish Museum of Modern Art, the Hugh Lane Municipal Gallery of Modern Art and other public collections. He is a member of Aosdána.

Patrick Hall

Moth

DESMOND FENNELL was born in Belfast. He studied history, economics and languages at University College, Dublin. He has lived and worked in Spain, Sweden and the United States. From 1976 to 1982 he taught history and politics at University College, Galway and from 1982 to 1993 English writing at the Dublin Institute of Technology. His books include *The State of the Nation: Ireland since the 1960s* (1983), *A Connacht Journey* (1987) and *Heresy: The Battle of Ideas in Modern Ireland* (1993).

Desmond Fennell

THE POSTWESTERN WEST

A civilisation is, essentially, a hierarchical set of rules about right behaviour which is subscribed to by rulers and ruled throughout an extensive territory for a long time. It lasts because it makes sense. In recent decades the West, led by the rulers of the USA, has rejected many characteristic rules of western civilisation and replaced them with new rules. Not merely 'postmodern', the present age is postwestern. The new collection of rules is chaotic, does not make sense. So people find sense, mainly, in the increase of money and of the things that this provides. Dependence for sense on something that will end makes the Ameropean system fragile. To preserve the essence of the life we have, when the money stops increasing, we must transform the senseless system into a civilisation: *organise its rules and values as a coherent hierarchy, and win authority and acceptance for this new sense.*

From *La Sfida della Civiltà Postoccidentale*, Rome, 1998

ANNE ENRIGHT was born in Earlsfort
Terrace, Dublin, on the first day of the
Second Vatican Council. She grew up in the
suburbs of Dublin. She has written two
books about all this, *The Portable Virgin* and
The Wig My Father Wore.

Anne Enright

THE HUNCHBACK WHO TOOK MY PICTURE

The hunchback who took my picture would not like me
to call him 'the hunchback who took my picture'
and he is right.

Though there is something old fashioned
about the hunch behind the lens,
    like the cloth they used to crouch under
to get a decent black, the five-legged thing with one eye
that asked my grandmother not to smile.

'You can smile,' he says. 'If you like,'
and I look at him through the lens, with a look
that is just myself.

'Too easy. Too easy,' says Raymond, the hunch man,
who never checks over his shoulder,
in the mirror, or in the street.

PETER REDDY was born in Dublin in 1971. He has always worked as a graphic designer and runs his own design company, Paintbox. He has won numerous international awards and is responsible for many well-known identities, including the Red Box, the Kitchen, the Mean Fiddler, Influx Records and Hobo clothing (for which he also designed the interior of the shop). He operates his own clothing label – Beatnik – which sells in Ireland, the UK and Europe.

Peter Reddy

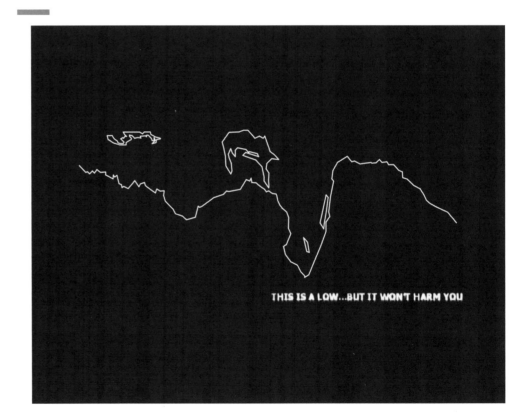

THIS IS A LOW...BUT IT WON'T HARM YOU

Maeve Binchy is a novelist and *Irish Times* columnist. Brought up in Dalkey, County Dublin, the eldest of four, she is married to the writer Gordon Snell. Her books have been translated into many languages and adapted as films and for television.

Maeve Binchy

I have always loved birthdays, everyone's birthdays, not just my own. I get excited when I see lists of famous people in the papers, some jazz singer or politician that I thought was forty turns out to be eighty. Someone I thought was dead for thirty years appears to be sixty-one. I love birthdays in restaurants even when I don't know the people, my heart soars when a cake comes out and someone's face lights up.

It comes from a very celebratory childhood where much was made of all birthdays in the house, people, cats, the tortoise and even the hens.

Once the month of May begins I still feel that it's not long now till my birthday. And sometimes strangers send me a card. It's childish, self-centred but basically harmless. And it's 28 May in case you were wondering.

BRIAN KENNEDY was born in Belfast. His first album, *The Great War of Words*, in 1990 introduced the world to his beautiful voice. By 1996 and his second solo album, *A Better Man*, his career had taken off and the album remained at the top of the Irish charts for many weeks. He has collaborated with many performers, including Van Morrison, with whom he toured and recorded. He can be heard on Morrison recordings 'A Night in San Francisco', 'Days Like This' and 'The Healing Game'. In 1996 he and Morrison sang for President Clinton in Belfast, an event that was televised worldwide.

Brian Kennedy

GALWAY SWANS

We're like those two swans you and me
Skimming over the surface of each other's lives
Staring straight ahead like we own the place
Like we couldn't possibly need anything
Let alone each other
Ready to strike if another curious soul gets too
    close for comfort
The perfect image for a matchbox cover
A beautiful, dangerous, indifferent weapon

At night we're like two stubborn clouds you
    and me
Far too good to be seen with the rest of the sky,
Heaven forbid, preferring the silent approval
    of the lough
Sure we don't even trust the sunset, well I
mean it can't be free, can it?
It must secretly expect something in return,

some kind of emotional debt outstanding
Nevertheless we're delighted by the excuse to
exile our heads beneath our wings for a few
hours of self imposed nothing
Like it was an afterthought

Yes, we're like those swans you and me
Those Galway swans, the ones last summer
that swam past the bread we threw from the
    bridge
Slowing only to look up at us briefly like we
    were mad,
As if to say 'Sure youse don't even know how to
look after yourselves, never mind anybody else.'

Biddy Jenkinson

Is le linn do Bhiddy Jenkinson agus Mireille Harnett a bheith ag rognú ainmneacha dá gcoileáin nua a tháinig an t–iarratas uaibh. Bichon Frisé atá ag Mireille. Ciarraíoch Mallaithe ag Biddy. Bhí beartaithe againn ainmneacha fiannaíochta a thabhairt orthu agus chuige sin bhí Laoithe na Féinne ar an mbord againn. Tá breis is céad cú luaite ansin. Bheartaíomar an gearrliosta a chur chugaibh – i nGaeilge agus i bhFraincis – lenár dea mhéin: Dordán–Grogneur. Mac an Truim–Fils de Surreau. Rith fada–Gallopeur. Caol–Maigrelet. Glórán–Aboyeur. Lom Bhall–Membre nu. Faraire–Gardien. Geall–Pari. An Cú Crón–Noireau. Steallaire–Pisseur. Marú na gCat–Tueur de Chat Dearg–Ruquet.

Céard a thugamar orthu ag deireadh? Fifi agus Púca.

JOHN BRENDAN KEANE was born in Listowel, County Kerry in 1928, where he has lived ever since, save for a two–year period spent in England. He owns a public house in Listowel and is regarded as the central character in the literary scene in County Kerry. His first play, *Sive* (1959), quickly established him as a new voice for the people. *The Field* (1965) is his most famous work and was filmed by Jim Sheridan and Noel Pearson in 1990. *Big Maggie* (1969) has been a perennial in Dublin theatre. Keane's numerous non–dramatic writings include *Letters of a Successful TD* (1967) and *The Bodhran Makers* (1986).

John B. Keane

Certainty

John B. Keane

This is the place I was told.
See the tall grass lie low.
They rested here and made bold.
Now for a certainty I know.

Take note of the bluebell broken,
The fern mangled and dead
And look at this for a token!
Here's a hair from her head

MERV GRIFFIN is the television genie who for twenty-four years hosted *The Merv Griffin Show*, one of America's most famous talkshows. He created American television's most popular gameshows, *Wheel of Fortune* and *Jeopardy!*, and is now chairman of the Griffin Group, which runs hotels (including St Clerans, near Galway), a television and film company, an events company and horseracing. Of Irish descent, he has been honoured by the American Ireland Fund.

Merv Griffin

Some years back, I interviewed the legendary American film director John Huston at this beautiful and historic estate, St Clerans. Of pure Irish ancestry myself, I envied him his magical manor. During that long-ago visit, the house rang with laughter from famous visitors, local gentry, and a delightful little girl named Anjelica who grew up to be an Oscar-winning actress.

When I learned in 1997 that St Clerans needed a new owner, I immediately knew – with the fabled Irish 'second sight' – that this house was part of my destiny. In Hollywood, I told Anjelica Huston how happy I was to open this special world to another delightful little girl, my granddaughter Farah Griffin, as well as the guests of my most personally meaningful Merv Griffin Hotel. Still as magical as the day I first saw it more than three decades ago, it opened officially on 1 June 1998.

PATRICIA SCANLAN's first novel, *City Girl*, was published in 1990, followed by *Apartment 3B, Finishing Touches, City Woman, Foreign Affairs, Promises Promises* and *Mirror Mirror*. She has also written adult literacy books. *The Bold Bad Girl* was her first children's book. She lives in Dublin.

Patricia Scanlan

—

Dear Reader,

Every time I write a novel I always insert a little epigram that will give a flavour of the book. I'm always on the lookout for something that touches me, or makes me laugh, or is perfectly suited to one or more of my characters. My favourite epigram is the one that I chose for *City Woman*. It needs no explanation. It is simple, profound and a good code to live by. It means a lot to me.

There is a destiny that makes us brothers.
None goes his way alone.
All that we put into the lives of others
Comes back into our own.

Warmest Wishes,

Patricia Scanlan.

BARRY DEVLIN was born and brought up in County Tyrone. He moved south in the late sixties and started the Celtic rock band Horslips in 1971. After ten years of touring, which wasn't actually Hell, he and the other members split and got on with part two. Part two consists, these days, of screenwriting and spending a lot of time with his wife, Caroline, and his monosyllables, Paul, Jack and Kate.

Barry Devlin

12 B. INT. THE BARN LOFT ON THE O'NEILLS' FARM. DAY.

He peers into the dusty loft. He blinks as his eyes grow accustomed to the dim interior, the light from outside burnishing the edges of things, old saddles and harnesses, a turnip mangle, a row of wooden barrels for grain. He steps inside, closes the half door behind him, pushes up a trapdoor and climbs into the hayloft above. Up here in the silent rafters, the mote–thick air hisses and burns. This is his private place. He pulls back a bale from the solid stack and enters his hide. Lying on his stomach, zebra striped by the bright sunlight from a slatted window, he surveys his secret world. There are books here, the Eagle Annual, the Wonder Book for Boys and Biggles. There is a cut–away of Dan Dare's craft Anastasia pinned to a broken board and a mirror and a Five Boys Club membership card and a gas mask. He sucks his thumb, cups his chin on his hands, pulls out a small red devotional pamphlet. It says, simply, 'Growing Up' and under that, 'A Guide for Teenage Boys' and at the bottom 'By Father William Nash, SJ'. He begins to read. After a moment he pauses, picks up the mirror and examines his upper lip intently. Relieved, he puts down the mirror and continues reading. Then, rolling over on his back, he sucks his thumb and stares at the roof.

Cut to...

From *All Things Bright and Beautiful*

MARSHA HUNT was commissioned to write her autobiography at age thirty–nine, when she had already been hailed as a sixties icon, had hit records, starred on stage and screen, been a model and a radio presenter and a member of the Royal National Theatre and the Royal Shakespeare Company. She has since written five books, including the internationally acclaimed *Joy* and *Repossessing Ernestine*. Her most recent novel, *Like Venus Fading*, was written from her home in the Wicklow Mountains. Marsha Hunt is founder/director of the SAGA Prize, a literary competition to encourage British– and Irish–born black novelists.

Marsha Hunt

Isabel Gilsenan was really enjoying that cigarette. Slipping the filtered tip between her dry, unpainted lips, she savoured each long drag. It was thrilling to see she could still draw such pleasure from one measly Silk Cut. Propped up by six pillows which were as snow white as her hair, she looked vibrant, cheeky even, sitting in her hospice bed. Only four days earlier when she'd been at St Vincent's and received the medical results explaining why her stomach had been bloated, she was also smoking a cigarette and said matter–of–factly, 'I'll have to go to Harold's Cross.' Like she was dying and there was going to be a bed at Our Lady's Hospice which was ready and waiting.

She was given the lovely corner room with windows on two sides which let the May sun stream in. Family and friends came and went at will and nobody complained about Isabel smoking. She reminded us to live each day like there will be no other.

MELANIE LE BROCQUY was born in Dublin in 1919 and studied at the National College of Art & Design, Dublin and the École des Beaux Arts, Geneva. A sculptor, her work has been purchased by the Arts Council, the Corporation of Dublin, Allied Irish Bank and Aer Rianta. It is represented in the Hugh Lane Municipal Gallery of Modern Art, Dublin, the National Self-Portrait Collection, Limerick, Trinity College, Dublin, the American College, Dublin and Magdalen College, Oxford, and in many private collections. She lives and works in Dublin.

Melanie le Brocquy

Bank Holiday

HARRY CLIFTON, a poet, was born in Dublin in 1952, but has travelled widely in Africa and Asia, as well as more recently in Europe. He has published five collections of poems, including *The Desert Route: Selected Poems 1973–88* and *Night Train through the* Brenner. His prose memoir is *The Children of Silone.* He divides his time between Paris and Dublin.

Harry Clifton

STEPS

for Deirdre

I would know you by your footsteps anywhere –
If, tomorrow, I was struck blind
And had to listen, in streets and corridors,
To the million feet in passing, to the sounds
Separating themselves, in casual conversations,
Snatches of laughter, jazz and hurly–burly,
Pandemoniums, and orchestrations,
Yours would be under them, making your way through
   the world.

Hesitant, nervous, now you start and stop –
Don't trip over your shadow, or drown in the river!
Blind though I am, I can make you up
As you go along, approaching me forever
On Achilles' heels of instinct or change,
Out of the otherworldly, out of the strange.

GERRY CAHILL was born in 1951 and educated at University College, Dublin and the Architectural Association, London. He is the author of *Back to the Street* (1980) and was co-ordinator of *Dublin City Quays* (1986), published by the School of Architecture at UCD, where he is a lecturer. These publications dealt with how integrated urban renewal could be achieved in Dublin's city centre. His practice, Gerry Cahill Architects, has worked extensively with voluntary organisations, housing associations and co-operatives.

Gerry Cahill

Page from a Sketchbook ....

The Place des Vosges in The Paris Morais is a beautiful urban space...
A park surrounded by trees railings and a colonnade which houses restaurants and shops...
Above apartments and offices look down on the shared world below .....

GC.

GORDON SNELL worked for much of his career as a radio and television broadcaster, before becoming a full-time writer. He has written over twenty books for children as well as plays, musicals and opera librettos. He lives in Dalkey, County Dublin and is married to the writer Maeve Binchy.

Gordon Snell

THE CONJUROR'S CANARY

'You see, there's nothing up my sleeve,'
He says, and that's what they believe,
    For I am neatly hidden.
Nothing I am, nothing remain,
Waiting to come to life again,
    As soon as I am bidden.

'ABRACADABRA!' Time to leave.
Now down the tunnel of his sleeve
    He sends me with a shove.
With ruffled wings and blinking eyes
I flutter out – surprise, surprise! –
    And perch upon his glove.

One day I'll see, beyond the glare,
Rows of Canaries sitting there
    Who'll flap and clap and cheer,
Exclaiming, 'How, for heaven's sake,
Did that Canary ever make
    The Conjuror disappear?'

JOE LEE is Professor of Modern History at University College, Cork. He has at various times been an administrative officer in the Department of Finance, Dublin, a Fellow of Peterhouse, Cambridge, and an Eisenhower Fellow. He has held visiting appointments in several European and American universities and was an Independent member of Seanad Éireann on the National University of Ireland panel. His book *Ireland 1912–1985* was awarded an *Irish Times*/Aer Lingus Prize, as well as the Donnelly Prize of the American Conference for Irish Studies.

Joe Lee

THE LOSS OF A GENTLE LION

For an educationalist, the funeral Mass of the late Bryan MacMahon was a bitter-sweet experience. Given his life of achievement, it was as much a celebration as a lament, at once intensely local, as it evoked his pride in Listowel and Listowel's pride in him, and yet essentially universal, not least in the assumptions about the literary standards of the congregation. The spontaneous applause that greeted the superb tribute by Fr James Linnane, PP, surely testified to an appreciation not only of the quality of insight but of the command of language that went into the making of it. But in how many other churches today – or for that matter, in how many university lecture theatres – could the eulogist have dared to assume that his listeners would warm to a reference to Cicero's *De Senectute* instead of it sailing straight over their heads? A sceptic might wonder if there has ever been a young generation with so much education as the one now growing up – and with so little learning.

Bryan MacMahon's death marks in certain respects the end of an era. It is partly that he carved out a unique path, even in his own time. But it is also that there are none who can follow in his footsteps. The Ireland whose essence he distilled, its virtues and vices, its riches and poverty, its triumphs and tragedies, is fading away. He celebrated, elevated, and represented the best of that Ireland. Something of that best has died with him forever. And Ireland is the poorer for it.

From an article which appeared in *The Sunday Tribune* on 22 February 1998

GEORGE O'BRIEN was brought up in Lismore, County Waterford. He left Ireland in 1965, after working in Dublin for two years, and attended Ruskin College, Oxford. He took his BA and Ph.D. at the University of Warwick, then he lectured in English at Vassar College in New York and in 1984 took up a similar position at Georgetown University, Washington DC. He was awarded a Hennessy/New Irish Writing Prize in 1973 for his short stories. *The Village of Longing* won the 1988 Irish Book Awards Silver Medal for Literature.

George O'Brien

When I was seven, I'd look up at heaven,
Reasoning you came to a good end.
But alleluia, I barely knew you.
It's long past time that we were friends.

So, were I a magus, never mind Orpheus,
Into your country I would surely fly,
And take you with me to that fair city,
Just for one session. Just you and I.

To Enniscorthy, where in the forties
A lonely teacher asked for your hand.
When to go courting meant modest disporting
— A stroll along Ballyvaldan strand.

Show me you lived there, the very place where
A kiss was stolen and a tyre went flat.
The Moyne, the Duffrey. 'Brave Father Murphy.'
The lorries passing and each dog and cat.

Let's walk the Slaney, and then, by Janey!
We'll eat fresh strawberries at the fair in June.
Or if you'd rather, we could drink lager,
The live–long length of an afternoon.

Up Vinegar Hill. Murphy–Flood's mixed grill.
Lashings and leavings, as the locals say.
Then into the gloaming I'd watch you homing,
No longer mourning. We'd have had our day.

From an unfinished work (*i.m. Nuala Royce O'Brien, 1917–46*)

SAM STEPHENSON was educated at Belvedere College and studied architecture at the College of Technology, Dublin, where he won the premier student award. Later he studied in Europe before returning to Dublin to set up his own practice. He is a Fellow of the RIAI and a member of the RIBA, ARCUK and the Chartered Society of Designers. He is also an Associate of the Royal Hibernian Academy and exhibits regularly. In 1985 he was awarded the Gold Medal for Architecture by the Royal Institute of the Architects of Ireland.

Sam Stephenson

PAT INGOLDSBY was born in Malahide,
County Dublin in 1942. On 23 June 1996 a
woman said to him in North Earl Street: 'I
thought you died years ago.' He apologised
and promised to try harder next time.

Pat Ingoldsby

SERENE

The sea receives purple light
when day is ending
and lets it in deep.

It never says look at me.

The sea smashes high
against black rock
and hisses back
into itself.

It never says look at me.

The sea leads shells
into perfect spirals
and puts
mother of pearl
into them.

It never says look at me.

BRIAN BOYDELL was born in Dublin in 1917 and educated at Cambridge University, the University of Heidelberg, the Royal College of Music and the Royal Irish Academy of Music. He was awarded the Mus.D. degree of Dublin University in 1959 and was Professor of Music at Trinity College, Dublin from 1962 to 1982. He is now a Fellow Emeritus of the college. His compositions include four string quartets, a violin concerto, and orchestral, chamber and choral works.

Brian Boydell

ROY FOSTER, born in Waterford in 1949, is Carroll Professor of Irish History at the University of Oxford. He has also held a chair of modern British history at Birkbeck College, University of London, and visiting appointments at Princeton University and St Antony's College, Oxford. His books include *Charles Stewart Parnell: The Man and His Family* (1976), *Lord Randolph Churchill: A Political Life* (1981), *Modern Ireland 1600–1972* (1988), *Paddy and Mr Punch: Connections in Irish and English History* (1993) and *W.B. Yeats, A Life: I, The Apprentice Mage 1865–1914* (1997).

Roy Foster

Intellectual freedom is a possession conferring the ability to face up to uncomfortable truths – for nations as for individuals. W.B. Yeats, in a speech of 1926, made a vital distinction between national vanity and national pride. 'When a nation is immature it is exceedingly vain, and does not believe in itself, and as long as it does not believe in itself it wants other people to think well of it in order that it might get a little reflected confidence. With success comes pride, and with pride comes indifference as to whether people are shown in a good or bad light on the stage. As a nation comes to intellectual maturity it realises the only thing that does it any credit is its intellect.' Here, I think that 'intellect' means culture. With maturity comes the recognition of cultural diversity. If we give up exclusive vanity (based on insecurity), we can achieve inclusive pride. Nor need cultural diversity imply political confrontation. People can learn to reconcile more than one cultural identity within themselves. And we Irish may have been doing so for longer than we think.

Brenda Fricker

Kiss slowly,
make-up quickly!
Brenda Fricker

DAVID NORRIS was born in 1944 and educated at St Andrew's College and the High School, Dublin before attending Trinity College, Dublin, where he was a senior lecturer in the English Department from 1968 to 1996. A member of Seanad Éireann, he has been nominated for the European Human Rights Prize and is chairman of both Dublin's James Joyce Cultural Centre and the North Great George's Street Preservation Society.

David Norris

WATCHING THE MOUNTAINS IN TIBET

Up there in the snow my past lies frozen
Clear and simple and sparkling.
As I look on its bright blankness I see
A Summer afternoon – my mother's damasked dressing table
Scent bottles casting a cut–glass lunch–time light:
Then bird–prints in a winter garden, while from back here
A speck in the snow might even be human,
Seeming to move, to stop, while the mind's eye designs, discerns.
As the bus turns the corner, it all
Vanishes forever like childhood.

Lhasa/Tsethang, April 1997

Gerald Barry was born in County Clare in 1952. He studied composition with Stockhausen and Kagel. His principal works include the orchestral piece *Chevaux de frise*, commissioned by the BBC for the 1988 Proms, and the operas *The Intelligence Park* and *The Triumph of Beauty and Deceit*. German radio commissioned *The Road in 1997* for the Frankfurt Radio Symphony Orchestra, and in 1998 the Bavarian Radio Symphony Orchestra gave the German premiere of his vocal/orchestral work *The Conquest of Ireland*. His music is published by the Oxford University Press and recorded on the NMC, Largo, Marco Polo, Black Box and Olympia labels.

Gerald Barry

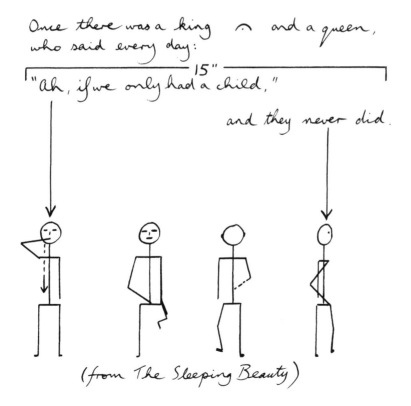

(from The Sleeping Beauty)

BRIAN FRIEL was born in Omagh, County Tyrone in 1929. He was educated in Derry at Long Tower School and at Maynooth College, County Kildare. He is the author of several collections of stories. His plays include *Philadelphia, Here I Come!* (1964), *Faith Healer* (1979), *Translations* (1980) and *Dancing at Lughnasa* (1990). His plays have been performed and translated throughout the world.

Brian Friel

I never met her father, the judge. Shortly after Gracie and I ran off together, he wrote me a letter; but I never met him. He said in it – the only part I remember – he used the phrase 'implicating my only child in your career of chicanery'. And I remember being angry and throwing the letter to her; and I remember her reading that line aloud and collapsing on the bed with laughing and kicking her heels in the air and repeating the phrase over and over again – I suppose to demonstrate her absolute loyalty to me. And I remember thinking how young she *did* look and how cruel her laughter at him was. Because by then my anger against him had died and I had some envy of the man who could use the word 'chicanery' with such confidence.

From *Faith Healer*

Sonja Landweer was born in Holland. During the early sixties she was part of the *6 Amsterdammers*, pioneering ceramics as an autonomous form of art. In 1964 she was awarded the Dutch Verzetsprize for her body of work. In 1965 she moved permanently to Ireland, where she became artist–in–residence in the Kilkenny Design Centre (1965–6) and helped start the Kilkenny Arts Week, presenting international ceramics exhibitions. Since 1982 she has been a member of Aosdána. She lives and works in County Kilkenny.

Sonja Landweer

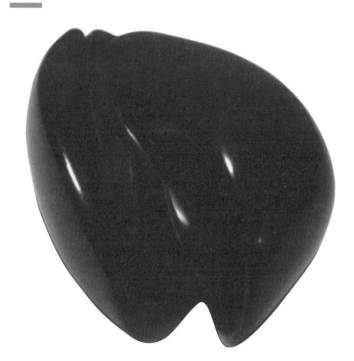

May the earth endure
to hold a future
for us all –

Seedform

MICHAEL HARDING, novelist and
playwright, was born in County Cavan in
1953, and now lives in County Leitrim. His
books and plays present a black and comic
picture of contemporary Ireland, its
religion and politics.

Michael Harding

As a child I dreamed of trees, of wind, and of doors opening and closing in the night. I grew up not far from the Church of Ireland Cathedral of Kilmore, a landscape of drumlins smooth as lapis lazuli, and neatly dotted with hard–wood trees. Lines of Beech along the ditches. And huge Chestnuts, just inside the high stone walls, hanging over the road, like the skirts of some giant auntie making canopies of shade. Past stone pillars and gothic gates, in the late summer evenings, we would cycle home from the lake, our carriers hung with branches of wild pike.

I stood below great trees and gazed up at their enormous elbows bending in storms of January. I saw them bending. I heard them screeching. The whoosh of drenching wind on leaf, and I would go home and dream of a door, flapping in the wind, with the flavour of emptiness.

MICHAEL DAVITT was born in Cork in 1950 and educated at University College, Cork. The journal INNTI, which he edited, set the scene for a new vibrant wave of Irish language poetry. Among his five poetry collections are *Scuais* and *Bligeard Sráide*. In 1994 he won the Butler Literary Award. He was co–editor of *Sruth na Maoile*, a trilingual anthology of poetry from Ireland and Scotland. As a senior producer/director with RTÉ television he has produced documentaries such as *Joe Heaney: Sing the Dark Away* and *John Montague: Rough Fields*.

Michael Davitt

DARTAIS

do John Waters

An Pabhar a chuir an lí sin ar an uisce
grian ghuairdeallach in airde
tá Sé eadrainn sa teagmháil...
díreach sara dtéann an DART thar bráid.

N'fheadar an bhfuil aon mhíniú daonna
ar chóras tarlaithe rudaí, ach go ngéillim
go bhfuil údarás a shocraíonn
nuair a dheinim iarracht a chruthú dhuit
go n–aithním foirm scartha an duine
thar an bhfoirm tháite
go dtéann an DART thar bráid
sara mbíonn deireadh ráite.

Á seo an samhradh bán
a gealladh dúinn fadó.
Seo an galar neamhdhubhach
gona bhiorán frithshuain
is a shúil imigéiniúil.
Slán ár gcarraig fúinn anseo in uachtar trá,
liúnn leaidín beag teanntásach an spáid

agus an DART ag dul thar bráid.

22.06.2000

June/Meitheamh

THURSDAY / DÉARDAOIN

PAUL MOSSE, painter, was born in Bennettsbridge, County Kilkenny in 1946. Having studied painting at the Chelsea School of Art, London, 1966–70, he returned to Ireland and now lives in south Kilkenny with his wife and son. He participated in a 1996 exhibition, *Innovation from Tradition*, and had a solo show, *Partial*, in 1997 at the Douglas Hyde Gallery. His work is included in ten public collections, including the Irish Museum of Modern Art.

Paul Mosse

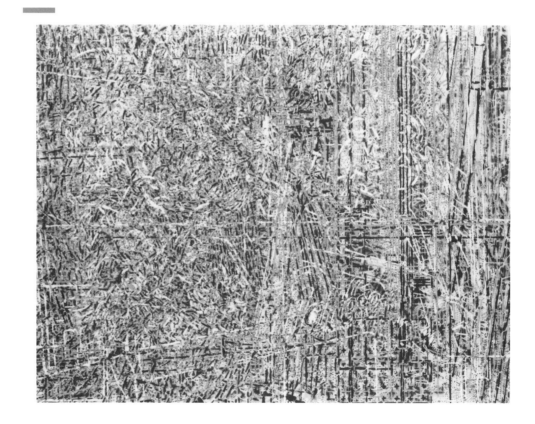

ÉILÍS NÍ DHUIBHNE, born in Dublin in 1954, is a short-story writer, novelist and poet. She studied at University College, Dublin, obtaining a Ph.D. in folklore, and has since lectured in medieval English and folklore and acted as an assistant keeper at the National Library, Dublin. She has written books for children as well as adults, while her short stories have appeared in a number of anthologies. In 1987 she was awarded an Arts Council bursary in literature. Her publications include *Eating Women is Not Recommended* and *The Bray House*.

Éilís Ní Dhuibhne

ST JOHN'S EVE

Stalking the rusty twig-thatched forest floor
looking for deer, I heard the thunderous
crackle and crack of my feet, thick feet
of a cumal breed. Generations of child-bearers,
ploughgirls, wielders of the heavy hammer
contrived those weighty ankles – legs
not fashioned
to stalk in silence
the sharp-eared doe.

I left the wood for the road
the man-made track where one bred in captivity
belongs and where shoes make no sound.
Trained by patterned papers, glossy paint
my eye can absorb yellow of buttercup
white of ox-eye, purple fox-glove —
a palette not too wild.

Then I saw you.

Reynard
Reynard.

red as flame
you flashed from the ditch

Your brush plumed up
your mouth full of victim.
Your redness glowed
redder than the forest
more golden than the buttercup.

Such a red
in thirty summers' chanting
'Maidrín a Rua Rua Rua Rua Rua'
I had not seen.
Swift as a fire you flashed past
Into the wood with your captive
Harmless farmyard mug.

Thirty summers,
Then just a second's sight.

For centuries, Reynard,
You have scorned such as me,
flat-footed cumals.
Seeing you for the first time,
My bonfire of Saint John,
I know why my fat-legged country cousins detest you,
And why some sell their souls to the devil.

RICHARD MURPHY was born in County Galway in 1927, brought up in Ceylon and Ireland and educated at Oxford University, where C.S. Lewis was his tutor. His books of poetry include *Sailing to an Island* (1963), The *Battle of Aughrim* (1968), *High Island* (1974), *The Price of Stone* (1985) and *The Mirror Wall* (1989). He lived at Cleggan, County Galway until 1980, when he moved to Dublin. Now he divides his time between Ireland and South Africa, where his daughter and grandchildren are living.

Richard Murphy

MOONSHINE

To think
I must be alone:
To love
We must be together.

I cannot think
Without loving
Or love
Without thinking.

I think I love you
When I'm alone
More than I think of you
When we're together.

Alone I love
To think of us together:
Together I think
I'd love to be alone.

THEO DORGAN is a poet, broadcaster, editor and scriptwriter. Born in Cork in 1953, he studied English and philosophy in University College, Cork and has an MA in English from that university. He now lives in Dublin, where he is director of the national poetry organisation Poetry Ireland/Éigse Éireann. Among his publications are: *The Ordinary House of Love* (1991), *Rosa Mundi* (1995) and *Sappho's Daughter* (1998). He is editor of *Irish Poetry since Kavanagh* (1995) and co-editor, with Máirin Ní Dhonnchadha, of *Revising the Rising* (1991). He is also, together with the painter Gene Lambert, co-editor of *The Great Book of Ireland/Leabhar Mór na hÉireann* (1991).

Theo Dorgan

INSTRUCTIONS

When the day comes, as it will, to lay me
down at last in the black, wet earth
choose what you will to remember,
let the rest fall away like leaves.

None of this will matter,
none of this will be important.

Speak for me:
           we lived, say this,
we loved, we were blessed
in each other and in our friends.

I am going nowhere.
I love this earth too much.
I can never love you enough but now
I have all the time there is to go on trying.

CHRISTY MOORE was born in 1945 to Andy Moore of Newbridge and Nancy Power of Yellow Furze, Navan. He was singing before he could talk, gave his first public performance as a folk singer in Clonmel, County Tipperary in 1964 and has been at it ever since. He lives in Dublin with his wife, Valerie, and their children, Andy, Juno and Pádraic.

Christy Moore

VERONICA.

IN THE BROAD DAYLIGHT OF A Summer's day
ON the CORK TO Dublin MOTORWAY
Suddenly the Singing BIRDS
WERE startled IN their Song
IN the SILENCE of that moment
OUR WORLD WENT OUT OF KILTER
IN THAT SPLIT Second
VERONICA WAS GONE

You, you'll never silence her
Your story will BE WRITTEN
HER SPIRIT wont REST Easy
UNTIL the JOB is done
WITH fists and BOOTS you BROKE her BONES,
you gunned her down at home,
As Soon as She WAS ABLE
She faced you up again.

VERONICA, VERONICA, VERONICA.
WARRIOR WOMAN
VERONICA, VERONICA, VERONICA,
I offer you this Song.

You who made the phone call
You who took the message down
You who hired the HITMAN
You who hatched the plan
YOU WHO DREW THE MONEY DOWN
YOU WHO KNOW THE STORY
& You who REMAIN SILENT
You are Guilty everyone.

I WAS ON Cape Clear ISLAND Co.CORK when
I heard the newsflash on RADIO na
nGaelTAcTA. I wrote most of this on the
afternoon that VERONICA died.

Christy Moore

AMELIA STEIN, the photographer, lives and works in Dublin, where she was born in 1958. She has worked for theatre companies including the Abbey, Druid, Rough Magic, Project Arts Centre and Wexford Festival Opera. Portraits and personal work have been used for album covers and she has participated in many group and solo shows. Most recently the *Mona Pictures* were bought by the Arts Council from a group portrait show at the Rubicon Gallery, Dublin.

Amelia Stein

27.06.2000
June/Meitheamh
TUESDAY / MÁIRT

LOUISE KENNEDY, originally from Thurles, County Tipperary, is one of Ireland's best-known fashion designers. After graduating from the Grafton Academy, Dublin, she set up business under her own name in 1986 and quickly acquired a loyal following at home and overseas. In 1990 she was chosen to design the inauguration outfit for incoming president Mary Robinson, who has since remained a client. Other well-known figures wearing Louise Kennedy include President Mary McAleese, the British prime minister's wife, Cherie Blair, and singer Enya. In 1998 Louise Kennedy designed new staff uniforms for Aer Lingus and a range of glass and tableware for Tipperary Crystal.

Louise Kennedy

EITHNE JORDAN was born in Dublin in 1954. An expressionist painter, she has spent extensive periods of time living and working at home and in London, Berlin and the south of France. She has exhibited consistently since the early 1980s and her work is represented in major public collections in Ireland, including the Irish Museum of Modern Art. She is a member of Aosdána.

Eithne Jordan

Gorge, Etching

SARA BERKELEY was born in 1967. She is a poet and short-story writer. She studied at Trinity College, Dublin and the University of California at Berkeley. Her volumes of poetry include *Penn* (1986) and *Facts About Water* (1994). Her first collection of stories, *The Swimmer in the Deep Blue Dream*, was published in 1991. She lives in California.

Sara Berkeley

APPROACHING THIRTY

On a journey to another country
deep into the untouched orchards
having exhausted sleep
I crouched in a chair till dawn
the world as a house around me
memory held impermanent.

It was not shown to me how to
move on, how to leap;
mid-air I was given the secret
words in their order.

But in time you have to go further
meet fire as a rival, maybe a salamander
not flinch at the small reminders
gravel thrown by the handful
age is irrecoverable
I will never be wiser.

Almost thirty
swimming in the deep pool
of my wife tears, honest and ordinary
I found in the many chambers of myself
with the fears connected to nothing
forty thousand reasons to go on living
I felt them collect, just out of my field of vision
and wait for me there, dark blue, dark green.

FERGUS MARTIN was born in Cork in 1955. He lived in Italy from 1979 to 1988. He had solo exhibitions at the Oliver Dowling Gallery in Dublin in 1990 and 1992. Since 1994 he has been represented by the Green on Red Gallery in Dublin. In 1996 his Six Paintings for the L'Imaginaire Irlandais festival were shown in Poitiers, Venice, Dublin and Limerick. His work is included in the collections of the Arts Council of Ireland and the Irish Museum of Modern Art.

Fergus Martin

Anjelica Huston, who was raised in Ireland, is the third generation of a renowned cinema family, following her grandfather, actor Walter Huston, and father, director John Huston. An internationally acclaimed actress, she received an Academy Award for Best Supporting Actress in *Prizzi's Honour* (1985), directed by her father; she also appeared in his last film, *The Dead*. Her other film credits include *Enemies: A Love Story*, *The Grifters*, *The Addams Family*, *Crimes and Misdemeanours* and *Manhattan Murder Mystery*. In 1998 she directed, executive-produced and performed the title role in *The Mammy*, which was filmed in Ireland. She lives in Los Angeles with her sculptor husband Robert Graham.

Anjelica Huston

dawn,
pale from her dark sleep
falls —
like our shadows from the sheets
lost as Icarus
from a dream
of flying.

Ronnie Hughes was born in Belfast in 1965 and studied fine art at the University of Ulster, Belfast. He has had numerous solo shows in Ireland and his work is in most Irish public and corporate collections, including the Irish Museum of Modern Art.

He has been a resident of PSI Museum, New York, Banff Arts Center, Canada and Bemis Arts Center, Nebraska. He now lives in County Sligo.

Ronnie Hughes

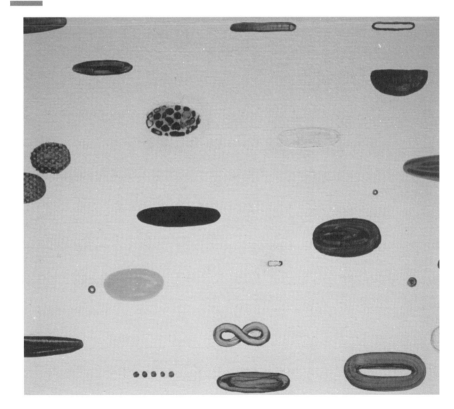

Butterfly

TOM MOLLOY, visual artist, was born in Waterford in 1964. He studied painting at the National College of Art & Design, Dublin, receiving a BA in 1987 and MA in 1992. Since then he has exhibited widely, including four shows at the Rubicon Gallery, Dublin. He now lives in Lisdoonvarna, County Clare.

Tom Molloy

05.07.2000

July/Iúil

WEDNESDAY / CÉADAOIN

MIKE MCCORMACK was born in London in 1965, grew up in Louisburgh, County Mayo and took a degree in English and philosophy at University College, Galway after working for a period as a gardener. He then worked in a butcher's shop in Galway while writing his first book, a collection of short stories called *Getting It in the Head* which was published in 1996 and won that year's Rooney Prize. In 1998 he published a novel, *Crowe's Requiem*. His writing, often using the first person singular, has been described as possessing 'an almost aggressive fluency', as well as a darkly surreal humour.

Mike McCormack

And further on as night was falling I met a man coming the opposite way. He told me he hadn't met another living soul in seven days and that he was hungry to talk. That was fine by me – I hadn't spoken myself to anyone since leaving home at the end of last month. That was two weeks ago. We built a fire and sat round it and spoke together long into the night. Among other things we discussed crop rotation, the plight of small farmers in the west, the shortcomings of the ontological argument, the separation of church and state, the third man tackle and the greatness of Maradona. By the time we had exhausted these topics the sun was coming up. This was my third consecutive night without sleep.

JOHN MONTAGUE was born in Brooklyn, New York in 1929, but returned as a child to his family's farm at Garvaghey, County Tyrone. He was educated at University College, Dublin and at the Universities of Yale and Iowa. Having lived for some years in Dublin and Paris, he became lecturer in poetry at University College, Cork in 1972. His collections of poetry include *Forms of Exile* (1958), *The Rough Field* (1972) and *Time in Armagh* (1993). His *Collected Poems* appeared in 1995.

John Montague

PATHS

We had two gardens.

A real flower garden
overhanging the road
(our miniature Babylon),
paths which I helped
to lay with Aunt Winifred,
riprapped with pebbles;
shards of painted delph;
an old potato boiler;
a blackened metal pot,
now bright with petals.

Hedges of laurel, palm.
A hovering scent of boxwood.
Crouched in the flowering
lilac, I could oversee

the main road, old Lynch
march to the well spring
with his bucket, whistling,
his carrotty sons herding
in and out their milch cows:
a growing whine of cars.

Then, the vegetable garden
behind, rows of broad beans
plumping their cushions,
the furled freshness of
tight little lettuce heads,
slim green pea pods above
early flowering potatoes,
gross clumps of carrots,
parsnips, a frailty of parsley,
a cool fragrance of mint.

HUGHIE O'DONOGHUE, the son of Irish emigrants, was born in Manchester in 1953 but spent his childhood summers on an aunt's farm in the west of Ireland. Much of his work is rooted in this Irish past, although the influence of classical masters such as Titian and El Greco is also powerful in many of his large-scale pieces. Originally trained as a teacher, he moved to London in 1979 and studied fine art at Goldsmiths College. Widely admired and exhibited throughout Europe, he first came to the notice of Irish critics during Kilkenny Arts Week 1991 and now works and lives with his family in County Kilkenny.

Hughie O'Donoghue

Wagons to Rouen

CHARLES HAUGHEY is a retired politician now living in Kinsealy in north County Dublin. He was a member of Dáil Éireann from 1957 to 1992 and held the offices of Minister for Justice, Agriculture and Fisheries, Finance, Health and Social Welfare, and the office of Taoiseach 1979–81, 1982, and 1987–92. Regarded by some as one of the principal architects of a successful modern Ireland, he devoted special attention to enhancing her artistic and cultural life.

Charles Haughey

SEAMUS HEANEY

THE GIVEN NOTE

On the most westerly Blasket
In a dry-stone hut
He got this air out of the night.

Strange noises were heard
By others who followed, bits of a tune
Coming in on loud weather

Though nothing like melody.
He blamed their fingers and ear
As unpractised, their fiddling easy

For he had gone alone into the island
And brought back the whole thing.
The house throbbed like his full violin.

So whether he calls it spirit music
Or not, I don't care. He took it
Out of wind off mid-Atlantic.

Still he maintains, from nowhere.
It comes off the bow gravely,
Rephrases itself into the air.

K

PATRICK SCOTT was born in January 1921 in Kilbrittain, County Cork, the son of a farmer. Although best known today as an artist, for many years he practised as an architect, working with Michael Scott after graduating from University College, Dublin. While in the Scott practice, where he became chief assistant in 1953 and a partner in 1960, he spent five years working on the building of Dublin's Busáras, where he carried out the striking mosaic decorations. First exhibiting pictures in 1944, he did not begin devoting the majority of his time to painting and tapestry design until 1961; in the previous year he represented Ireland at the Venice Biennale.

Patrick Scott

JOSEPHINE HART was born in Mullingar. She worked in London in publishing before producing West End plays. In 1985 she created Gallery Poets, which produced poetry performances in major theatres. She also presented a series of Thames Television's *Books by My Bedside*. She is the author of *Damage*, which sold over one million copies and was filmed by Louis Malle, *Sin*, *Oblivion* and, most recently, *The Stillest Day*.

Josephine Hart

We are here to add to the sum of human goodness. To prove the thing exists. And however futile each individual act of courage or generosity, self–sacrifice or grace – it still proves the thing exists. Each act adds to the fund. It needs replenishment. Not only because evil flourishes, and is, most indefensibly, defended. But because goodness is no longer a respectable aim in life. The hound of hell, envy, has driven it from the house.

We two, Charles and I, once united by the powerful bond of sin, now float towards each other across a sea of sorrow. Above the faces of the boys, who rise and fall, to watery graves, again and again.

And as we move towards each other, the face of Elizabeth also rises. Again and again.

And if I had never met her? What then? Did she create me? Or I her? Am I Elizabeth? Now?

From *Sin*

Nóirín Ní Riain, an internationally renowned spiritual singer, was born in Caherconlish, County Limerick in 1951. She studied music in University College, Cork, graduating with a master's degree on traditional song in Irish in 1980. Her CD repertoire includes a trilogy of recordings with the Benedictine monks of Glenstal Abbey. She is the author of three books, the most recent being *Gregorian Chant Experience*. She has shared performances with Gregory Peck, Anjelica Huston, Sinéad O'Connor, John Cage, and the Dalai Lama, and has sung at four United Nations conferences. She lives in County Tipperary with her husband, Mícheál Ó Súilleabháin, and their two sons.

Nóirín Ní Riain

On this day, the feastday of St Benedict, founder of Western monasticism and Patron of Europe, three millennium 'seanfhocals' or wise words from Benedict's Rule:

Videte ne graventur corda vestra crapula.
Take care that your hearts are not weighed down with overindulgence.
CHAPTER 39

Et sic stemus ad psallendum ut mens nostra concordet voci nostrae.
And so sing the psalms that mind and voice may be in harmony.
CHAPTER 19

Otiositas inimica est animae.
Idleness is the enemy of the soul.
CHAPTER 48

MARIANNE ELLIOTT is Professor of Modern History and director of the Institute of Irish Studies at the University of Liverpool. Born near Belfast, she was educated at Queen's University there and at the University of Oxford. She is one of the leading historians of Ireland, her best-known books being *Partners in Revolution: The United Irishmen and France* (1982) and *Wolfe Tone: Prophet of Irish Independence* (1989). Her *History of the Catholics of Ulster* will be published in 2000. She was a member of the 1993 Opsahl Commission on Northern Ireland, and co-authored its report: *A Citizens' Inquiry*.

Marianne Elliott

It looked smaller, the street on which I grew up. White houses, laid out four by four between Belfast Lough and the Cave Hill. It had been a happy, mixed-religion housing estate, the pride of post-war Housing Trust redevelopment. Only around the Twelfth did friends become remote. Now it was being bulldozed and rebuilt 1990s-style. One house remained occupied. Luckily it was our old one. The people were kind. They let us step inside to say goodbye. The following week, it was no more. The new houses went up quickly. But they were no longer peopled by a diversity of creeds. The Catholics had not returned. Now a peace-wall separates them from their old neighbours. Two hundred years on, I wondered what Wolfe Tone, Thomas Russell and Henry Joy McCracken, watching from McArt's Fort, would have made of it all.

ROBERT GREACEN was born in Derry in 1920 and educated at Trinity College, Dublin. Having lived in England for many years, he returned to Ireland in the mid-1980s and settled in Dublin. His *Collected Poems 1944–1994* won the Irish Times Prize for Poetry in 1995.

Robert Greacen

Irene, goddess of peace, had been a symbol of light in a dark and threatening world. The flesh–and–blood person who once existed for me becomes less and less real as the years blur the image. Have not most of us, one way and another, had an Irene in our lives? She is the girl we once saw in a train and loved instantly, but never even spoke to. She is the person we have lost. For poets and dreamers, because they trade in images and magic, the Irenes, the Maud Gonnes, are not so much women as enchantresses.

From the autobiography, *The Sash My Father Wore*

Seóirse Bodley was born in Dublin in 1933. His compositions include five symphonies (his Symphony No. 2 was commissioned by the Irish government in commemoration of Padraig Pearse), large orchestral works, choral compositions, two string quartets, song cycles (for poems by Brendan Kennelly and Micheal O'Siadhail), solo piano works and chamber music. He is Associate Professor of Music at University College, Dublin, as well as a conductor, a lecturer on music and an accompanist.

Seóirse Bodley

SPAZIERGANG [1]

A street in Witten, Germany
Caught unawares
Unexpected the interior gust
The wind of energy: day–flares.

How feel youth's thrust?
Unprepared joy
Man and boy
Truth?

Last night's cafe
We talked, drank, all of us
Music, food –
But not this good

'Das Ewigweibliche
Zieht uns hinan'[2] –
What's done is done.
Into the sun,
Icarus...

1. A walk. 2. The eternal–womanly draws us upward (Goethe).

ELIZABETH MAGILL was born in Ontario in 1959. Her family returned to Northern Ireland in the early sixties, and she studied painting at Belfast College of Art, graduating in 1982. From 1982 to 1984 she was a postgraduate student at the Slade School of Fine Art in London, where she still lives and works. She has had several one-person shows in Ireland and abroad and has participated in many group exhibitions. She was shortlisted for the IMMA–Glen Dimplex Award in 1995.

Elizabeth Magill

Berlin

PATRICK O'REILLY is an artist living and working in Dublin. He works in various media, constantly seeking to expand the boundaries of visual art. He has exhibited widely in Ireland and has been well received abroad. In Dublin his work can be seen in the Hugh Lane Municipal Gallery of Modern Art.

Patrick O'Reilly

Dear Michael,

Delighted to hear you are well.

My Australian Exhibition opens tomorrow. Should I stay overnight?

I enclose a recent article about Ireland's (long overdue) Renaissance in Visual Art which you might find interesting.

James has started in that new Computer Free, Nature School in Connemara. How quickly computers came and went – although I was never comfortable with the soulless experience of learning through a screen.

My latest scan says that I should have been a Fireman! What amazing faith we all had in DNA believing we had reached the centre, only to find just another layer of skin.

Met John this morning in Derry. He never mentions past dramatic events there – then again nobody does. It's all peaceful now.

After the painful removal of all that dead wood, religion here has had such vigorous growth. No longer afraid of science it continues to thrive and relieves so much fear for those like myself nearing the end.

Write again soon.

Regards

Patrick, July 2038.

ALICE TAYLOR was born in 1938 in County Cork, was educated there and still lives there, in Inishannon. In her three memoirs, *To School through the Fields* (1988), *Quench the Lamp* (1990) and *The Village* (1992), she recounts the changing lifestyles of her village and herself and Ireland's move from the 1950s into modern times. *Close to the Earth* (1989) is a collection of her poetry.

Alice Taylor

FRESH FLOWERS

Give me a bunch
Of dew fresh flowers,
What if they will not last:
I cannot live in the future
The present is all I ask.

MARY LELAND, a writer and journalist, was born in Cork. Her short stories have been widely anthologised, the most recent appearing in *If Only* and the *American Literary Review*. Her first novel, *The Killeen*, appeared in 1985 and her second, *Approaching Priests*, in 1991. A collection of short stories, *The Little Galloway Girls*, was published in 1986.

Mary Leland

The two girls went off together to the old henhouses. They had to find that smell, that dry must of childhood summers, of shelter from the rain and imperious adults or siblings, the almost animal sense of sanctuary they still cannot identify although they know, they know so well, how it felt. They had to find it, believing that they could store it like a deposit in the bank of their senses.

Is this all they need bring with them to the house of tomorrow? Beth stands on the path as if trapped by an intimation of a future to which she does not belong. Do all our stories end here?

All our stories! Who are we? What have we become? This is only one garden of the many in our lives. If this path, mossy, stone-edged, overhung with Lady's Mantle, Snow in Summer, Tradescantia and Lavender and London Pride could radiate beyond its walls where would it find us, at which point of its compass would we have come to rest? The pear tree, the apples, the cherry have shaded our existence; for these last years we have lived immured if not immune, like a harem, visited by the journeymen of our lives but no-one, nothing, else.

From *Thorn Jam*, a work in progress, 1998

PADDY MOLONEY's passion for traditional Irish music led to the formation of The Chieftains, who have to date won five Grammies and played all over the world, including China. Paddy has also recorded with mainstream artists such as Mick Jagger, Eric Clapton, Frank Zappa and Sting. In 1988 he was awarded an honorary doctorate of music from Trinity College, Dublin for his contribution to Irish traditional music. He lives in County Wicklow.

Paddy Moloney

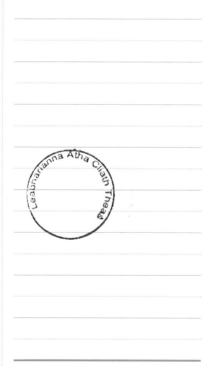

Pat (Papa) O'Neill – shopkeeper, Rita's (my wife) grandfather, and Aedin Moloney (our daughter), actress. Taken in The Stores, Milltown Bridge, Dundrum Road, 1977. Photograph by Paddy Moloney.

HUGH WALLACE qualified from Dublin Institute of Technology, Bolton Street with a degree in architecture. He is managing director of Douglas/Wallace Architects and Designers, which he established in 1982 and which now has offices in Dublin and Galway. As president of the Institute of Designers in Ireland in 1999, he intends to ensure that the organisation represents the design profession and lobbies in Ireland for its proper recognition.

Hugh Wallace

I am always amazed at how particular smells can evoke memories. Recently I stumbled across a box of poster paints and found myself sitting in my old classroom in the middle of a bunch of six year old boys and girls. There was my old primary school teacher at the top of the class room busily chewing her way through her favourite box of coloured elastic bands casting her beady eye over us. She would bribe us — if we were good boys or girls we would have the chance to prepare her eleven o'clock break — oh! the joy of spreading her Calvita Triangle of cheese between two crackers and unsteadily pouring her pre-milked coffee from a flask.... unfortunately, I was never a very good boy or girl!!

MARIE FOLEY, sculptor, was born in Kanturk, County Cork and trained at the Crawford College of Art in Cork city. This was followed by further study in Cardiff and at the University of London, Goldsmiths College. She now lives in Thomastown, County Kilkenny. A member of Aosdána, she is best known for the use of porcelain in her work, seen to effect in a solo exhibition at Dublin's Project Arts Centre in 1989. However, she also frequently incorporates *objets trouvés*, such as feathers and animal bones, in certain pieces, reflecting a preoccupation with death and spirituality.

Marie Foley

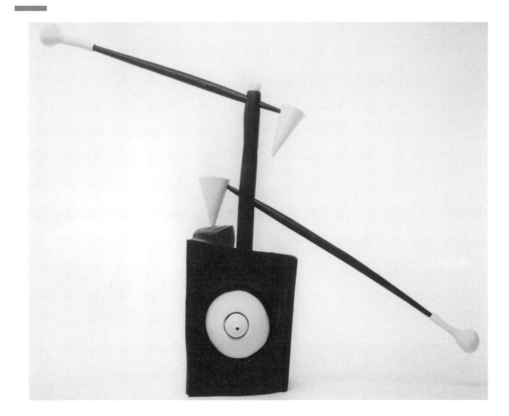

Breathing Earth

MATTHEW SWEENEY was born in Donegal
in 1952 and moved to London twenty-one
years later. He has published several books
of poetry, including *Blue Shoes*, *Cacti* and,
most recently, *The Bridal Suite*. He has also
co-edited several anthologies. He
frequently gives readings and workshops
and works regularly in schools. A member
of Aosdána, he was writer-in-residence at
London's South Bank Centre in 1994-5 and
in 1997-8 on the Internet for electronic
publisher Chadwyck-Healey.

Matthew Sweeney

DO NOT THROW STONES AT THIS SIGN

Do not throw stones at this sign
which stands here, in a stony field
a stone's throw from the sea
whose beach is a mess of pebbles
since the sand was stolen for building,
and the few people who dawdle there,
rods in hand, catch nothing,
not even a shoe – might as well
bombard the waves with golfballs,
or wade in and hold their breath,
or bend, as they do, and grab a handful
of pebbles to throw at the sign,
and each time they hit it they cheer
and chalk up another beer, especially
the man who thought up the sign,
who got his paintbrush and wrote
'Do Not Throw Stones At This Sign'
on a piece of driftwood which he stuck
in this useless field, then, laughing,
danced his way to the house of beer.

COLM O'GAORA was born in Dublin in 1966. His short stories have been widely published and broadcast, and his debut collection, *Giving Ground*, appeared in 1993. His first novel, *A Crooked Field*, was published in 1999.

Colm O'Gaora

It is in the rain of Portnew that I will always see her, a hood pulled down over her eyes, drops hanging on the fringe, bare legs half–blue beneath a cotton skirt. Yet there is nothing to hide the silken skin that rainwater beads upon, the dark hair, the green eyes, the wide mouth, the quick and mischievous smile, the smooth limbs of a princess. Time has not dimmed her, but with each memory she is taken further from me, smaller and smaller so that she is summoned, still perfect but with greater effort.

From *Closer*

CHARLES TYRRELL was born in Trim, County Meath in 1950. He studied painting at the National College of Art & Design, Dublin. After graduating in 1974, he continued living in Dublin until 1984 when he moved with his family to Allihies on the Beara peninsula in County Cork. He has had numerous solo exhibitions in Dublin, London and Cork since his first one at the Project Arts Centre in 1974. He has represented Ireland in international exhibitions and has works in the major Irish public collections. He is a member of Aosdána.

Charles Tyrrell

MARY O'MALLEY was born and grew up in Connemara. She graduated from University College, Galway and taught at the University of Lisbon for eight years. Her first collection of poetry, *A Consideration of* *Silk*, was published in 1990, and she received a Hennessy Award the same year. In 1992 she edited a book of children's writing. For several years she has been a member of the Cúirt Poetry Festival organising committee and responsible for its educational programme. She lives in the Moycullen Gaeltacht with her husband and two children.

Mary O'Malley

My pain is hungry and lean.

It licks the skin, eats shame slowly

and wolfs through to the bone

but the real work, the slow burn

is in the sinews, like a poem.

That's what the man said – a bit slight

but sinewy all the same. Not tough enough, I felt.

The wolf is tearing at my chest.

Men with knives surround me.

It is half past one.

They will come at two

for the third time to cut into my chest

and release a thousand roses.

The instructions – between the fourth

and fifth ribs – are precise.

It is all done without screaming,

without making a fuss.

I am not brave. 'I can't.'

It is my own thin voice.

I have no shame, no control.

You will not stitch breath

with such blunt instruments.

Use salve, some unguent made with herbs.

Pray to Hygeia, Apollo, Panacea

For a drug to help us tolerate

the mercury heavy air.

From *Miss Panacea Regrets*. For A.G.

DERVLA MURPHY was born to Dublin parents in County Waterford in 1931. Her first book, *Full Tilt*, described a 1963 cycle trip from Dunkirk to New Delhi. She has since written about numerous countries on four continents. Her non-travel books include *A Place Apart* (about Northern Ireland), *Race to the Finish?* (about the nuclear power industry) and *Tales from Two Cities* (about race relations in Britain). She has one daughter and two granddaughters and still lives in Lismore, County Waterford.

Dervla Murphy

Once upon a time Granny gave her spouse enough cash to buy himself a very necessary pair of everyday trousers. (He was not normally entrusted with such large sums of money.) Wearing his Sunday suit, because he had nothing else fit to wear, he set off for wherever the cheapest men's clothing was to be had. But unluckily his route took him onto the quays and there he chanced to notice the ten-volume 1840 edition of Sismondi's *Histoire des Républiques Italiennes*, elegantly bound and without a blemish. It cost considerably more than he had in his pocket, but he judged it to be a bargain and acted with a decisiveness that had it been otherwise directed might have made him a rich man. Nearby was a second-hand clothes shop where he quickly flogged his Sunday suit and bought threadbare trousers for a few shillings. The substantial balance, added to his original allowance, just about paid for Sismondi and he arrived home in a state of advanced euphoria. He was also in his shirt-sleeves, and very nearly indecently exposed, and Granny did not appreciate his purchase.

From *Wheels within Wheels: An Autobiography*

HAMMON JOURNEAUX was born in Wyndham, New Zealand in 1964 and now lives in Ballydehob, County Cork with her partner and their children. She has exhibited paintings in New Zealand, London and Ireland over the past ten years, specialising in drawing writers. Her work has been published in literary magazines. To celebrate the poet John Heath-Stubbs's eightieth birthday in 1988, a solo exhibition was held in London, and an exhibition on Samuel Beckett was mounted in the Mill Gallery, west Cork in 1998.

Hammon Journeaux

NEIL JORDAN was born in Sligo in 1950. After graduating from University College, Dublin, he worked as a teacher and began his creative career by writing short stories. *Night in Tunisia* won the *Guardian* Fiction Prize. He has published three novels: *The Past*, *The Dream of a Beast* and *Sunrise with Sea Monster*. He is an internationally celebrated screenwriter and director, whose films include *Angel*, *The Company of Wolves*, *Mona Lisa*, *The Crying Game* – for which he won an Oscar for Best Screenplay, *Michael Collins* and *The Butcher Boy*. He lives in Dalkey, County Dublin.

Neil Jordan

From the first, heedless of the masculine call, Mary had within himself that urge to please, the well of sweetness, those moist eyes that at the time were labelled feminine and hence the name. Jane, lonesome for the company of her kind, gladdened in this tendency, dressed the elephantine child in gingham and lace, plastered back his bustop ears with sellotape and developed his curls. As broad as his brother was long, Mary would stand at the edge of the freezing pitch, coo with each bounce of the ball, deliver him slivers of oranges and mend his jersey. Whipperlip was named because of the same, i.e. the upper lip, more a whorl than a hare–lip, a huge scimitar of red beneath the button of his nose. The profound melancholy of the profoundly ugly resided inside him and the eyes were saucers of a soul that was bound for oblivion. Lucifer and Thompson, his youngers, understood this from the start and grew up full of the necessary sympathy. They mercilessly battered their younger, Manno, blonde–haired and tiny, with the eyes and face of an angel, if only to compensate. And the Brat, being the youngest, was left from the start to his own devices. That is, he howled for attention and when it wasn't forthcoming, he dreamt.

From a work in progress

COLM HENRY was born in Dublin in 1953. He received a diploma in photography in London and began by documenting social and living conditions in Dublin city in the mid-seventies. His reportage photographs were first published in *The Irish Times* and German magazines. When the Dublin music explosion occurred in the late seventies he became its chronicler. He has photographed most major rock artists who pass through Dublin. In the nineties he broadened his subject matter to include the social set, environmental portraiture, opera, dance and children. He has had many exhibitions of his work in Irish galleries.

Colm Henry

...to my knowledge the only photo of the two men playing music together – Phil Lynott and Rory Gallagher, with Bono lurking in the background

RONAN BENNETT was brought up in Belfast and now lives in London. His most recent novel is *The Catastrophist* (1998). Screenplays for films include *Face* and *A Further Gesture*. He is a regular contributor to the *London Review of Books* and *The Guardian*, among other publications.

Ronan Bennett

STOPPED WORDS

I write to you
I have tricks
This is a trick
I know what I'm doing
So do you.

It's hard, this is a hard thing to do
To commend myself to you
When I know the words
And so do you
I've used them, you've heard them
You've used them, I've heard them
Only the tongue–tied are honest
And mumbling is real.

Your good looks
For you are good–looking
Your good looks –
We cannot pretend they don't exist
I have never been honest.

Still I write
Some anger
Things buried
I know this is something I should not do
But I want to recommend myself to you
And be thought of highly by you
Be in your regard
Wanted by you –
Held.

None of this is going my way
Stop. Stop here.

GERARD FANNING, born in Dublin in 1952, studied philosophy and economics at University College, Dublin. He began publishing poetry in the seventies and his work appeared regularly in David Marcus's 'New Irish Writing' page in *The Irish Press* and in *Soundings*, edited by Seamus Heaney. *Easter Snow* won the 1992 Rooney Prize for Literature and the Brendan Behan Prize for Poetry. His second collection is *Working for the Government*.

Gerard Fanning

ALMA AGAIN

My father has travelled down for the weekend
He tip–toes from the scullery, yearning I suppose
For his smoky rooms where men exhale,
Talking of horses, guineas, Redbreast
Or the whiff of shag tobacco in an ox–tail.

His pipe snorts like a little pot stove,
As he sneaks over the sleepers to the far bedroom.
Linen flaps the rust–embroidered air,
End of July 1951, he comes into his own,
And I almost feel I am there.

Only my mother can say this wasn't true,
Though when she closes her eyes chanting vespers
She reveals my snow–blind tattoo.

JOHN STEPHENSON was born in Dublin in 1951 and educated at Trinity College, Dublin. He has worked as producer and provocateur in the arts for over twenty years. He ran the Project Arts Centre in the 1970s and directed the first major Irish arts festival abroad, A Sense of Ireland, in London in 1980. Later, he worked in film production in England, having graduated from its National Film and TV School. More recently he created The Flaming Door for the seventy-fifth anniversary of the 1916 Rising and the Féile Bríde festival in Kildare, and in 1996 was projects manager for the first St Patrick's Day Festival. He is currently concocting magic for the millennium.

John Stephenson

Remembering	Illuminating	Imagining
	CRÉ EARTH / AER AIR	
Samhain Nov 1		Imbolc Feb 1
Winter	OILEÁN 2000 ISLAND	Spring
Autumn		Summer
Aug 1 Lughnasa	FIRE TINE / WATER UISCE	May 1 Bealtaine
Past	Present	Future

CHARLIE MCCREEVY, TD was born in County Kildare and educated at University College, Dublin. He was elected to Dáil Éireann in 1977, was Minister for Social Welfare 1992–3, Minister for Tourism and Trade 1993–4, front bench spokesperson on Finance 1995–7 and appointed Minister for Finance in June 1997.

Charlie McCreevy

WHOSE WIN

Whose win was it anyway?
It felt like it was mine.
Forty–two years waiting.
Waiting and watching.

Oh what exhilaration.
What a great feeling,
Never in my life before,
Never have I felt such joy.

Joy and pain, life and death.
We rose again,
Gradually,
Gradually from death,
Bore life into the lily and bloomed,
Bloomed in August.

But, whose win was it anyway,
IT WAS KILDARE'S!

Kildare Leinster Gaelic Football Champions 1998 (Also known as the Lilywhites) last won in 1956

03.08.2000

August/Lúnasa

THURSDAY / DÉARDAOIN

EAMON DUNPHY was born and brought up in Dublin. A writer and broadcaster, he has written controversially for many Irish newspapers and currently hosts a lively current affairs radio programme. He played professional soccer in England for seventeen years (five of them for Manchester United) and is the author of the classic football book *Only a Game?* He also wrote two biographies: *Unforgettable Fire: The Story of U2* and *Sir Matt Busby & Manchester United: A Strange Kind of Glory.*

Eamon Dunphy

Like most I fear the future. The next millennium will be awful, of that I'm certain. Mostly fear of the future reflects fear of the unknown. Alas we are only too familiar with what lies ahead for our children and theirs.

Fast food. Noise. Sex on the Internet. Terrorists with nuclear weapons. And terrorists in suits called marketing men. There is nothing original in this analysis. Sadly originality, already dying, will disappear in a world moving ever closer to universal conformity.

Therefore the task of writing for this worthy collection is pretty grim. Unless one glances backwards into the glorious twentieth century to which we are now about to bid adieu. Sinatra. Picasso. The Beatles. Colour printing. The slow emancipation of women. Sexual longing. Periods of celibacy. The practice of earnest devotion to a God one could believe in. Innocent children.

Pelé, Lester Piggott, Muhammad Ali, George Best. Drug–free sport. Bernard Shaw, George Orwell, Patrick Kavanagh, Philip Larkin, John Betjeman.

Scott Fitzgerald.

Billie Holiday.

Few tourists.

Aeroplanes that seemed the height of luxury. Empty airport.

Manners. Books. Humility as a virtue rather than a character defect.

STEPHEN AVERILL, a graphic designer and music enthusiast, was born in 1950. His aim in life was always to combine his two passions, design and music. This he has done most notably as founder member of legendary punk band The Radiators (from Space) and with his ongoing design work with U2, and in a day–to–day context with Averill Brophy Associates, the company he co–founded ten years ago. The photograph below, a testament to the fragility of modernism and the power of beer and shotgun shell, was taken in the Nevada desert.

Stephen Averill

FRANK ORMSBY was born in County Fermanagh in 1947 and educated at Queen's University, Belfast. His collections of poetry include *A Northern Spring*, *A Store of Candles* and *The Ghost Train*. He won a Gregory Award for Poetry in 1974. He now teaches English at the Royal Belfast Academical Institution and edits *The Honest Ulsterman*.

Frank Ormsby

THE BUILDER

Even at fifty you were in demand,
three hayfields of your handiwork on show
each summer where your father's farm sloped
to the main road. So often we watched you step

into that rough circle. Your arms swept
round the prongs of dangerous pitchforks.
You seemed to embrace entire meadows,
patting them like aprons about your knees.

As you rose on your own foundation, people waved
from bus windows. The more you spread and trod,
above head–height, above hedge–height, the further we
had to step back not to lose sight of you.

You never looked like falling. Braced at the top,
you fielded the two hayropes, threw them back
nonchalantly between your legs
and prepared to return to the earth.

No memory now to match this: you gather your skirts
and slide with a girlish flourish
down the rick face,
land like a gymnast among our outstretched arms.

DERMOT SEYMOUR, a painter, was born in Belfast in 1956. He studied at the University of Ulster. Since his first solo exhibition in Belfast in 1981, he has exhibited widely throughout Ireland, had solo shows in Berlin and New York, and taken part in numerous international group shows. He has received many awards, including the PSI international studio fellowship in New York in 1987 and the Marten Toonder Award in 1996, and was elected a member of Aosdána in 1997. He now lives and works in County Mayo.

Dermot Seymour

The Mistrust of Matter

BRENDAN McWILLIAMS, one of the *Irish Times*'s most popular columnists, has been producing his daily 'Weather Eye' column for the newspaper since August 1988. Born in Cahirsiveen, County Kerry in 1944, he has followed his father into the profession of meteorologist after briefly working as a teacher. During the 1970s he was a weather forecaster on television before becoming head of administration for the Irish Meteorological Service in Glasnevin, Dublin. In addition to his work with this organisation and *The Irish Times*, in recent years he also edited a report on the implications of climate change for Ireland. He now works for EUMETSAT, the European Meteorological Satellite Organisation, and lives with his wife, Anne, in Darmstadt, Germany.

Brendan McWilliams

SHAWONDASEE'S SUMMER

Sometimes, in the twilight of the year, the weather gives us one last chance. The term Indian Summer is of native American origin, and according to Longfellow in *The Song of Hiawatha*, is brought by Shawondasee, the personification of the South Wind – a languid, warm and easygoing spirit.

> Shawondasee, fat and lazy,
> Had his dwelling far to southward,
> In the drowsy, dreamy sunshine,
> In the never–ending Summer.

Shawondasee was benign. He sent the migratory birds northward in the springtime, and provided the right conditions for fertile crops and rich hunting. And before the real onset of winter each year...

> From his pipe the smoke ascending
> Filled the sky with haze and vapour,
> Filled the air with dreamy softness,
> Gave a twinkle to the water,
> Touched the rugged hills with smoothness,
> Brought the tender Indian Summer
> To the melancholy North–land,
> In the dreary Moon of Snow–shoes.

Tom Murphy, playwright, was born
in Tuam, County Galway. He lives in
Dublin. He is a member of Aosdána and the
Irish Academy of Letters and among his
various awards is an honorary D.Litt. from
the University of Dublin. Works include
A Whistle in the Dark, *The Sanctuary Lamp*,
Famine, *Conversations on a Homecoming*,
Bailegangaire, *The Gigli Concert*, *The Wake*
and *She Stoops to Folly*.

Tom Murphy

CHRISTY: Yeh know Robin Hood, Mrs de Burca? Your man with the feather, bow–and–arrow, Sherwood Forest.

MRS DE BURCA: I do.

CHRISTY: Well, he's dying yah see, and he's very bad, feeble, and he's in bed in his room, and Friar Tuck is with him. And says he to Friar Tuck: 'Pull back that curtain, open that window so that I can behold my beloved Sherwood Forest for one last time.' And Friar Tuck does everything he's told. 'Now,' says Robin, and the hands on him are very shaky, 'hand me down my bow and arrow. And now,' says he, aiming the bow at the window, 'wherever this arrow falls, it's on that spot I'm to be buried by my merry men.' And he fires. And d'you know where they buried him? On top of the wardrobe.

From a work in progress

RONNIE DREW was born in Glasthule, County Dublin in 1934. He attended the Christian Brothers' School in Dun Laoghaire until the age of seventeen and there followed a few years of dead-end jobs. In 1956 he became a telephonist in Dublin's Telephone Exchange but he left after a year and went to Seville, to teach English and to learn some flamenco guitar. On a visit home, he was invited by John Molloy to take part in a show in the Gate Theatre and a few years later he was a founder member of The Dubliners, where he remained for thirty-three years. He left the group in 1995 'but I'm still available for work'.

Ronnie Drew

Well! he got burned at last. 'Good enough for him. He burned us for long enough' – always a penny dearer than anybody else.

This was said to me on a Dublin street in or about February 1969, by a well-known Dublin oul fella as he pointed to a few lads who were carrying from a pub the charred remains of chairs, stools, etc., the result of a non-life-threatening interior fire.

Feeling that I was, of course, wiser in the ways of the world than this 'oul fella', I said to him, 'There's no fear of him, Joe. I'd swear he had the place well backed and that the insurance would cover all his losses.'

'I know him for forty years,' said Joe, 'and when he goes home tonight and he has no pound notes to count it'll break his miserable heart.'

BILLY ROCHE, playwrite, actor and author, was born in Wexford in 1949. His first novel, *Tumbling Down*, was published in 1986. The plays *A Handful of Stars*, *Poor Beast in the Rain* and *Belfry* make up what is known as the Wexford Trilogy. Other plays include *Amphibians* and *The Cavalcaders*. His first film, *Trojan Eddie*, was screened in 1996.

Billy Roche

I LET MY HAIR DOWN

I Let My Hair Down
I Slipped My Shoes Off
Danced Like An Angel
But I Still Didn't Win His Heart

Leaves Of A Willow
Under My Pillow
Calling Him Softly
As I Slumbered

I Saw The Sun Rise
I Saw The Moonshine
I Heard His Name Linked
To Every Rumour

I Saw Him Laughing
From A Distance
I Heard Him Whistling
In The Evening

I Let My Hair Down
I Slipped My Shoes Off
Danced Like An Angel...

'Bridie's Song' from the stage play *Amphibians*

T.K. (KEN) WHITAKER, public servant, was born in Rostrevor, County Down in 1916. He was educated by Christian Brothers, Drogheda, and obtained, by private study, the degrees of B.Sc. (Econ.) and M.Sc. (Econ.) of London University. Secretary, Department of Finance, 1956–69, governor, Central Bank of Ireland, 1969–76, senator, 1977–82, Chancellor, National University of Ireland, 1976–96. He was the principal author of *Economic Development* (1958). He chaired the Committee of Inquiry into the Penal System, 1984–5 and the Constitution Review Group, 1995–6.

T.K. Whitaker

FROM DIARY JOTTINGS

The door to happiness opens outwards

L'amour ne se paie que par l'amour. (St Thérèse)
(Love's only recompense is love)

Make of the stones of the place
A pillow for thy head
And thou shalt see angels
Ascending and descending. (Unknown)

Níl pian, níl peannaid
Níl galar chó trom–chráite
Le héag na gcarad
Nó scaradh na gcompánach. (Cathaoir Mac Cába)

I beseech you, in the bowels of Christ, think it possible you may be mistaken. (Cromwell)

FROM PERSONAL REFLECTION

A full–time job is your best protection against overwork.

An unpaid job is the hardest to resign from.

A reputation is rarely enhanced by an autobiography.

La gloire est la somme des malentendus qui se forment autour d'un nom. (Rilke)

GUGGI ROWEN was born in 1959 in Dublin. The second of ten children, he began drawing and painting as a child. A rebel then and a rebel now, he shied away from formal art training and embraced the punk movement at the age of seventeen. He was a founder member of The Virgin Prunes, the cult Dublin band, which combined music with the visual arts to create performance punk art. In 1986 Guggi returned to full-time painting. His work is on permanent display in the Clarence Hotel in Temple Bar, Dublin. He is married to the artist Sibylle Ungers.

Guggi

A Jug for Sibylle

Guggi 98.

ANTHONY CRONIN was born in Enniscorthy, County Wexford and has lived mainly in Dublin, but also in London and Spain. He is a poet, novelist, critic and biographer. His book *Dead as Doornails*, an account of a friendship with Brendan Behan, Flann O'Brien, Patrick Kavanagh and others, is considered a classic. He has written biographies of Flann O'Brien and Samuel Beckett, as well as the novels *The Life of Riley* and *Identity Papers*.

Anthony Cronin

SONG

(for Robert MacBryde)

All things tend to completion,
Towards a resultant end.
The heat of a harvest noonday
With an August night will blend.

The rose burns out in its calyx.
The leaf yields to the ground.
Almost every appearance
Is with disappearance crowned.

VAL MULKERNS was born in Dublin in 1925. Her first novel, *A Time Outworn*, was followed by *A Peacock Cry*, *The Summerhouse* and *Very Like a Whale*. She won the AIB Prize for Literature in 1984. She was a weekly columnist on the *Evening Press* from 1968 to 1983, and in 1997–8 was was writer-in-residence at Mayo County Library, where she edited an anthology, *New Writings from the West*.

Val Mulkerns

He remembered the day when he had come closest to his commanding officer after the week's fiercest battle when they found the six mown–down Tommies in a heap together near the head of Church St, like boys who had tumbled over in a game. He knew that Ned Daly and himself were united in not seeing them any more as the ancient enemy but as sons and brothers who would not go home any more and who hadn't even the glory of dying out in Flanders. Their families and friends would see this as death in a brawl in Ireland, stupid and ignoble and soon to be forgotten.

BENEDICT KIELY was born in 1919 in Omagh, County Tyrone but has spent most of his life in Dublin, where he studied at University College. His long and successful career spans the writing of novels, short stories and memoirs. His novels include *The Cards of the Gambler*, *The Captain with the Whiskers*, *Dogs Enjoy the Morning*, and *Nothing Happens in Carmincross*. His short-story collections include *A Journey to the Seven Streams* and *A Ball of Malt and Madame Butterfly*. The second volume of his memoirs, *The Waves Behind Us*, was published in 1999. In 1996 he was presented with the golden torc of a Saoi of the Aosdána by President Robinson.

Benedict Kiely

My father died in a seaside town in the County Donegal, forty miles from the town I was reared in. The road his funeral followed back to the home places led along the Erne shore by the Stone Fiddle of Castlecauldwell and the glistening water, across the Boa Island where there are no longer crossroads dances. Every roadside house has a television aerial. It led by a meadowland saucer of the Minnieburns where the river still springs from seven magic sources. That brooding place is still much as it was but no longer did it seem to me to be as vast as Siberia. To the left now the low sullen outline of Cornavara and Pigeon Top, the hurdle that our Bucephalus refused to take. To the right was Drumlish. The old schoolhouse was gone and, in its place, a white building, ten times as large, with drying rooms for wet coats, fine warm lunches for children, and even a gymnasium. But the belt of trees that he and Paddy Hamish planted to break the wind and shelter the children is still there.

Somebody tells me, too, that the engine of Hookey Baxter's car is still with us, turning a circular saw for a farmer in the vicinity of Clanabogan. As the Irish proverb says: It's the little thing doesn't last longer than a man.

From *A Journey to the Seven Streams*

BRIDGET O'CONNOR was born in London to Irish parents. She studied English at Lancaster University. She was included in *The Picador Book of Contemporary Irish Fiction* and her story 'Harp' won the *Time Out* Writing Competition. Her books include *Here Comes John* and *Tell Her You Love Her*. In 1993 she was shortlisted for the *Irish Times* Literature Prize for a First Book.

Bridget O'Connor

'Banna Beach, County Kerry. The Summer Elvis Died.' From left to right: Peggy, Kathleen, James, Bridget and Rosie O'Connor.

16.08.2000

August/Lúnasa

WEDNESDAY / CÉADAOIN

DAVID BYRNE studied at the Abbey Theatre's National School of Drama and worked extensively as performer with both the Abbey Company and Edwards/MacLiammóir Gate Theatre Company. In 1975 he joined Radio Telefís Éireann Young People's Programming as writer/producer. A founder member of Wet Paint Arts, and artistic director since its inception, he wrote and directed six works, winning in 1985 the Arts Council's Experimental Theatre Award. In 1991 he was appointed new writing editor at the Abbey Theatre. He has won a number of national and international awards, including Fringe Firsts in the 1990 and 1995 Edinburgh Festivals.

David Byrne

I stood at the bottom of the garden watching my seven–year–old son, Robert, climbing a tree.

Now, he wasn't very high, I could step in, reach up and lift him down. But, I stood watching.

There was a crack as the branch broke.

I tried, but his falling body burst through my outstretched arms and I heard the thud of his small body hitting the ground.

As he stood up he looked at me, I supposed, wondering if I would say something about the broken branch.

I wanted to say 'I broke your fall.' But I hadn't.

Last week he came out the front door, put his two arms around my waist and lifted me clean off the ground.

Don't, I said, don't, please. I have a sore back.

BASIL BLACKSHAW was born in County Antrim in 1932 and studied at the Belfast College of Art. His work has been exhibited in many one-person and group shows, beginning in 1952 in the Donegall Place Gallery in Belfast and including the Living Art, Rosc, the Kerlin Gallery in Dublin, the Arnolfini in Bristol, the Tate in London and the Watergate Gallery in Washington DC. A major retrospective of his work opened in Belfast in 1995 and toured to several venues in Ireland and the United States. Between 1986 and 1990 he designed the posters for the productions of the Field Day Company. He is a member of Aosdána.

Basil Blackshaw

MÁIRÍN JOHNSTON was born in the Liberties, Dublin. She is the author of *Around the Banks of Pimlico*, a best-seller, published in 1985. *Dublin Belles* (1988), retitled *Alive, Alive, O*, is a collection of conversations with Dublin women. Her first children's book, *The Pony Express*, won the Bisto Book of the Year Merit Award in 1993. She is co-author of *These Obstreperous Lassies* (1945), a play on the laundrywomen's strike of 1945, produced by Theatreworks in Dublin. Her second children's book is *Rebel on the Run*.

Máirín Johnston

Lying there in the quiet solitude of the forest, there was nothing for me to do but think. My thoughts wandered randomly over all the events that had taken place since I'd left home yesterday. So much had happened it seemed as though I'd managed to squeeze a lifetime's experiences into a few hours – experiences I could well and truly have done without.

Living wild on the run was definitely not for me. I desperately wanted to go home. I missed Rory. I missed my regular meals. I missed my creature comforts. For Rebel it was different. He was wild, untrained, a free spirit. I vowed that tomorrow I would make my way to the canal and sail home on Jack's barge with Trixie.

From *Rebel on the Run*

RACHEL JOYNT, born in County Kerry in 1966, graduated from the National College of Art & Design in Dublin in 1989 with a degree in sculpture. The year before this, she received her first commission, for *People's Island* near O'Connell Bridge, Dublin. Her first solo exhibition, *Selene*, was shown at the capital's Project Arts Centre and the Arts Council Gallery, Belfast in 1994, and in the same year she was awarded the Arts Council Macaulay Fellowship. A residency and exhibition in Marseilles were her contribution to the L'Imaginaire Irlandais festival in 1996 and she is currently working on a public commission for the Dun Laoghaire seafront.

Rachel Joynt

Work in Progress

CARLO GÉBLER was born in Dublin in 1954, educated in England and now lives in Enniskillen, Northern Ireland, where he is married with five children. He has made several documentaries for television, and published a non-fiction book about Northern Ireland, *The Glass Curtain*, but he is best known for his novels, which include *The Eleventh Summer* (1985), *The Cure* (1994) and *How to Murder a Man* (1998). He is writer-in-residence at H.M.P. Maghaberry.

Carlo Gébler

For the next half-hour, while the storm raged, the metropolis was going to be awash with rain. But then, the rain would stop and the clouds would move on, hurried off by the wind, and the rainwater would drain away, along the gutters and down the drains and into the rivers, taking all the heat and the dust of the city along with itself; and the rainwater would flow on, bearing its cargo, until eventually, it tumbled out into the sea.

And then, when the people of the city awoke, they would find their streets were clean and cool; they would find that the air was dry, and that it was possible to breathe again; they would find the sky was blue and clean and open; and they would find that the sun, where it fell, was warming the chilly world with its touch.

From the story 'W9'

ARTHUR MATHEWS was born in County Meath in 1959. He studied graphic design in the College of Marketing and Design before becoming a designer for Hot Press magazine. He was one-third of the 'joke U2 tribute' band, The Joshua Trio, and was a regular cartoonist for the New Musical Express. With writer Graham Linehan, he created the television comedy series Father Ted.

Arthur Mathews

EAVAN BOLAND was born in Dublin in 1944 and educated in Ireland, England and the United States. She taught English at Trinity College, Dublin between 1966 and 1968. Her first book of poetry, *New Territory*, appeared in 1967. Three subsequent volumes have been the Poetry Book Society Choice: *The Journey and Other Poems* (1986), *Outside History* (1990) and *In a Time of Violence* (1994). She holds the chair of poetry at Stanford in California, but lives mainly in Dublin.

Eavan Boland

THIS MOMENT

A neighbourhood
at dusk.

Things are getting ready
to happen
out of sight –

Stars and moths and rinds slanting
around fruit.

One tree is black.
One window is yellow as butter.

A woman leans down to catch a child
who has run into her arms
this moment.

Stars rise.
Moths flutter. Apples sweeten in the dark.

SIBYLLE UNGERS, born in Cologne in 1960, studied fine arts at Cornell University, New York. In 1984 she joined the Max Hetzler Gallery in Cologne. She was the youngest winner of the Schmidt–Rottluff Award. She moved to Ireland for a six–month stay which became permanent when she married the painter Guggi Rowen in 1992. She now lives in Dublin but returns frequently to Cologne to exhibit.

Sibylle Ungers

24.08.2000

August/Lúnasa

THURSDAY / DÉARDAOIN

PATRICK O'BRIEN was born in Claremorris, County Mayo in 1951. He was ordained a priest in 1979, has served on Clare Island and Skehana and is currently in Kilmeena. A collection of poetry, *A Book of Genesis*, appeared in 1988. He edited the *Selected Poems* of Daniel Berrigan and is preparing a selected Thomas Merton. He also edited a book on the poetry of Padraic Fallon and is working on a cultural history of the Tuam diocese, for the millennium.

Patrick O'Brien

FIRST STEP

What I first remember is the end – blood
sponging through the fluff feathers of a day–
old–chick, and on the kitchen floor a mood
broken forever. I was suddenly
on the edge of unknowns. Time sets the scene:
a white raeburn range mothering the heat,
a cardboard box nestling some half dozen
chicks, a child, me, about to find first feet.
And not finding them, or to only live
for a moment the thin air of new heights.
Somewhere a voice counts: 'One. Two. Three. Four. Five.'
Silence pools in the pulped flesh of the sixth.
And I will always be that child, in fear
that each first step of man is weighed in tears.

RODDY DOYLE was born in Dublin in 1958 and educated at University College, Dublin. He is the author of five novels and a number of plays. The first three novels, known as the Barrytown Trilogy, have each been filmed. In 1993 his novel *Paddy Clarke Ha Ha Ha* won the Booker Prize.

Roddy Doyle

So the city was crawling with Tommies and Irish-born squaddies, and lots of them were broke and desperate enough to sell their rifles to us. Officers, even Unionist officers, came looking for us once word got round that ready cash could be had from the Shinners in exchange for working weapons. We gave four quid each for Lee-Enfields. And we upped it to a fiver when a colonel in the Munster Rifles threw in his Official Army Military Manual with the gun, as well as a box of bullets and a map of Dublin Castle. We carried the Manual around inside the covers of a book, *Uncle Tom's Cabin*, one of the few that Granny Nash hadn't wanted.

'I had an Uncle Tom,' she said. 'I don't want to waste my time reading about another one.'

From a novel in slow progress

DESMOND O'GRADY, poet, was born in Limerick in 1935. He left to teach and write in Paris, Rome, the United States and Egypt. During the late 1950s in Rome he was a founder member of the European Community of Writers, editor of *The Transatlantic Review* and English editor of *Europa Letteraria*. He lives in Kinsale, County Cork and has published sixteen collections of poetry, including *The Road Taken, 1956–1996*, nine collections of translated poetry, including *Trawling Tradition, 1954–1994*, and prose memoirs. He is a member of Aosdána.

Desmond O'Grady

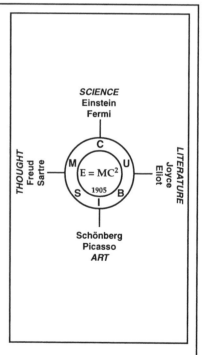

Millennium Elegy

Skeletons in those vaults of man's barbaric past
rattle. The millennium's end disturbs their rest.

Uniforms in their castles of our fearsome present
reflect on their truthful mirrors' content:

"What does the Emperor command?" mouths the visage.
"To mould you all in my deathless image."

We are not who we think; solely what we do:
remembered if our life moves some rare few.

The mirror shows the best and worst of our dark past
millennium as ruler, thinker, artist.

Rulers offer us their now or their abstract hereafter,
either may nourish life, prevent disaster.

Poet and prosist implode all place and time in now.
Thinkers help us grow, heal as best we know.

The artist shows us all our features combine as one
however placed; composers the same.

Those reflected perspectives that face myself shock
me dumb. The Bang that made us all will suck

us back to 0. All life began, will end in naught.
Physics theory in three letters spells that.

The Ides of March, 1998

SCIENCE
Einstein
Fermi

THOUGHT
Freud
Sartre

LITERATURE
Joyce
Eliot

Schönberg
Picasso
ART

$E = MC^2$
1905

LOUIS MARCUS, a documentary–maker, was born in Cork in 1936. Since moving to Dublin in 1960, he has made over seventy films and television programmes, winning twenty international festival awards, including two Academy Award nominations. A long–time activist for an Irish film industry, he is currently chairperson of Bord Scannán na hÉireann/The Irish Film Board.

Louis Marcus

A few years ago, I made a bilingual television
documentary on the Hospice movement called
'Saol go Deire – Living to the End'.

I approached it with some trepidation – for myself
and for the audience. People with terminal illness
seemed a gloomy prospect for both maker and viewers.

As it turned out, I could not have been more wrong.
Under Hospice care, whether institutional or in their
own homes, the patients had discovered that dying
could be a rich part of living – for some, perhaps,
the richest they had known!

So, with only a few weeks to live, they took part
with enthusiasm in a programme that they hoped
would convey this life–affirming message to others.

Contrary to my initial forebodings, they attracted
and held an audience of half a million.

CIARÁN BENSON was born in 1950 in Dun Laoghaire, County Dublin. He is Professor of Psychology in University College, Dublin and a former chairman of An Chomhairle Ealaíon/The Arts Council of the Republic of Ireland (1993–8). He lives in Dublin.

Ciarán Benson

Narcissus or Echo?

Early spring they met
Eyes, Gulls adrift in sunlight.
A tide coming in.

A summer rock pool,
Anemones closing. The
Pupils of her eyes.

He used see himself
In her eyes. Now the mirror's
Broken, he's shattered.

JEAN KENNEDY SMITH served as the United
States Ambassador to Ireland from 1993 to
1998, and was awarded Irish citizenship for
her service to the country.

Jean Kennedy Smith

'I am certain that after the dust of centuries has passed over our
cities, we, too, will be remembered not for our victories or defeats in
battle or in politics but for our contribution to the human spirit.'

PRESIDENT JOHN F. KENNEDY

VAN MORRISON was born in 1945 in Belfast; his father was an avid collector of blues and jazz records. Van first began performing with Irish showbands and later in the sixties fronted the R&B group Them. After Them split up, he recorded the solo album *Astral Weeks* in 1968, an album which is still regarded as a landmark achievement. He has since released almost thirty albums, with styles ranging from jazz and blues to soul, plus his own unique sound of music, during a career spanning more than three decades. He continues to perform and record regularly, to critical acclaim.

Van Morrison

ON HYNDFORD STREET

Take me back, take me way, way, way back
On Hyndford Street
Where you could feel the silence at half past eleven
On long summer nights
As the wireless played Radio Luxembourg
And the voices whispered across Beechie River
In the quietness
As we sank into restful slumber
In the silence
And carried on dreaming in God

ANNE MADDEN was born to Irish and Anglo–Chilean parents and has spent most of her life between Ireland and France. She has held more than forty personal exhibitions and her work is represented in many public and private collections internationally. She is married to the artist Louis le Brocquy and they share a studio in France and Dublin. A permanent space in the Château Musée in Carros is dedicated to their work. She published *Louis le Brocquy: Seeing His Way* in 1994. Anne Madden is a member of Aosdána.

Anne Madden

MARTIN MCDONAGH was born in London to Irish parents. As a child he visited Irish relations and became fascinated by their stories and speech patterns. The Leenane Trilogy, comprising *The Beauty Queen of Leenane*, *A Skull in Connemara* and *The Lonesome West*, was a theatrical sensation, *Beauty Queen* winning four Tony Awards in 1998. He has also written *The Cripple of Inishmaan* and *The Pillowman*.

Martin McDonagh

THE TALE OF THE TOWN ON THE RIVER

Once upon a time in a tiny cobbled-streeted town on the banks of a fast-flowing river, there lived a little boy who did not get along with the other children of the town; they teased and picked on and bullied him, because he was poor and his parents were drunkards and his clothes were rags and he walked around barefoot. The little boy, however, was of a happy and dreamy disposition, and he did not mind the taunts and the beatings and the unending solitude. He knew that he was kind-hearted and full of love and that someday someone somewhere would surely see this love inside of him and repay him in kind. Then, one night, as he sat nursing his newest bruises at the foot of the wooden bridge that crossed the river and led out of town, he heard, then saw, the approach of a horse and cart along the dark, cobbled street, and as it neared he saw that its driver was dressed in the darkest of robes, the black hood of which bathed the whole of his craggy face in shadow and sent a shiver of fear through the little boy's body. Putting his fear aside, the boy took out the small sandwich that was to be his supper that night and, just as the cart was about to pass onto and over the bridge, offered it up to the hooded driver to see if he would like some. The cart stopped and the driver nodded, got down and sat beside the little boy for a while, sharing the sandwich and discussing this and that. The driver asked the boy why he was barefoot and ragged and all alone, and as the boy told the driver of his poor, hard life, he eyed the back of the driver's cart; it was piled high with small, empty animal cages, all foul-smelling and dirt-lined, and just as the boy was about to ask what kind of animals it was had been inside them, the driver stood up, having finished his food, and announced that he had to be on his way. 'But before I go,' the driver whispered, 'because you have been so kindly to an old weary traveller in offering half of your already meagre portions like this, I would like to give you something now, the worth of which today you may not realise, but one day, when you are a little older perhaps, I think you will truly value and thank me for. Now close your eyes.' And so the little boy closed his eyes, and from a secret inner pocket of his robes the driver pulled out a long, sharp and shiny meat cleaver, raised it high in the air and brought it scything down onto the boy's right foot, severing all five of his muddy little toes. And as the little boy sat there in gaping, silent shock, staring blankly off into the far distance, the driver gathered up his bloody toes, tossed them away to the gaggle of rats that had begun to gather in the gutters around, got back onto his cart again, and quietly rode on over the bridge, leaving the boy, the rats, the river and the darkening town of Hamelin far behind him.

SHAY HEALY, a multimedia artist, was born in Dublin in 1943. He is the director of television documentaries (*Small World, Dr Courageous*), a songwriter (Eurovision Song Contest winner in 1980 with 'What's Another Year?') and novelist (*The Stunt, Greencard Blues*). He is also a photographer (exhibitions: *America in 60 Minutes, Dublin in 60 Minutes*), journalist and television host (*Nighthawks, Beastly Behaviour*).

Shay Healy

MARIAN KEYES was born in Limerick and brought up in Cavan, Cork, Galway and Dublin. She spent her twenties in London and is now living in Dun Laoghaire. Her novels *Watermelon, Lucy Sullivan is Getting Married* and *Rachel's Holiday* are all best-sellers in Ireland and Britain. She also writes monthly columns and one-offs for various magazines. She is working on her fourth novel and a multi-authored project for Amnesty International.

Marian Keyes

SANSKRIT PROVERB

Look to this day
For it is life
The very life of life.
In its brief course lie all
The realities and verities of existence,
The bliss of growth,
The splendour of action,
The glory of power –

For yesterday is but a dream,
And tomorrow is only a vision,
But today, well lived,
Makes every yesterday a dream of happiness
And every tomorrow a vision of hope.

Look well, therefore, to this day.

REMCO DE FOUW was born in 1962. Since graduating with a degree in sculpture from the National College of Art & Design in Dublin, he has shown work in many group exhibitions. He recently received the Alexandra Wejchert Sculpture Award. As part of several months' travel in Asia, he completed a residency at the Sanskriti Kendra in India in 1994; in the same year, he had his first solo exhibition, *Reservoir*, at the Project Arts Centre, Dublin. More recently, he held a show called *Undercurrent* at the Temple Bar Gallery and the Model Arts Centre, Sligo. He has completed a number of public commissions and is currently concentrating mainly on photographic projects.

Remco de Fouw

From *Infinity + 1 Series*

ITA DALY was born in County Leitrim, but her family moved to Dublin when she was thirteen. She took a degree in English and Spanish at University College, Dublin, where she also did postgraduate work in English. She taught for eleven years until the birth of her daughter in 1979. Her novels include *Ellen* and *A Singular Attraction*.

Ita Daly

At six months, Nellie's head began to grow faster than the rest of her. At nine months it was too heavy for her to lift off the pillow and Dr McGinley, summoned from Fintown, had diagnosed some condition, incurable and with a many-syllabled name.

No second opinion was sought, no quack or seventh son called in, for Nellie's deformity was now seen as something shameful, something which must be kept hidden as far as that was possible. Lily was warned not to talk about her at school and when she died a month past her fourth birthday it was taken as an indication of God's infinite mercy.

Lily was not so sure as she witnessed her mother's leaden inertia and the *Táilliúr*'s increasingly lengthy absences from home. It was then too that his drinking began to get out of control.

Lily thought it a curious fashion in which God chose to manifest His mercy.

From a novel in progress

GWEN O'DOWD was born in 1957 in Dublin, where she now lives and works. She graduated from the National College of Art & Design, Dublin in 1980 and since then has been painting full-time. She had her first solo show in the Project Arts Centre in 1984 to much acclaim, establishing her among the leading younger generation of artists at the time. Since then, she has had numerous exhibitions both in Ireland and abroad and is represented in major collections. Her work originated with landscape but seems to encapsulate not only the physical but the emotional and spiritual environments. She has been a member of Aosdána since 1991.

Gwen O'Dowd

RICHARD KEARNEY was born in Cork in 1954. Professor of Philosophy at University College, Dublin, he has written many books on philosophy and literature, including *The Wake of Imagination* and *Poétique du Possible*. He was founder editor of *The Crane Bag*, a review of arts, politics and philosophy. He is also the author of a collection of poetry, *Angel of Patrick's Hill*, and two novels, *Sam's Fall* and *Walking at Sea Level*.

Richard Kearney

It is here and now, in the very darkness of the post–modern labyrinth, that we must begin again to listen to the story of imagination. For it is perhaps in its tale of the self relating to the other, that we will discover a golden thread which leads beyond the labyrinth. Might we not surmise an ethical summons lodged at the very heart of our post–modern culture? And also a poetic summons: to see that imagination continues playfully to create and recreate even at the moment it is announcing its own disappearance? Even when it can't go on, the post–modern imagination goes on. A child making traces at the edge of the sea. Imagining otherwise. Imagination's wake. Dying? Awakening?

From *The Wake of Imagination*

Brian Keenan was born in Belfast in 1950 and studied at Coleraine University, where he took an MA in Anglo–Irish literature. He taught in northern Spain before returning to Belfast, where he worked as a teacher and later a community development officer. In 1985 he went to teach in the American University at Beirut. After three months he was taken hostage and held by Islamic fundamentalists for almost five years. On his release in 1990 he wrote a journal of his captivity, *An Evil Cradling*. He is currently working on a book on Turlough Carolan and another on his travels in Chile.

Brian Keenan

nothing *escapes the sound of time.*
Its resonance marks out the boundary
for all human activity,
provoking
the irrevocable decision
that life must be lived
within that line,
or nothing at all.

'I firmly believe
there is always
an end and a
beginning, a purpose
in all things. If
we choose to make
it so and choose
to believe
that it will be so.'

Christmas without Chains, 1996

GENE KERRIGAN was born in Dublin in 1949 and raised in Cabra west. He has worked for *Magill* magazine, *The Sunday Tribune* and *The Sunday Independent* and has written five books: *Round up the Usual Suspects* (1984) with the late Derek Dunne, *Nothing but the Truth* (1990), the text of *Goodbye to All That* (1992) with Derek Speirs's photographs, *Hard Cases* (1996) and *Another Country* (1998). He is married to Julie Lordan and has a daughter, Cathleen.

Gene Kerrigan

She was buried in the same grave as Eileen, which is the grave in which their parents are buried, in Glasnevin cemetery. Their brother Joe lies quite close and not too far away is the grave of my Uncle Larry and his wife Mary.

On the morning my mother was buried I stood beside the priest, a kind man who had often visited my mother during her last years. He leaned forward and looked down into the grave. Then, purely as a matter of observed fact, just making small talk, he turned to me and he said, 'There's room for one more.' I looked into the grave and I nodded and I said, 'So there is.'

From *Another Country*

RICHARD HARRIS was born in Limerick in 1930 and educated in Ireland and at the London Academy of Music and Dramatic Art. He made his stage debut in 1956 in *The Quare Fellow*. A larger–than–life personality translated well on to screen in such films as Lindsay Anderson's *This Sporting Life* (1963), *A Man Called Horse* (1969) and Jim Sheridan's *The Field* (1990), for which he was nominated for an Academy Award.

Richard Harris

EXCUSE ME, while I disappear
Actually I was NOT HERE
NEITHER WAS I THERE
NOR WAS I SOMEWHERE
BETWEEN HERE AND THERE

MAY BE I WAS WHERE
HERE AND THERE never meet
LOST
BETWEEN THE IF'S AND BUT'S
of mind and Body
I IN THE four SEASONS of a perfect VAPOUR

MAY BE I WAS
maybe I WASN'T
MAY BE I WAS NEVER I
MAY BE I WAS NEVER ME
MAY BE ME WAS NEVER I
MAY BE I OR ME WAS NEVER THERE OR HERE
to disappear in the perfection of VAPOUR.

BERTIE AHERN, TD was born in Dublin in September 1951 and, as a member of the Fianna Fáil party, was first elected to Dáil Éireann in 1977. After being an Assistant Whip in 1980–81, he became Minister of State at the Departments of the Taoiseach and Defence and Government Chief Whip in 1982. He was appointed Minister for Labour five years later and again in 1989. Dublin's Lord Mayor for 1986–7, he has been Minister for Finance three times, first in 1991. In November 1994 he was unanimously elected Leader of Fianna Fáil and in June 1997 was elected An Taoiseach.

Bertie Ahern

WHOSEDAY IS IT TODAY?

Whoseday is it today?
to cry arrive, or slip away
From shadowland to light and then to dark,
Each one to make their presence felt
And mark.

Deep in the ancient springs of Irishness
Great talents spin and bubble to the top
In glint of eye, in tart–tang tongue
And sweet euphonious ear –
To sing what we hold dear, and
Celebrate from year to year.

New ship upon the bay, new boat
On old Styx way
Penny–bridge for your thoughts.
Whoseday is it today?

ANNE DEVLIN was born in Belfast in 1951. She has written two plays for the theatre: *Ourselves Alone* (Royal Court, 1985) and *After Easter* (Royal Shakespeare Company, 1994). A collection of short stories, *The Way–Paver*, was published in 1985. As well as writing several plays for radio and TV, she adapted *Wuthering Heights* for Paramount in 1991. She now lives in London with her husband and son.

Anne Devlin

I am three,
I have just got my new three–wheeled bike.
I am riding along the hall. I pass the parlour
door, the walnut piano is up against the wall.
My grandmother is standing in the doorway to
the livingroom. She is talking about playing
the piano: you have to press on the pedals,
you have to know when to use them. I turn my
bike around and pedal down the hall to the
bolted door: a letter cage hangs on it to catch
the letters. A meat safe hangs on the wall by
the backyard door: fat flies settle on the
tight mesh. These are the boundaries of the
house. Uncollected letters lie in the cage
on the closed front door, I wonder if when
I am four I will be able to explain to her
that safe and cage are not the same
and a bike is really a piano.

13 September 1954: A Memory

PAULA MEEHAN was born and reared in the city of Dublin. She has published four collections of poetry; her most recent work is available from Gallery Press. She has also written for the stage, for both children and adults.

Paula Meehan

In Memory, John Borrowman

All things move through me:
the wind that shakes the willow;
my old friend's last breath.

In memory of all my family and friends who didn't make it to the Millennium

MICHAEL LONGLEY was born in Belfast in 1939 and educated at the Royal Belfast Academical Institution and Trinity College, Dublin, where he read classics. For twenty–five years he worked for the Arts Council of Northern Ireland, where he initiated the programmes for literature, the traditional arts and arts–in–education. His poetry collections include *Poems 1963–1983*, *Gorse Fires*, which won the Whitbread Prize for Poetry, and *The Ghost Orchid*. He is married to the critic Edna Longley and lives in Belfast.

Michael Longley

A TOUCH
after the Irish

She is the touch of pink
On crab apple blossom
And hawthorn, and she melts
Frostflowers with her finger.

Michael Longley

JOHN HORGAN was born in County Kerry in 1940. A journalist, author and teacher, he has worked for the *Evening Press*, the *Catholic Herald* and *The Irish Times*, where he was editor of *The Education Times* from 1973 to 1976. In 1969 he was elected to the Seanad, becoming subsequently a Labour TD and MEP. Since 1982 he has been teaching journalism at Dublin City University. He is the author of a number of books, most recently political biographies of Mary Robinson and Seán Lemass.

John Horgan

CUBAN MISSILE CRISIS, 1962

Only the typesetters will have time to read
Banner headlines half unrolled
And the shocked certainty of war revealed.
Yesterday's rumours blow about the streets –
Tattered confetti for a shotgun spree –
Past the crowded corners
Where their readers wait, furled,
Dead leaves on a terrible tree.

SAMUEL WALSH, born in London in 1951 to Irish parents, moved to Limerick in 1968. He came to prominence as an artist through his one-man exhibitions with the Oliver Dowling Gallery in Dublin and now shows with the Rubicon Gallery, Dublin. His work is notably included in the collection of the Irish Museum of Modern Art and he is the founder of the National Collection of Contemporary Drawing in Limerick. He is a member of Aosdána and now lives and works in County Clare.

Samuel Walsh

JOHN CONNOLLY was born in Rialto, Dublin in 1968. He studied English at Trinity College, Dublin and journalism in Dublin City University before becoming a freelance journalist with *The Irish Times*. His first novel, *Every Dead Thing*, published in 1999, concerns the efforts of a former New York detective, 'Bird' Parker, to find the murderer of his wife and child, a serial killer known only as 'The Travelling Man'.

John Connolly

And I will sit on my porch as the wind takes the evergreens in hand, pressing and moulding their branches into new shapes, creating a song from their leaves. And I will listen for the sound of a dog barking, its paws scraping on the worn boards, its tail moving lazily in the cool evening air; or the tap–tap–tap on the rail as my grandfather prepares to tamp the tobacco into his pipe, a glass of whiskey beside him warm and tender as a familiar kiss; or the rustle of my mother's dress against the kitchen table as she lays out plates for the evening meal, blue on white, older than she is, older than the house.

Or the sound of plastic–soled shoes fading into the distance, disappearing into the darkness, embracing the peace that comes at last to every dead thing.

From *Every Dead Thing*

Mick O'Kelly was born in Dublin, where he attended the College of Technology, Bolton Street before going to art college, first in Dun Laoghaire and subsequently in Dublin. In 1997 he received an MFA from the California Institute of the Arts. He worked for a period in the 1970s as an architectural technician and has taught at both Ballyfermot Senior College and St Patrick's College, Drumcondra. He exhibited work in Paris as part of the 1996 L'Imaginaire Irlandais festival and has also shown in Scotland, England and Germany, as well as Ireland.

Mick O'Kelly

MISSING

MICHAEL FARRELL
Date of Birth 10-12-1963
Went Missing on the 19th September 1994.

At approximately 10.30p.m. on the 19th September 1994, 31 year old Michael Farrell was seen walking towards his cabin on a B & I ship en route to Pembroke from Rosslare, Ireland. The next morning there was no sign of him. Michael's family are completely mystified as to what can have happened to him and cannot believe he could have fallen overboard. The family find it very hard to deal with the fact that he has gone missing as there is nothing to suggest where he could be.

Michael was the cinema projectionist on board the B & I ferry. His home is in Donaghmede in Dublin.
Michael is 5ft 4ins tall, of medium build, blue eyes, moustache, and an earring in his left ear.

IF YOU SEE THIS PERSON
PLEASE CONTACT 1 800 616617
THE MISSING PERSONS HELPLINE

ARTHUR DUFF had the good fortune to have been born into a large family which provided him with an excellent education into the ways of people. Having survived that baptism, he studied architecture in Dublin and Ahmadabad, India. After becoming far too involved over there, he finally returned home for good and went into partnership with Greg Tisdall, a rock of sense. They take great delight in design at every level: the practice of architecture, manufacturing furniture, interiors, lighting, set design...they really have lost the run of themselves.

Arthur Duff

A recipe for delight:
Throwing design and caution to the wind I sneaked off yesterday afternoon under the cover of a 'high-level meeting' and drove a group of friends down to New Ross to see the OTC's production of *The Lighthouse*. A breezy drive with bars of chocolate and fizzy drinks. Countryside soaked with colour, sky so huge and no matter that we got stuck behind a series of articulated lorries for most of the way. Shadowed streets of the town and then the glistering water at the quayside, a great splashy mix of light and sound, a feast!

Here's to high-level meetings!!

DAPHNE WRIGHT was born in 1963 and educated in Sligo, at the National College of Art & Design in Dublin and the Newcastle–upon–Tyne Polytechnic. In 1991 she won the Cheltenham Fellowship, the first of many awards for her sculpture and installations. Her work contains and defines space. She has exhibited in Ireland, Britain and New York and her work can be seen in the Towner Art Gallery in Eastbourne, England.

Daphne Wright

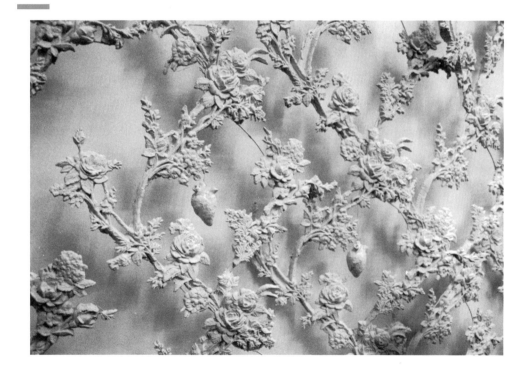

Domestic Shrubbery

MICHAEL CRAIG–MARTIN was born in Dublin in 1941. He grew up and was educated in America, studying fine art at Yale University. In 1966 he moved to England. He has exhibited internationally in solo and group shows. A retrospective of his work was held at the Whitechapel Art Gallery in 1989. He is the Millard Professor of Fine Art at Goldsmiths College, London.

Michael Craig–Martin

I was appointed artist–in–residence at King's College Cambridge for two years from 1970 to 1972. I was provided with a beautiful large room to use as a studio in the College. I could withdraw there and, for the first time in years, work without worrying about teaching or how to pay the bills.

During my first year I was invited to an annual formal dinner in the College. I dreaded going, as I was still learning to cope with the verbal sparring and aggressive philistinism that often characterised conversation at high table. As an artist, and at my hippiest with hair to my shoulders, I was of course an easy mark.

Seated to my right was a small Asian man, very modest and shy, who hardly spoke during dinner. Towards the end of the evening we started to converse. He asked what I did. I said I was the artist–in–residence. He had never heard of this position and asked me to explain. I tried to describe what I was doing with milk bottles and shelves, with clipboards and mirrors, my play at the time with the relationships of ordinary objects. He expressed interest.

I asked about his work. He said he was an astrophysicist, and I said, 'Oh, you look at the stars.' 'Only when I go out into the garden at night,' he smiled; 'my work is mainly mathematical.' I asked him what he was working on at present, and he replied quietly, 'I am trying to discover the origin of the Universe.' Stunned, I said, 'How are you doing?' and he replied, 'I am very close to the solution.'

JOHN BEHAN was born in Dublin in 1938. He studied at the National College of Art & Design, Dublin, Ealing Art College, London and the Royal Academy School, Oslo. In 1967 he was one of the founding members of the Project Arts Centre and in 1970 he established the Dublin Art Foundry. A retrospective of his work was held at the Galway Arts Centre in 1994 and travelled to the RHA Gallagher Gallery in 1995. John Behan lives and works in Galway.

John Behan

ON a visit to TURKISH CYPRUS two years ago I DISCOVERED a second hand bookshop near the main mosque. It had a stock of OLD Penguin books from the fifties.

The owner was a charming Levantine gentleman in an alpaca coat and a skull cap a local intellectual.

He smiled and invited me to explore upstairs. TWO PLACES I cannot pass, a bar or a book shop. Having made my purchase we chatted. He had known LAWRENCE DURRELL when DURRELL taught nearby in the 50's. He said DURRELL was like me, a gentleman. "Do you mind a person-al question? no" He said "you look just like Benny Hill!" collapse of stout party!

ANGELA BOURKE, a Dubliner, writes in Irish and English. Her publications include *Caoineadh na dTrí Muire: Téama na Páise i bhFilíocht Bhéil na Gaeilge* (1983), a short–story collection, *By Salt Water* (1996), The *Burning of Bridget Cleary* (1999), and many essays on Irish literature and oral tradition. A member of the Department of Modern Irish at University College, Dublin, she has lectured and taught at several universities. This poem commemorates her father, Tim Bourke (born 25 August 1913), who died in Our Lady's Hospice, Harold's Cross, on 19 September 1986.

Angela Bourke

19 September 1986

On an afternoon of sunshine,
the sky a clear and unimpeded blue,
you lay in one small room,
the window open.

The milk–and–water of your skin,
the coolness of your wrists,
the bubbles at your lips,
told us
that soon you would be done with breathing air.

It seemed that you were changing elements,
as though a panting salmon,
veteran of migrations,
gave up the ghost,
or some great struggling water bird –
a gannet or a swan –
lay washed up on a shore.

Maighinis, Co. na Gaillimhe, 24.ix.1986

GERRY ADAMS was born into a Belfast Republican family, and was an active Republican by the time of the 1968 civil rights explosion. One of the key figures involved in setting up the Provisional movement following the split of 1970, he was later interned in Long Kesh, an experience credited with his transformation from activist to politician. As president of Sinn Féin, he began secret talks with the SDLP leader, John Hume, which culminated in the Hume/Adams initiative, and subsequently led to the paramilitary ceasefires of 1994 and the Belfast Agreement of Good Friday 1998. He has published several books, including memoirs, non-fiction and short stories. He married in 1971 and has one son.

Gerry Adams

JUST A GAME

As he moved to clear his lines for the second time, while wee Eoin screamed from behind the posts, 'Help him, help him, somebody help him!' his shot was expertly blocked down.

The loose ball bounced back towards the goal and dribbled slowly – almost in slow motion – into the back of the net. For a split second there was silence. Then as the ball settled in the dust the long piercing scream of the final whistle brought the game to an end.

Mickey embraced each of the exhausted youngsters as they came off the field to the cheers of the spectators still ringing from the sidelines. Big Charlie began to sob when Mickey grabbed him. He shook himself free and stood facing the three team mentors. He was covered in sweat, smeared with mud and his hair was plastered to his forehead. His hurling stick jutted defiantly from his clenched fist.

'They won,' he blubbered, 'but they never beat us.'

Mickey grabbed him again. Leo and wee Eoin patted them both on the back.

'They'll never beat yous, son,' Leo said. 'Never.'

DEREK MAHON was born in Belfast in 1941, studied at Trinity College, Dublin and the Sorbonne, and has worked as a journalist and screenwriter in London and New York, where he also taught at Barnard and NYU. A member of Aosdána, he lives in Dublin.

His books include *Selected Poems* (1991), *The Hudson Letter* (1995), *Racine's Phaedra* (1996), *Journalism* (1996) and *The Yellow Book* (1997).

Derek Mahon

KINSALE

The kind of rain we knew is a thing of the past –
deep–delving, dark, deliberate you would say,
browsing on spire and bogland; but today
our sky–blue slates are steaming in the sun,
our yachts tinkling and dancing in the bay
like race–horses. We contemplate at last
shining windows, a future forbidden to no–one.

From *Selected Poems*

MARK FRANCIS was born in Newtownards, County Down in 1962. He studied painting at St Martin's School of Art and Chelsea. He has had solo exhibitions in Dublin, London, Paris, Frankfurt, New York and Los Angeles. His work was included in *Sensation*, work from the Saatchi Collection, at the Royal Academy in London in 1997.

Mark Francis

Various Boletes, Aberdeenshire, Scotland 27–9–96

J.P. DONLEAVY was born in New York City in 1926 and educated there and at Trinity College, Dublin. Thus began a lifelong love affair with Ireland. His novel *The Ginger Man* drew on his college days in Dublin and he settled down to the life of a squire in the Irish countryside. His works include the novels *A Singular Man*, *The Beastly Beatitudes of Balthazar B.*, *A Fairy Tale of New York* and *The Destinies of Darcy Dancer, Gentleman*, the short-story collection *Meet My Maker the Mad Molecule* and six plays.

J.P. Donleavy

Stand here on Knightsbridge pavement in the public domain. Where so much of one's life began. To wait for a taxi to take me just a little further away. Aboard the train. Out of London and England. Across the grey Channel. To bury a mother. And chase others gone goodbye in my years. Calling after their names. Come back again. Where that countryside sings over your grasses matted by wind and rains fall in sunshine. Don't fear when some nights rise up wild. Go walk in heather along a narrow path. Seagulls glide and curlews cry. Reach up and gather all this world. Before dark or any other people should ever come. And find you sheltering. As all hearts are. Worried lonely. Your eyes quiet. By the waters cold. Where the sadness lurks so deep.

> It doth
> Make you
> Still.

From *The Beastly Beatitudes of Balthazar B.*

STEPHEN MCKENNA, painter, was born in London to Irish parents in 1939 and studied at the Slade School of Fine Art. He now divides his time between homes in Tuscany and Donegal and has had his work shown throughout Europe. Among the many exhibitions in which he has been included were *British Art 1940–1980* at London's Tate Gallery and the touring *Europe Eighty*, which came to Dublin as well as Strasbourg and Milan. A figurative artist with distinctive neoclassical tendencies, in 1997 he curated a show called *The Pursuit of Painting* at Dublin's Irish Museum of Modern Art, which included work by twenty-six artists, living and dead.

Stephen McKenna

JUNE CONSIDINE was born in Dublin in 1945. She was educated at Finglas, where she lived until 1969. She works as a freelance journalist and magazine editor and is the author of twelve books for teenagers and young adults. Her first book, *When the* *Luvenders Came to Merrick Town*, was published in 1989. This became part of the Luvender Trilogy, followed by *View from a Blind Bridge* and *The Glass Triangle*. Married with a family of three, she lives in Malahide, County Dublin.

June Considine

BURIED MEMORIES

The rivers have been buried under glass–domed shopping centres. They run silent now, channelled beneath rows of suburban houses. A dual carriageway, hot with the pulse of traffic, cuts a swathe through the memories of my childhood.

I was born under the sign of Cancer and, true to my birth sign, spent the first four years of my life within sight and sound of the Grand Canal. One day my mother began painting pictures with words. She saw beyond the high–ceilinged flat where we lived in Herbert Place, past the hum of city life to a quiet rural village called Finglas.

Outside the window I could hear the deep throb of barges going past with their cargo of turf and flour. I wondered if the canal would flow past our new home.

'No,' said my mother. 'But there will be rivers, clear and free–flowing, everywhere you look.'

From the anthology *Invisible Cities*

MARIA SIMONDS-GOODING, artist, was born in 1939. The primitive, ethereal qualities of remote landscapes have captured her imagination from her earliest recollections. Memories of childhood years in India and the sparse landscape of the Dingle Peninsula near her home in County Kerry are strong influences. Simonds-Gooding works in a measured way and a piece can take up to three months to complete.

Maria Simonds–Gooding

Lone sheep of the Dingle Peninsula

KATIE DONOVAN was born in 1962 and spent her early youth on a farm in County Wexford. She studied at Trinity College, Dublin and at the University of California at Berkeley. She taught English in Hungary and now works as a journalist with *The Irish Times*. She has published two collections of poetry *Watermelon Man* (1993) and *Entering the Mare* (1997). With Brendan Kennelly and A. Norman Jeffares, she is the co-editor of the anthology *Ireland's Women: Writings Past and Present*.

Katie Donovan

PRAYER OF THE WANDERER
(TO BRIGIT)

Racoons shriek
and alligators creep
beneath my window.

Trees are lapped
by waterlog,
their arms bearded
with the tangled grey
of Spanish moss.

My hands
are wrinkled
and lost.

I wish for a mooncow
to carry me home
to the land of apples.

I would lure her
to my house
with sweet grass.
I would press my face
against her fragrant belly
and try for milk.

I have left her sign
of woven rushes
over my door,
while I roam this place
of swamps and broken shells.

I pray she keeps all safe
'til my return:

let my house not be fallen,
nor eaten in flame,
let my loved ones flourish,
and my garden thrive.

One glimpse
of the white star
on her great head
would give me peace.

Even her hoofprint
in the night sky
would tell of home.

JAMES MCDAID was born in County Donegal in 1949. He was the eldest of five children, whose father died when he was six years old. He studied medicine at University College, Galway, qualifying in 1974. A co-founder of the Donegal Hospice Movement in 1988, he has been its chairman for ten years. He was elected to Dáil Éireann as Fianna Fáil deputy for Donegal North-East in 1989 and was appointed Minister for Tourism, Sport and Recreation in 1997.

James McDaid

My hope for the Millennium is the end of Global McMurdochism. I want to see a media where journalists will be able to relentlessly pursue the truth and not be pack animals in the building of a private global dynasty founded on prurient titillation. Journalists will refuse to do this dirty work and to allow democracy to be swapped for the building of a private empire that has truth as its chief commodity. Journalist and film-maker John Pilger has written many articles on this subject. He recalls how Alfred Hugenberg in the 1920s enjoyed control over nearly half of Germany's press with his right-wing nationalist views. With his hypothesis of 'Supply and Demand' he helped block the spread of democracy which allowed Hitler to give many people what they thought they 'wanted' to read. As we enter the Millennium in the current era of global media monopolies, does this mean that journalists must always be looking over their shoulders wondering if they are giving people what 'they want', regardless of the demands of principle and of honest journalism? The freedom of the press should not be about what the people 'want' but about truth and contributing to democracy. I look to journalists in the Millennium for leadership and truth. Is that too much to ask?

LELAND BARDWELL, novelist, poet and playwright, was born in India in 1928, but grew up in County Kildare. She has since lived in Dublin, Monaghan and Sligo. Her fiction includes *Girl on a Bicycle*, *There We Have Been* and *Different Kinds of Love*. Among her poetry collections are *The Mad Cyclist*, *The Fly and the Bedbug* and *Dostoevsky's Grave: New and Selected Poems*. Her work combines a comic tone with a clear-eyed sharpness. She is a member of Aosdána.

Leland Bardwell

TWO LESSONS IN ANATOMY: YORK STREET, DUBLIN

Lesson I. I.M. The X Case

The father of the pregnant girl
has lost his temper – their bodies
reflected in the armour of rush hour traffic.
Two people from one kitchen.

She rubs her eyes like a cat
polishing its face with a single paw.
His anger spins from the bones of his shoulders
with the crescendo of his curses.

She backs away, knocking into students,
bruising her ankle on the pedal of a bike.
She will go to that nowhere place
where decisions bang around in her head.
I wonder will she remember the time
the moth was banging against the electric bulb
and how she climbed on that wobbly chair
to cup the insect in her palm
to throw it from the open window.

Lesson II

The woman upstairs is being beaten.
Her screams jangle across the street
where windows in the College of Surgeons
black out one by one. Students
are filtering home to their digs
in Rathmines or Ranelagh
and the air is left untroubled
by the cry for help
that no lessons in anatomy can fathom.

DEREK SPEIRS was born in Dublin in 1952. He trained as a photographer in London with Simon Guttman, founder of the Report agency. Since his return to Ireland in 1978 he has become a leading photojournalist, working in news and features. Exhibitions: *Speirs at Large* (1988–92), *Pavee Pictures* (1991), produced with the Dublin Travellers' Education and Development Group, *Ireland Yesterday and Today* (1993), *At Work* (1994), IMMA. Since 1995 he has been working with the Agency for Personal Service Overseas, documenting the work of volunteers. He has published two books: *Pavee Pictures* and *Goodbye to All That*.

Derek Speirs

La Garrucha, Zapatista Community, Chiapas, Mexico 1996

PAM BRIGHTON was born in Yorkshire and has worked in Ireland for a number of years. She settled in Northern Ireland in 1989. Two years later she founded DubbelJoint Productions with Marie Jones and Mark Lambert. Among her productions are *A Night in November, Women on the Verge of HRT, Bin Lids* and *Mother of All the Behans*.

Pam Brighton

In October 1917 the Russian Revolution occurred – it was an amazing achievement, one of the largest and most backward states in the world turning itself round to face the future. It began with huge ideas about fair distribution of wealth, land, education, health for all, excitement in the Arts and Sciences. It was probably the greatest achievement of the twentieth century. Its subsequent collapse possibly the most profoundly sad event.

How much we need in the new millennium an equal achievement that will hold out the hope of productivity for the social good rather than profit, social generosity rather than selfishness. Growing up in the 1960s, I had a sense that the world could be a quite, quite different place; talking to kids in the late 1990s, their cynicism and despair that the world they live in is the only way it can ever be is heartbreaking.

ANDREW KEARNEY, a mixed–media installation artist, was born in Limerick in 1961. He studied fine art at Limerick College of Art and Design and worked as a photographer for three years before going to Chelsea College of Art and Design, where he obtained an MA in sculpture. He won the Barclays Young Artist award in the Serpentine Gallery, London in 1992. Later that year, he was awarded a fellowship in the PS1 Studios of Contemporary Art in New York. In 1993 he moved back to London, where he currently lives. He has exhibited extensively in Ireland, England, the United States and Canada. In 1995 he was shortlisted for the IMMA/Glen Dimplex award.

Andrew Kearney

Mondo LA '98

SEÁN Ó TUAMA, born in Cork in 1926, was Professor of Modern Irish Literature in University College, Cork and has been a visiting professor at the universities of Harvard, Oxford and Toronto. His publications include three books of his own verse and four plays, as well as literary criticism, literary history, and a number of academic works. He served as a member of the Irish Arts Council from 1975 to 1981 and was chairman of the working party which produced a report entitled *The Arts in Irish Education*. In 1982 he was appointed chairman of Bord na Gaeilge.

Seán Ó Tuama

CEOL FÓMHAIR

Is ceol téad im chluais
na duilleoga buí fáin
ag titim gan fuaim
ar an díon dearg stáin.

From *Death in the Land of Youth*

SHEILA O'DONNELL was born in Dublin in 1953, studied architecture at University College, Dublin and later took an MA at the Royal College of Art in London, where she lived for five years.

JOHN TUOMEY was born in Tralee in 1954, studied architecture at University College, Dublin and worked for five years in London with James Stirling. His partnership with Sheila O'Donnell was established in 1988.

O'Donnell and Tuomey's buildings include the Irish Film Centre, the Irish Pavilion at IMMA, the National Photography Centre and Ranelagh School. They have won the AAI Downes Medal four times.

Sheila O'Donnell & John Tuomey

Music makes proportions in time
Gerald Victory '94 —

ROSITA BOLAND, poet, travel writer and short-story writer, was born in Ennis, County Clare in 1965. Her first collection of poems, *Muscle Creek*, was published in 1991. A travel book, *Sea Legs: Hitch-Hiking the Coast of Ireland Alone*, was published in 1992. In the same year she was awarded a Bursary in literature from the Arts Council and in 1997, she won the *Sunday Tribune/Hennessy* First Fiction Award. She now lives in Dublin, where she works as a journalist for *The Irish Times*.

Rosita Boland

THE SEALION'S STOMACH

The sealion swallowed the pebbles to
   ballast itself,
Like a diver's weightbelt; preventing itself
From coming up to the surface too soon.

A Victorian curiosity, the petrified stomach
Is now displayed
Under the water-clear surface of a glass case
In the Edinburgh Museum.

Leaning over it,
We counted two-score or more smooth stones
Spilling from the split bag
Of the sealion's too-small stomach.

All the rest of that afternoon, I thought
About the sealion, slowly swallowing its way
   towards oblivion,
Risking too much with every dive.

It is like this between us yet, sometimes
Misjudging the ballast,
Diving clumsily into the uncertain depths
Of separate pasts,
Distending something vital in the process: Let us
Always come back to the surface, still breathing,
Still buoyant.

Desmond Egan was born in Athlone in 1936. He has published fourteen collections of poetry and his work has been translated into many languages. In 1983 he received the National Poetry Foundation of USA Award and in 1986 an honorary doctorate in literature from Washburn University in the United States. He lives near Newbridge, County Kildare.

Desmond Egan

LEGACY
to my daughters Kate and Béibhinn

Some other tomorrow

The sun will shine again
along our path through the orchard

Desmond Egan

From Elegies (1972–97)

BRENDAN KENNELLY was born in Ballylongford, County Kerry in 1936. A poet, dramatist and critic, he received the AE Memorial Award in 1967. Since 1973 he has been Professor of Modern Literature at Trinity College, Dublin. He has published many books of poetry, including *My Dark Fathers*, *The Voices*, *Moloney Up and At It* and *Selected Poems*. His dramatisations include *Antigone*, *Medea* and *The Trojan Women*.

Brendan Kennelly

MARY KENNELLY AT 97

I want to go down to the house in the glen, she said,
         lock the door
           and sit
              in the peace of God.

— *Brendan Kennelly*

PAUL O'CONNOR, a graphic designer, was born in Cambridge in 1972 and educated at the University of Portsmouth. He has based himself in Dublin where, after a brief period at Dynamo Design, he founded the Light Surgeons. Using a technique of layering a number of 16 mm film and 35 mm slide projectors onto large screens, the Light Surgeons produced eclectic visual installations for a wide range of music events and venues. They are now experimenting with digital mixing and title sequences for television and film.

Paul O'Connor

Tela, Honduras. 1996

LIAM Ó MUIRTHILE was born in the South Parish, Cork city in 1950. His novel *Ar Bhruach na Laoi* is set in this neighbourhood and in west Cork. He began writing in Irish at University College, Cork, in association with the poetry journal INNTI. Having worked as a broadcaster for RTÉ (1972–90), he now lives on his writing. He contributes a weekly column in Irish to *The Irish Times* and his work encompasses poetry, novels, plays and screenplays.

Liam Ó Muirthile

INNIU IN ÉIRINN

Dreas den teas aneas
suth den bhruth i gcéin
inniu in Éirinn.

Leoithne ardú meanman áin
gliondar ar na héin féin
inniu in Éirinn.

Eitilt obann fáinleog mear
gile uile bhrollaigh le gréin
inniu in Éirinn.

Scuainí aonta aoibhne ar muir
sciatháin in earr ar ár gcoiscéim
inniu in Éirinn.

15.10.2000
October/Deireadh Fómhair
SUNDAY / DOMHNACH

ALICE HANRATTY was born in Dublin and studied at the National College of Art & Design, Dublin and Hornsey College of Art, London. A pioneer of specialised printmaking, she travelled to Africa and lived and worked there for two years. When she returned to Dublin in the early seventies, she taught in the National College of Art & Design, the School of Architecture in Bolton Street and the Dublin Institute of Technology. She has exhibited widely in Ireland, London, Europe, the United States and Japan, and is a member of Aosdána.

Alice Hanratty

The Lads III

PAUL DURCAN, poet, was born in Dublin in 1944, to County Mayo parents, and studied archaeology and medieval history at University College, Cork. Since 1967 he has published sixteen books of poetry. These include *The Berlin Wall Café* (1985), *Daddy,* *Daddy* (1990), which won the Whitbread Award for Poetry, *Crazy About Women* (1991), *Give Me Your Hand* (1994), *A Snail in My Prime: New and Selected Poems* (1993) and *Christmas Day* (1996). He is a member of Aosdána and lives in Dublin.

Paul Durcan

For the great gate of night stands painted red —
And all of heaven lies waiting to be fed.

MARY AVRIL GILLAN, artist, was born in Waterford in 1964. She studied at the National College of Art & Design in Dublin. Her first solo show, *Nostalgia for Industry*, was held at the Rubicon Gallery, Dublin in 1994. In 1997 she was featured as the emerging Irish artist at Éigse, Carlow Arts Festival, with a show entitled *Journey Out* which later went to the Rubicon Gallery. Her work has been included in several major group shows throughout Ireland and is held in many public and private collections in Ireland. She lives and works in Dublin.

Mary Avril Gillan

Untitled – computer drawing

18.10.2000

October/Deireadh Fómhair

WEDNESDAY / CÉADAOIN

CON HOULIHAN attempted to grow up in Kerry in the aftermath of the Civil War; he needed a sense of humour as a survival kit. He attended three schools and did not leave them of his own volition; he got much of his education by field and wood and stream. He has wandered in many lands and worked at many trades. Sometime in the early 1970s he settled, more or less, in Dublin's south side, where he lives with good neighbours and numerous pigeons.

Con Houlihan

Whoever coined the label 'birdbrain' wasn't too clever: our avian fellows are very bright – and their domesticated cousins, the hens, are not only bright but cunning.

If you are ever watching a hen that wishes to lay out, you need only turn your head for a moment and she will vanish.

Hens have a great sense of fun: they delight in flying amidst the branches of a fallen tree; their race memory takes them back to the wild.

And they dream: at night they utter little sounds of pleasure and fear.

Not all hens follow the flock instinct: I knew a little black Anconi that loved to forage farther than her companions and stay out later. One evening I feared that Reynard had got her as I searched in vain in nooks and crannies.

At last I noticed a ray from the afterglow brightening a patch of sand by a stream – there she was digging.

She reminded me of Ernest Hemingway: 'Matadors live their lives all the way up.'

That hen did; to keep fowl in captivity is a crime against humanity.

He prayeth best, who loveth best
All things both great and small;
For the dear God who loveth us,
He made and loveth all.

EAMON DELANEY, the novelist, was born in Dublin in 1962 and brought up by the sea in Dun Laoghaire and by another sea in Carraroe, County Galway. As a diplomat in the Department of Foreign Affairs, he served in New York and at the United Nations. His novel *The Casting of Mr O'Shaughnessy* was published in 1995 and he is now working on a mysterious sequel. An active writer and freelance journalist, he contributes to *The Sunday Times* and *IT* magazine. When not at his desk, he is often to be seen wandering Herbert Park looking for chestnuts – out of season.

Eamon Delaney

She was a laughing girl with a mane of black curls and a cream beaded dress which clung to her big–hipped figure, like the one Marilyn Monroe wore when she sang for JFK. It's funny but even the younger Irish in this atmosphere seemed old–fashioned, a little formal. And yet sometimes he had to rein back his South Dublin perspective. Later on, he got to know Rosie and she was anything but formal. She was bawdy and good crack, and she was all of the things he wouldn't see in Dublin 4. It may seem patronising but it was true. In Irish America, he saw an America many young Irish wouldn't see – indeed, many young Americans wouldn't see – but he also discovered an Ireland he didn't know at home.

From *The Sharing of the Green*, work in progress

FIONNUALA NÍ CHIOSÁIN was born in Dublin in 1966 and educated at St Martin's School of Art, London and the National College of Art & Design, Dublin. Her work can be seen in the Irish Museum of Modern Art, the Hugh Lane Municipal Gallery of Modern Art and the National Self–Portrait Collection of Ireland. A young, vibrant, abstract painter, she lives and works in Dublin.

Fionnuala Ní Chiosáin

Gutter, Rome 1997

JOHN MINIHAN, photographer, was born in Dublin in 1946. He worked for thirty-five years as a photojournalist in London. His photography of Athy, County Kildare, *Shadows from the Pale* (1996), and his Samuel Beckett photographs from the previous year were described by John Calder thus: 'His love of his native Ireland, its people, landscapes, homes and geniuses is apparent in all his work. His camera never lies.'

His most recent book *An Unweaving of Rainbows: Images of Irish Writers* was published in 1998.

John Minihan

Mary Byrne, Athy, Co. Kildare, 1972

IVOR BROWNE was born on 18 March 1928 in the front bedroom of number one Sandycove Avenue East, County Dublin. He underwent his psychiatric training in Dublin, Oxford, London and Harvard. He dreamed of being a professional musician, but until his retirement in 1994 he was Professor of Psychiatry at University College, Dublin and chief psychiatrist of the Eastern Health Board. He now focuses on psychological trauma and how the brain processes traumatic experience. He is in charge of the Irish Centre of Sarg Marg Meditation.

Ivor Browne

Our rented field was an enclosed world in which we lived out our fantasies or rather my father's fantasies, one being of the trenches in the First World War. It beat work in the bank which he hated. With his help we excavated dugouts, covering the roof with corrugated iron camouflaged with fresh sods.

I spent hours hiding in the dugout watching the lane, ready to repel attacks from marauding gangs. There were no gangs, Sandycove in those days being so isolated that there were few young people and they were our friends.

My father was strongly attached to the history of Wexford and his Norman ancestry. On one of our Sunday walks we came upon the Castle on Dalkey Hill. The County Council was doing some repair work on it and a workman came down to warn us off. However, I distinctly remember him as a Norman soldier in full armour with the tight leggings, and helmet. My heart was bursting as I fled from this man coming after us with crossbow.

From a work in progress

MARTIN GALE was born in Worcester in 1949. Educated in Ireland, he received a diploma in painting from the National College of Art & Design in Dublin in 1973. He has had several solo exhibitions and taken part in all the major group shows in Ireland, and he represented the country at the Biennale de Paris in 1980. In 1982 he was elected a member of Aosdána and in 1996 a member of the Royal Hibernian Academy. He is represented by the Taylor Galleries in Dublin.

Martin Gale

DAVID WHEATLEY was born in Dublin in 1970 and studied at Trinity College, Dublin. He won the Friends Provident National Poetry Competition in 1994, and was awarded the Rooney Prize for Literature for his poetry collection *Thirst* (1997).

He co-edits *Metre* magazine and is a widely published critic, writing for *The Times Literary Supplement* and *The Irish Times*, among others. He has worked as writer-in-residence in County Wicklow.

David Wheatley

SECONDS, BEAUBOURG

The first thing I couldn't believe was how dirty it was,
though I may have suspected the dirt, too, was 'modern'.
Beaubourg was toutes tripes dehors, all its guts hanging out,
pumping its gobbled-up tourists along
the escalator for the view from the roof –
Hôtel de Ville, Sacré Cœur, Défense –
like one long crazed digestive tract.

Below in the square a clock was counting down
to the year 2000 in seconds,
four hundred million give or take,
with fruit-machine rolls to conjure its jackpot.
I set the time delay on my camera, stood back
from the ledge to wait and started to count:
10, 9, 8, 7, 6, 5, 4, 3, 2, 1...

From *Thirst*

Dermot Bolger, poet, novelist, playwright, editor and publisher, was born in Finglas in Dublin in 1959. He began as a poet, with collections such as *Internal Exiles* (1986) and *Leinster Street Ghosts* (1989). His novels include *The Journey Home* (1990), *A Second Life* (1994) and *Father's Music* (1997). His plays, among them *The Lament for Arthur Cleary* and *April Bright*, have received many awards, including the Samuel Beckett Prize. He founded Raven Arts Press in 1979 and New Island Books in 1992.

Dermot Bolger

Prayer

I have come this long way without finding you
Or losing your reflection,

I've tried a dozen obsessions without cleansing
Your taste from my tongue.

Oldest friend and adversary, fugitive brother,
We recognise each other

In carriages of express trains which pass:
Your hands beat on the glass.

Nick Kelly was born in Dublin in 1962. Between 1986 and its split in 1994, his band, The Fat Lady Sings, released a series of highly acclaimed singles and two albums, *Twist* and *Johnson*. In 1997 Kelly ended a three-year self-imposed exile from the music industry with the release of his debut solo album. Funded by contributions from 260 fans and released on his own Self Possessed label, *Between Trapezes* was hailed by *Hot Press* magazine as 'album of the decade'. In 1998 Kelly was voted Best Solo Male Artist at the annual Heineken/*Hot Press* Awards.

Nick Kelly

Republic: my world has grown inside your world my feet followed yours I lay secure in your embrace I curled my face in towards yours **but I declare myself a Republic I must leave you and you must let me go I have no choice** my voice is not your voice your seeds have grown a different tree you should not be scared you should rejoice in the difference that rings out between you and me **I declare myself a Republic I stand alone and you must stand aside I have my wings** to fly to the edge of what I can be to sing my life to sing my own needs to see days that you will never see and though I move away from you these borders I define link us together in a chain that winds out far beyond us holds us united nations in the face of time **I declare myself a Republic a Republic I am my own.**

JOHN KINDNESS was born in Belfast in 1951 and studied fine art at the College of Art in Belfast. It took him ten years to recover. He became involved in underground comics and television graphics. He married Danae Campbell in 1978 and went back to making art full-time in 1986. An influential year was 1989–90, spent in New York on a PS1 Fellowship. He moved to Dublin in 1991 and began working on large-scale public commissions. His work can be seen in IMMA, Dublin, Boston Museum of Fine Art, Imperial War Museum, London, Ulster Museum, Hugh Lane Municipal Gallery of Modern Art, Dublin and the Victoria & Albert Museum, London.

.

John Kindness

Spider Lace Cuff, 1997 – from: The Museum of the Old Lady who Swallowed a Fly (Geraldine Clarke, Lacemaker)

28.10.2000

October/Deireadh Fómhair

SATURDAY / SATHARN

TIM ROBINSON was born in England in 1935, studied mathematics at Cambridge and taught in Istanbul before taking up a career as an artist, first in Vienna and then in London. In 1972 he moved to the Aran Islands, where he began to write and to make a map of the islands. His two-volume work *Stones of Aran* was published in 1986 and 1995. In 1984 he settled in Roundstone, where he and his wife, Máiréad, run Folding Landscapes, which publishes his maps of Aran, the Burren and Connemara.

Tim Robinson

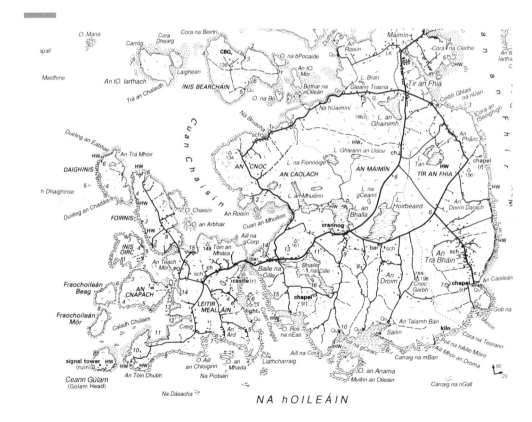

BLAISE DRUMMOND was born in Liverpool in 1967 and studied philosophy and classics at the University of Edinburgh and then fine art at the National College of Art & Design in Dublin. His solo shows include *The Natural Order of Things* at the Rubicon Gallery in Dublin in 1997 and *A Short Discourse on Nature and Culture* at the Crawford Municipal Gallery in Cork in 1996. His work is included in collections such as the British Council and the Walker Art Gallery, Liverpool. He is currently doing postgraduate work at Chelsea College of Art and Design in London.

Blaise Drummond

A PROJECT FOR THE ENDS OF THE EARTH

To gather patiently the odd exotic pods that wash up upon our western margins. Strays borne by the waves from the Caribbean on the same currents that bring us our weather. Nurturing gently, craftily the seeds into leaf in order to fill a glass house with greenery from the ends of the earth. A hothouse in Connemara, coast to coast a botanical ark adrift on our cool wind–blown shores.

MARY DORCEY was born in County Dublin. In 1990 she won the Rooney Prize for Literature for her short-story collection, *A Noise from the Woodshed*. She has published three volumes of poetry: *Kindling, Moving into the Space Cleared by Our Mothers* and *The River that Carries Me*. She has also published a novel, *Biography of Desire*. Since 1996 she has given seminars at Trinity College, Dublin.

Mary Dorcey

With each new day behind you
you ask
do you remember when...?
and I do –
almost all of it
and more.

You were not always good.
You threatened with a wooden spoon,
cursed me when there was no one else to curse.
At sea in your kitchen
you did not counsel or console,
you turned your eyes from trouble
having known too much of it
uncomforted yourself.

Going down the stairs now
behind your anxious, baby steps
I want to pick you up and carry you
or launch you down the banister
as you did me
in this house
when we were children together.

But you must take every step first
along this passage
we daughters follow after
each one of us
moving into the space
cleared by our mothers.

And with what fine nerve,
what unthanked grace,
you confront this last world
you will discover before me.

I see your shy, jaunty smile
at the mirror –
see you say
what do you think?
As if death
were a foolish, extravagant hat
you were trying on for size.

From 'Trying on for Size'

TONY HIGGINS, born in 1939, attended national school in Celbridge and Denmark Street Technical College, Dublin, where he trained as a carpenter. He abandoned tongue-in-groove for photography in the early 1960s, working first in Con Conor's studio and in 1967 opening his own. Since then he has received numerous photographic awards, his work has appeared in international fashion magazines and over three decades he has photographed most of our major public figures: politicians, writers, actors, singers, entertainers and a president or two.

Tony Higgins

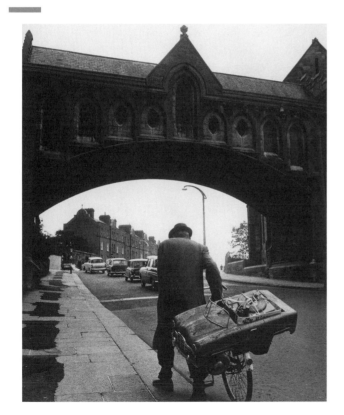

Man with Bike and Child's Car

AIDAN MATHEWS was born in Dublin in 1956. He has written poetry (*Windfalls, Minding Ruth*), plays (*The Diamond Body, Exit–Entrance*) and fiction (*Adventures in a Bathyscope, Muesli at Midnight, Lipstick on the Host*). His most recent work is the book of poems *According to the Small Hours*. He is married to Patricia Bourden, a history teacher. They have two daughters, Laura and Lucy.

Aidan Mathews

THE COMMUNION OF SAINTS

The true Doomsday Book was not about omens
But about families: Domus, the Latin for home.
It was an inventory of fireplaces, a candle–mass.
My daughter drew her granddaddy at his wake
As a blackhaired youngster. Crayons cannot do white.
They cannot do newsprint or parchment or papyrus.

My eighty–year–old father is pointing still like Moses
To a sepia of a baby on his chest of drawers.
That is my mother, he says. She fed me for years and years.
He tells me: I wish that I had asked you to my wedding.
I show him the hospital scans of his great grandchildren
The colour of the corpse in the Holy Shroud of Turin.

ALICE MAHER was born in Tipperary in 1956. She graduated from the University of Ulster with a master's degree in fine arts in 1986 and has been a full-time working artist since then. She has exhibited widely in Ireland, Europe and the United States, and represented Ireland at the 1994 São Paulo Bienal. Her work often engages with the subject of memory, using a wide variety of materials and processes and employing a wicked sense of humour.

Alice Maher

Talking to My Hair

HUGH CARR was born in Dunkineely and grew up in the Donegal Gaeltacht. Having moved to Dublin, he studied at the Royal Irish Academy of Music and later with Frederick May. In 1962 he entered the Irish Civil Service, where he worked in the District Court until taking early retirement in 1988 to write full-time. He has had plays presented at the Peacock, the Abbey, the Gate, in several Dublin Theatre Festivals, in London and in New York. His novel *Voices from a Far Country* was published in 1995.

Hugh Carr

TO NEIL IN THE FRENCH FOREIGN LEGION

At first I thought your leaving was rebellion:
'Fuck you all, I'm off to join the Legion!'
Rejection of a family which you found
Composing, writing, painting all around
You, while you were probing fire and thunder.
Action–Man. But now I wonder.
Always you stood apart.
Was it to take the measure of our art?
Until, without knowing why, you reach
To life for what art could never teach;
Joining with rogues and vagabonds to gain
The authentic note of ecstasy or pain,
And blast our affectations – Man alive!
If only you survive.

EILÍS O'CONNELL was born in Derry in 1953 and studied sculpture at the Crawford School of Art, Cork and at the Massachusetts College of Art in Boston. Her first solo show was in Dublin in 1981 and she has exhibited extensively in Europe and America. She represented Ireland in the Paris Biennale and the São Paulo Bienal. The recipient of the *Sunday Tribune* Visual Artist of the Year and the UK Art and Work Award, she also won fellowships to the British School at Rome and PSI in New York.

Eilís O'Connell

Secret Station, 1992

MARY MORRISSY was born in Dublin in 1957. She won a Hennessy Award in 1984 and her stories have been anthologised widely. Her first collection, *A Lazy Eye*, was published in 1993 and her novel *Mother of Pearl* (1996) was shortlisted for the Whitbread Prize. In 1995 she was awarded a Lannan Literary Award. She lives in Dublin and works as a journalist for *The Irish Times*.

Mary Morrissy

CEILING

Your tongued and grooved, the timber merchant said,
his hinged lorry dropping by our door
a batch of lapping wood.
Each lath had a lip
which sought another's cleft
in sated consummation overhead.
Pine shone when we looked up
But in the shed among the coals
leftovers lie,
sad strays that would not lock together.

CIARÁN LENNON, one of twelve children, was born in 1947 and grew up in Inchicore, Dublin. Until the age of fourteen he was a keen boxer. The following year he saw an exhibition of American artists such as Pollock and Rothko and he traces his own interest in painting from that time. His large abstract canvases show an affinity with American modernism, at the same time often returning to a series of folded-paper drawings he produced in the mid-1980s. An exhibition of his paintings was held at the Irish Museum of Modern Art in 1995.

Ciarán Lennon

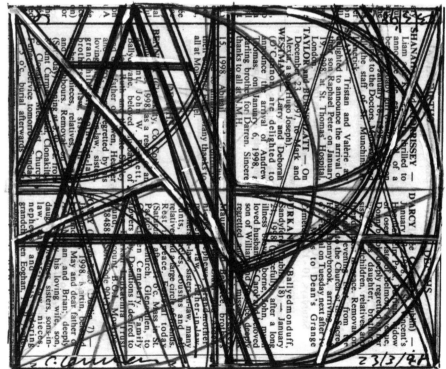

Births & Deaths

NEIL HANNON, aka The Divine Comedy, was born in Derry in 1970 and grew up in Enniskillen. When still teenagers, his band went to London and signed with Setanta Records. They released one album before Neil became a solo artist. His first two albums, *Liberation* (1993) and *Promenade* (1994), were both critically acclaimed. However, commercial recognition came with the release of *Casanova* (1996), which attained gold status in the UK and Ireland. It was followed by *A Short Album about Love* (1997) and *Fin de Siècle* (1998). Neil continues to write music from his new home in London.

Neil Hannon

THE HEART OF ROCK & ROLL IS BROKEN

Humpty Dumpty got so drunk he
Thought he could sing
Now every rag and glossy mag
Think he's the next Big Thing
Watch the floodgates swinging open
Now the heart of Rock & Roll is broken.

Mary Mary, only rarely
Have I heard such shit
But still the DJs give you 3 plays
Every nine minutes
Shall the truth be left unspoken
Now the heart of Rock & Roll is broken.

Jack and Jill popped every pill
Till the thrill was gone
They looked inside and could not find
The will to carry on
My worst fears have re–awoken
Now the heart of Rock & Roll is broken.

CHARLES CULLEN, artist, was born in Longford in 1939. He studied at the National College of Art & Design in Dublin from 1957 to 1960. He spent the following year working and travelling in Spain and, on returning to Ireland, became one of the founder members of the Project Arts Centre in Dublin. He has taken part in numerous group shows and solo exhibitions in the intervening years. In 1997 he staged a retrospective at the Hugh Lane Municipal Gallery of Modern Art. He is head of painting at the National College of Art & Design.

Charles Cullen

EOIN MCNAMEE was born in Kilkeel, County Down and educated in various schools in Northern Ireland and at Trinity College, Dublin. He has written two short novels, *The Last of Deeds* (1989) and *Love in History* (1992), the first of which was shortlisted for the *Irish Times*/Aer Lingus Literature Prize. *Resurrection Man* (1994) deals with a series of sectarian killings in Belfast. His collection of poetry, *The Language of Birds*, appeared in 1995. Screenplays include *Resurrection Man*, directed by Marc Evans, and *I Want You*, directed by Michael Winterbottom. He lives in Sligo.

Eoin McNamee

SOFT GOING

Onscreen
Through the fog at Sandown
The fence rails gleam
White, exalted, eerie.

Moody dusk.
What does the horse love?
Soft going.
Holding close to the rail.

Men's hearts that force
Loneliness upon it.
A year after his death
I came across the yellow slips.

Hughes Turf Accountant.
Yankees, trebles –
A dialect at risk
From tales of the fallen.

It is Winter there
At Epsom, at ghostly Sandown
And the horses
Verify it.

FRANK HARTE, described as one of the most important figures in the Irish song revival, is an architect, born and reared in Dublin and living on the banks of the Liffey at Chapelizod. His introduction to traditional Irish songs came from hearing a traveller who was singing and selling his ballad sheets at a fair in the town of Boyle many years ago. He admits to having been obsessed ever since with songs that tell stories. He has amassed a very large collection and says that in many cases these songs are the unwritten history of our people.

Frank Harte

TED MCCARTHY, writer and teacher, was born in Clones, County Monaghan in 1957 and has lived and taught there since completing his degree. His work has been published in Ireland, Europe and the United States. His first collection of poems, *November Wedding*, was published in 1998. He is working on a second collection, as well as a German edition of both.

Ted McCarthy

MUSIC ROOM

The metronome is still; neutral
the co-ordinates of that other triangle,
lamp, seat, keys. The score waits;
peaks and troughs, that run of distant notes.

(Don't walk under ladders, its small sky–
corner cut, the Trinity
offended. Spirit lurks where unwary
thought or step is meshed in air.)

It was here I was taught the rudiments
and learned, in spite of all was meant
to show me otherwise,
truth was beyond the brink of hand and eye;

the left line by itself had a togetherness
more pure for having made no sense. That bass
a paradigm
of all I've done since. Harmony seems

to flee my hands' clumsy hovering,
quavers on the stave weave,
stand petrified and die
as fingers blink then break atonally.

Beyond the brain now, the room
and its every artifact dumb,
music in the broken air
dissipated, but still whole somewhere.

PAKI SMITH, born in 1963, is a painter and occasionally an art director on films. He was the production designer with Nathan Crowley on Stephen Bradley's *Sweets Bassett*. In 1999 he showed four years of painting at the Taylor Galleries in Dublin.

Paki Smith

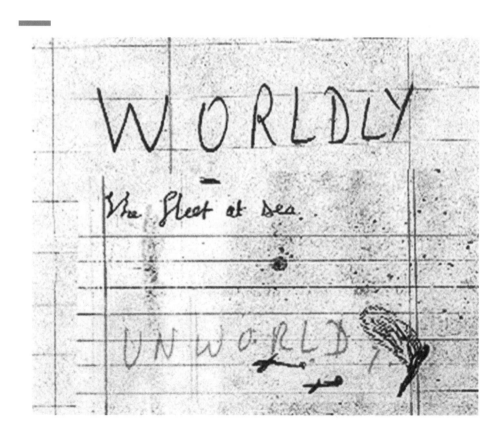

1999

JOHN ROCHA, the fashion designer, was born in Hong Kong of Chinese and Portuguese descent. His graduation collection from Croydon College of Art & Design featured Irish linen and inspired him to visit Ireland. He has lived in Dublin since 1979 and works from a large, modern studio in Temple Bar with his wife and business partner, Odette. In 1994 he was named British Designer of the Year. The influence of Chinese and Celtic traditions and his natural love of textiles form the inspiration for his clothes' collections. In 1997 he designed a range of Waterford Crystal.

John Rocha

FINTAN O'TOOLE was born in Dublin in 1958 and educated at University College, Dublin. He is a columnist with *The Irish Times* and has been drama critic for the New York *Daily News*. His collections of essays include *A Mass for Jesse James* (1990) and *The Ex–Isle of Erin* (1996). *The Politics of Magic: The Work and Times of Tom Murphy* appeared in 1987. His acclaimed biography of Richard Brinsley Sheridan was published in 1997.

Fintan O'Toole

In November 1995, the Minor Planet Centre in Cambridge, Massachusetts decided to name Minor Planet 5029, an asteroid recently discovered somewhere between Mars and Jupiter, 'Ireland'. Minor Planet Ireland is far away and virtually invisible to the naked eye and almost nothing is known about its composition. It bears, in other words, a similar relationship to the terrestrial Ireland as the emergent Ireland of imaginative connections does to the physical Ireland in the Atlantic. Spinning in the dark, held in place by the pull of invisible gravity, it is still solid, full of possibilities, and, perhaps, habitable.

In another sense, though, Minor Planet Ireland is not so dreamily comforting. Ireland has long had its human satellites, its exiled communities orbiting the motherland. But it is not so long since some people thought that all the planets went round the earth, and had to suffer the psychic shock of finding that it was the other way around. These days, it gets harder to shake off the thought, absurd but insistent, that Minor Planet Ireland, the distant place called after the familiar one, is not an imagined asteroid but the real, green island that used to be at the edge of Europe.

From *The Ex–Isle of Erin*

PAULINE BEWICK was born in 1935 in Newcastle and was raised in County Kerry. A major retrospective of her paintings was organised at the Guinness Hop Store in 1985. From September 1989 Bewick spent two years living and working in Polynesia and she subsequently wrote and illustrated a book about her South Seas experience. A member of the RHA and Aosdána, she lives and works in Kerry.

Pauline Bewick

Catching a Seagull

ROBERT BERNEN, artist and writer, was born in New York in 1928. He received degrees in classics from Cornell and Harvard Universities. His books include *Tales from the Blue Stacks* (1978) and *The Hills* (1984), based on fourteen years of farming sheep in County Donegal, and *Myth & Religion in European Painting* (1973), co-authored with his wife, Satia Bernen. His thirty-three issues of a newsletter, *Parkinsonian Speak-Out* (1987–93), were written from a patient's point of view. *In the Heat of the Sun*, travel sketches of France, has been issued in Braille by the Library of Congress. *The Hills* is on the American Library Association Notable Book List for 1984. He lives with his wife in Providence, Rhode Island.

Robert Bernen

I watched the heavy cows, their great broad solemn heads swaying as they advanced, walking and chewing as they went. As they chewed their lower jaws swung down and to one side, then up and across, and so over and over again sharing the swaying undulating movement of their heads, and of their great sides, swollen with the embryos of calves and with their day's grazing. Even their forward movement had something intermittent and periodic about it. So they moved forward, graceful clumsy heavy delicate large timid beasts, about twenty of them, some with calves following, all steeped in that heavy but transparent dusk of a November day in Donegal.

HUGH LEONARD was born in Dublin in 1926. He worked in the Civil Service for a time before moving to London but he returned annually for the Dublin Theatre Festival. He settled in Dalkey, County Dublin in 1970. His plays include *The Au Pair Man*, *Da*, which won a Tony Award in 1978, *Summer* and *A Life*. He has written two volumes of autobiography, *Home Before Night* and *Out After Dark*.

Hugh Leonard

MAC:

A true story, then. (He opens a jar of cold cream and begins removing his make-up.) Fifteen or so years ago, around the time the talking pictures came in, may their inventor sizzle on the nethermost hob of hell, there was an actor of the old school named Quintus Colquhoun. I played with him in my London days before I journeyed westward in every sense of the word. He had the most resounding 'Harrump' in the business (he demonstrates), and that, together with a way of peering inimitably over his glasses, enabled him to corner the market in judges. Nobody could wear a black cap or say 'Three clear Sundays' as vivaciously as he. So, five or six times a year old Quintus trotted off to the studios of Pinewood or Shepperton – may one stone of them cease to rest upon another – where in a facsimile of a courtroom he sat on his inflatable rubber ring and harrumped for a week or so. He had no need of other work; even so, when he was not pulling faces for the camera, he toured the east coast seaside towns in the role of a somewhat geriatric Sir Percy Blakeney/the Scarborough Pimpernel, you know. A colleague of his had the misfortune not only to be in Cleethorpes, but in Cleethorpes on a February night when snow came swirling in from the North Sea, and there was old Quintus playing the Theatre Royal. So he presented his Equity card, saw the play and went back afterwards. 'Call this a dressing room?' he said. 'There's cracked lino on the floor. A pane of glass is gone out of that window. You make up by the light of one 40-watt bulb, and there's fly-shit on the mirror. There can't have been more than fifty people out front this evening, in a house that holds fifteen hundred. The other one thousand, four hundred and fifty of them are off at the picture palaces, the Bijou and the Gaumont, watching Greta Garbo or Wallace sodding Beery. So what's it all in aid of? You aren't short of a few bob, and because you're as queer as a coot you don't have a wife to squander it. Look at you, your hands are so blue with the cold you can't even hold a stick of Leichner. You get no thanks, no comfort. And you know what they say are the three most useless things in the world? A nun's tits, the Pope's balls and a rave notice in the "Cleethorpes Chronicle". So why do you do it? Why?' And old Quintus peered back at him out of that...that looking glass darkly. He said: 'Well, you see, old darling, how can I possibly give it up? It's the magic.'

From *Magic*

THOMAS RYAN, painter, was born in 1929 in Limerick, where he attended the School of Art, followed by the National College of Art & Design in Dublin. President of the Royal Hibernian Academy of Arts from 1982 to 1992, he was the designer of the Irish one–pound coin and the Dublin Millennium fifty–pence piece. An established artist whose work hangs in many major collections, he is an honorary member of both the Royal Academy, London and the Royal Scottish Academy, Edinburgh, as well as an Associate of NCAD and a council member of the Watercolour Society of Ireland.

Thomas Ryan

The Hospice Kitchen (Woman at Range)

GERALD DAWE was born in Belfast. He studied at the University of Ulster and at University College, Galway, where he taught for many years. His books of poetry include *The Lundys Letter*, for which he was awarded a Macaulay Fellowship in Literature, *Sunday School*, *Heart of Hearts* and *The Visible World*. He has also published two collections of essays: *Against Piety* and *The Rest is History*. He lives in Dublin and teaches at Trinity College.

Gerald Dawe

PROMISES

To wake like this in the middle of the night
and hear a bird, I'm not sure which,
in solo run; then pad down to the kitchen
and notice the blue light of the moon
give way to the dawn, is OK too.

In private gardens and apartment blocks
they are already up and showered.
From Valhalla, Greenfields, Haven,
the gates remain open; gravel
spits out from under the twisted wheel.

That flash of thigh at the downstairs'
front window when I get into the car –
her hair bells and she has a quick look
at what kind of day it promises to be.

A chilly light takes hold of clothes,
lotions, little bottles of perfume.
By chance, too, a necklace is hanging there.

CAROLYN MULHOLLAND was born in
Lurgan, County Armagh in 1944. She
studied ceramics and sculpture in Belfast
College of Art and moved to Dublin in 1991.
She has worked as a sculptor since leaving
college and her favourite material is bronze.

Public commissions include *The Poet's Chair*
and *The Man on the Trestle* in Dublin.

Carolyn Mulholland

WILLIAM CROZIER was born in Yoker, Scotland in 1930, to Irish parents, and studied at Glasgow School of Art. An expressionist painter of landscapes, he has exhibited in major London galleries since 1958 and has worked and lived in Malaga, Paris, London, Venice and west Cork. His work is in the national galleries of Canada, England, Australia, the USA, France, Ireland, Germany and Scotland.

William Crozier

Still Life 1998

EVELYN CONLON, born in County
Monaghan, is a short-story writer and
novelist. Her stories have been widely
anthologised. Publications include *My Head
is Opening*, *Stars in the Daytime*, *Taking Scarlet
as a Real Colour* and *A Glassful of Letters*.

Evelyn Conlon

We liked walking on the ditch because when we were sent to the shop, particularly at night, my mother said, don't walk on the ditch, you might fall into the shuck. And we shone the light, when it worked, all over the sky, up and down from the tip of the earth to our wellington boots, dancing over the Milky Way, teasing it as we passed. It was probably the flashlight one of the band saw and then came out to tell us that President John F. Kennedy was shot. Killed stone dead. They must have had a wireless on all the time, which would be odd because you couldn't hear it over the drone of the practising bagpipers. It's more likely that one of them was late and had just arrived with the news. Or maybe they had known it for a long time and saw us and thought that by the look of us we didn't know Kennedy was dead and felt that they'd better tell us.

From *Taking Scarlet as a Real Colour*

PAOLO TULLIO was born in 1949 in Scotland, to Italian parents. He came to Ireland in 1968 to study at Trinity College, Dublin and never left. He is a writer, actor and journalist, and his book *North of Naples, South of Rome* was made into a television series which has been shown around the world. His last book is a novel called *mushroom.man*. He lives in County Wicklow with his wife, Susan Morley, and their two children.

Paolo Tullio

From the keyboard to the screen, to the window, to the roses, to the lawn, to the drive, to the trees, to the river, to the mountains, to the sky – my eye finds its horizon and defines my world; inside and out.

Felim Dunne is an architect living and
working in Ireland.

Felim Dunne

Illustrated is a worm's eye–view of a proposal for
housing, a meeting–hall and public gardens in Kilcoole,
County Wicklow. This assembly of buildings establishes
itself on the existing mass walk to Kilquade. This cross–
country path is manipulated through the new public
gardens revealing a Piranesian silhouette of the Great
Sugarloaf Mountain.

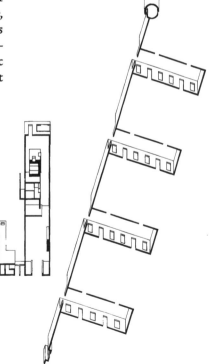

MARY HIGGINS CLARK was born and raised in New York, of Irish descent. Her father died when she was ten, and after high school she went to work to help with the family finances. In 1964 her first husband died of a heart attack and she began writing to support their five children. She has since written nineteen best-selling suspense novels, including *Where are the Children?* (1975), *A Stranger is Watching* (1978), *The Cradle Will Fall* (1980) and *Moonlight Becomes You* (1996). Her Christmas novel, *All Through the Night*, was published in 1998.

Mary Higgins Clark

This is my self-portrait

Pen in hand –

Always in a rush

and

Looking for a plot

KEVIN ROCHE was born in Dublin in 1922 and grew up in Mitchelstown, County Cork. He graduated in architecture from University College, Dublin in 1945 and moved to the United States in 1948. He has an international architectural practice. In addition to buildings all over the United States, he has built in Japan, Singapore, Malaysia, China, India, Turkey, Spain, France and England. He has served as president of the American Academy of Arts and Letters and been the recipient of many international awards.

Kevin Roche

27.11.2000

November/Samhain

MONDAY / LUAN

GABRIEL ROSENSTOCK, poet, haikuist, is the author/translator of some eighty books, including the selected poems in Irish of Francisco X. Alarcón, Seamus Heaney, J.W. Hackett, Robert Bebek, Günter Grass, Peter Huchel, Willem M. Roggeman, Georg Trakl and Georg Heym. He is a former chairman of Poetry Ireland/Éigse Éireann, a member of the British Haiku Society, Society of Irish Playwrights, and the Irish Writers' Union, and an honorary life member of the Irish Translators' Association. His daughter Héilean, who shares this page, is a student of photography.

Gabriel Rosenstock

atitim
aingeal
an uabhair

once more
to earth
the fallen angel

Photograph by Héilean Rosenstock

PAUL MCGUINNESS was born in 1951 in Germany. His father was an RAF navigator from Liverpool and his mother is a schoolteacher from County Kerry. He was educated at Clongowes Wood College and Trinity College, Dublin. In 1978, after working as an assistant director on various films and many TV commercials, he became the manager of U2. He also manages P.J. Harvey and is a partner in McGuinness Whelan Music, the publishers of Riverdance. His other businesses include Ardmore Studios and TV3. He has been a member of the Arts Council/An Chomhairle Ealaíon since 1988.

Paul McGuinness

We Irish are good at this cultural stuff; probably better at it than we are at some of the things we like to think we're good at, like tourism and farming. What kind of arts do we want? Sponsorship–driven arts? Tourism–led arts? We're uncomfortable when most of the seats in a theatre have been sold to coach companies and the audience don't know what they're coming to see. And let's not get carried away by this idea that everyone can be an artist if they say so. What about excellence? Is the guy who stitches on the scales as much an artist as the man in the head of the dragon? Or is the director the artist? Ask Macnas.

Our greatest national asset is that most generous gift of history, the English language. How lucky to speak English without the dreadful responsibility of being English. Or American for that matter. And we can be honorary Jews of course. In the movie business, the music industry and book publishing we are more welcome than WASPs. In U2 we always understood that. When we first toured in small clubs in America, Bono would say from the stage, 'We're not just another English band passing through: We're Irish and we'll be back.' The crowd would cheer and that welcome was echoed by the instinctive hospitality extended by lawyers, promoters and hustlers mostly Jewish, to members of another victim race.

So we can be heroes now. Grammies, Oscars, Emmies, BAFTAs, Tonys, Nobels, Bookers. Isn't it great?

THOMAS KILROY was born in County Kilkenny in 1934. He has written both original and adapted stage plays, the most recent being his version of Pirandello's *Six Characters in Search of an Author* (1996) and *The Secret Fall of Constance Wilde* (1997), both at the Abbey Theatre. His novel *The Big Chapel* won the *Guardian* Fiction Prize and, the Heinemann Award for Literature and was shortlisted for the Booker Prize. He is a former Professor of Modern English at University College, Galway, a member of Aosdána and the Irish Academy of Letters and a Fellow of the Royal Society of Literature.

Thomas Kilroy

(FROM : THE SECRET FALL OF CONSTANCE WILDE)

OSCAR WILDE: Do you know, I dread the thought of living beyond the century. The very thought of putting nineteen hundred & something atop one's notepaper gives one the willies! And yet! There are times when I see the mists of the future life. I see them there, in rows. Standing. And you know something? They are applauding me ————

(Oscar Wilde, died. November 30th, 1900)

MERLIN HOLLAND, the only grandson of Oscar Wilde, is a writer and journalist living in London. Following Oscar's conviction in 1895, his wife, Constance, and their two sons changed their name to Holland after being refused accommodation at a Swiss hotel. For the last twenty years, Merlin Holland has been researching his grandfather's life and works and he now lectures, writes and broadcasts regularly on the subject. He is preparing an enlarged and reworked edition of Wilde's letters for the centenary of Oscar Wilde's death on this day in 2000.

Merlin Holland

It was when he was fifteen that I knew my son would appreciate the rain, the craic, the odd sunset and 'the purple mountains and silver rivers' of Connemara, as Oscar once described them. So we went to dig up our Irish roots, first in the West at the Wildes' fishing lodge on Lough Fee; then at Sir William's rather grander country retreat, Moytura, on the shores of Lough Corrib; and finally to the Georgian splendour of the Wilde family home in Merrion Square. 'Do you mean to say,' asked Lucian as we came down the steps of the last, 'that all this could have been ours if Oscar had behaved himself?' 'No,' I replied, thinking how the Victorians had resented Wilde's Irish brilliance as much as they had hated his aesthetic decadence; 'it was a bit more complicated than that.'

Iris Murdoch was born in Dublin in 1919, grew up in London and received her university education at Oxford and later at Cambridge. Since 1948 she has been a Fellow of St Anne's College, Oxford, where for many years she taught philosophy.

A prolific and protean writer, her twenty-five novels include *The Bell* and the Booker-winning *The Sea, The Sea*. She has written works of philosophy and stage and radio plays, and has published a volume of poetry, *A Year of Birds*.

Iris Murdoch

DECEMBER

When the dark hawberries hang down and drip like blood
And the old man's beard has climbed up high in the wood
And the golden bracken has been broken by the snows
And Jesus Christ has come again to heal and pardon,
Then the little robin follows me through the garden,
In the dark days his breast is like a rose.

Tom de Paor was born in 1967.
He is an architect.

Tom de Paor

——

```
                    striped ready-mix lorries (in motion) bring to mind that
childhood exercise of simultaneously rubbing stomach clockwise and top of head
anti-clockwise
```

EUGENE McCABE was born in Glasgow in 1930 and went to secondary school in Dublin and to University College, Cork. He was a farmer before he began writing. His plays for theatre are *King of the Castle*, *Breakdown* and *Swift*. He has also written, for television, a trilogy called *Cancer*. Other writings include *Heritage and Other Stories*, *Roma* and *Death and Nightingales*. He still farms the family holding in County Monaghan.

Eugene McCabe

GLORIA MUNDI

High over all that harmony
Of Wintry light and tidal beauty
The guide was pointing down
At the pillared lion guarding
The Doges palace. 'Look for yourselves;
Amongst cities, we say here: Unique
The glory of the world.' Far out – on
The Adriatic we heard a siren shriek.
'Below is the Riva Degli Schiavoni
So called because for centuries
Slaves were our main commodity;
Bought and sold along the fondamenta
There before the Church of the Pietà.'

If you look now across the Grand Canal
You'll see the Lido. A great French army
Of the fourth crusade camped there in 1202
Awaiting orders: on the mainsail of
The pilot ship cravened and batiked
A giant Redeemer with a flaming
Sword, flanked by angels armed to conquer Israel.
He talked on; art and architecture, dates, names
No mention of the man from Stratford
Who penned that subtle suspect portrait of
The unforgiving Jew and who some scholars
Argue must have been here to see with those
All seeing eyes, Shylock at the Rialto

Badged in the yellow cap of his race
Or in the fish market with Jessica.
A yellow ribbon to her breast,
Must have known that for a hundred years
They were curfewed strictly behind steel gates;
By day all trades forbidden but discarded
Clothes and money lending; the penalty
For contravention: death, by hanging, without mercy.
After a silence he was heard to say
If anyone has any questions...Please?
Someone did ask this or that,
answers were given with ease till a voice
American; asked: *Where is the ghetto?*
Ah! the ghetto Yes:...again in Venice
Here we have the first ghetto in Europe,
From the old Venetian dialect word
Geto...G.E.T.O. meaning foundry
Furnace or iron works.
He blinked half smiling and all could hear
Black madrigals of bellowheeze
And oven blast, the hiss of dunked axles
Sharp ringing canticles of sword and spear
Along with anvilgong of chariot wheels
And high on the list of that golgothic forge
The iron cross processed and cauldron cast
For Cathedral spires and domes
Linking every field in Christendom.

BRIAN MOORE was born in Belfast in 1921 and educated at St Malachy's College. He joined the British Ministry of War Transport in 1943. In 1948 he emigrated to Canada where he became a journalist and eventually a Canadian citizen. He won wide acclaim for his novel *The Lonely Passion of Judith Hearne* (1955) and subsequently established a secure reputation as a writer of fiction. His twenty novels include *An Answer from Limbo* (1962), *I Am Mary Dunne* (1968), *Catholics* (1972), *Black Robe* (1985) and *The Statement* (1995). He also wrote film scripts, including *Torn Curtain* for Alfred Hitchcock. Brian Moore was shortlisted three times for the Booker Prize and twice won the Governor General's Award for fiction in Canada. In 1959 he settled in Malibu, California. He died there on 11 January 1999.

Brian Moore

Roland Barthes writing of Chateaubriand

"Memory is the beginning of writing and writing is, in its turn, the beginning of death."

Brian Moore

RUAIRÍ QUINN was born in Dublin in 1946 and educated at University College, Dublin. He trained as an architect and practised as such until 1993. He entered politics in 1976 when he became a member of Seanad Éireann. Elected to Dáil Éireann in 1977 as a member of the Labour Party, he has since held five ministerial posts and is now party leader. He is married to Liz Allman, with one son, and has two children by a previous marriage.

Ruairí Quinn

On Wednesday, 1 July 1998 Seamus Mallon, who speaks quietly with clear authority, responded to his nomination as Deputy First Minister in the Northern Ireland New Assembly.

The rectangular space was cramped, more like an office room than the chamber of a Democratic Parliament. His hesitant delivery underlined the conviction that infused his extempore address. Many members of the Assembly had been implacably opposed to the views held by Seamus Mallon in the past. Some still were and showed no sign of change.

But it was of change he spoke with the passion of a man who had worked for little else. At last he had come here to welcome that change in his own place and in his own time. His people and their people had spoken. Together they had voted for the same change. At last, not just after thirty years, or eighty years or even two hundred years, he was telling them that it was going to work.

GERRY ROBINSON was born in Donegal and educated at St Mary's Seminary, Castlehead. He began his career in the cost office of Lesney Products (Matchbox Toys). By 1980 he had become finance director of Grand Metropolitan's UK Coca–Cola business and went on to become chief executive of the whole contract services division. He joined Granada in 1991 and took over as chairman in 1996. He has also been chairman of BSkyB plc and of ITN. He is currently chairman of the Arts Council of England.

Gerry Robinson

This is a note from April, my daughter, at age five and a half. I'd not allowed her something. I can't remember what. She went off in great irritation and reappeared with this, much settled and obviously feeling better for it. It made me laugh but also made me feel good about her courage and ability to express her feelings so clearly.

(You a pig and a smelly dad, I hate you, hate from April)

TADHG MAC DHONNAGÁIN was born in Aghamore, County Mayo in 1961. He has been writing songs in Irish and English since the age of sixteen. His first album, *Solas Gorm*, was released in 1988. Some of the songs from that album have since made their way onto the Irish Junior Certificate exam syllabus, an unusual accolade for a contemporary songwriter. *Raifteirí san Underground* was released in 1993 and in 1997 he set up his own record company to release a CD for children (and former children) on the theme of the seasons, under the pseudonym Futa Fata Féasóg.

Tadhg Mac Dhonnagáin

SEO AN TALAMH

Ag teacht abhaile thar Chnoc an Bhainne
Siar go Duagaire is Doire Ghé
Tá chuile ardán is chuile ísleán
Ag fógairt chugam a ainm fhéin
Seo anois mé ar bhóithrín portaigh
Tá ceannabháin bhána ag rince leo
Anseo im' pháiste a ghróiginn móin dubh
Anois is cuimhní atá gróigthe romham

Curfá
Seo an talamh a shaothraigh mo mhuintir
Ar an talamh seo a tógadh mé
Go seasta síoraí, de ló is d'oíche
Molaim agus móraim é.

Ba chéimín beag é a thóg an chéad fhear
Nuair a leag sé cois ar ghealach lán
Siúd sa spéir uaidh an plainéad gléghorm
Mé fhéin 's mo mhuintir ar fud an domhain
Ag teacht anuas dó bhí cnoic is sléibhte
Le feiceáil síos uaidh i bhfad i gcéin
Bhí chuile ardán is chuile ísleán
Ag fógairt chuige a ainm fhéin

Curfá

Droichead
Ó Chnoc an Bhainne go Fujiyama
Ón Mississippi go hInis Gé
Ar na hardáin, ar na hísleáin
Ar an talamh seo a tóigeadh sinn go léir

Curfá

MÁIRE BRENNAN is best known as the lead singer of Clannad. Her haunting voice has added a poignant, ethereal quality to the unique sound that the band has developed over two decades, winning it many accolades and awards in the process. In more recent years Máire Brennan has made great strides in her own musical progression. Her third solo album, *Perfect Time*, was released in 1998. She comes from a large musical family in Donegal, and now lives in Dublin with her husband, Tim, and two children.

Máire Brennan

Wonderful children destined to be
climbing in darkness
ashamed for you and me
Prayers can be answered
Let's move mountains high
God we reach for ancient skies
Let our faith never die.

"Heal this land" Máire Brennan

Is é an Tiarna mo sholas is mo shlánú
Cé a chuirfidh eagla orm?

Is é an Tiarna daingean m'anama
Cé a chuirfidh ar crith mé?

psalm 27:1-2

JOHN BOORMAN is a film director and writer. His films include *Point Blank*, *Deliverance*, *Excalibur*, *Hope and Glory* and *The General*. He is author of *Money into Light* and co-editor of the annual publication *Projections*. He has lived for thirty years in County Wicklow, where he has planted 15,000 trees.

John Boorman

I started planting too late in life
but one acorn sown is now a sturdy oak
and I am not yet too old to climb it.
Cradled in its branches,
an old fool smiles proudly down
at the earth receding by a foot each year.

JOHN HUME was born in Derry in 1937. As a public representative for the Foyle constituency and leader of the Social Democratic and Labour Party, he has been the voice of moderate, constitutional nationalism in Northern Ireland through the thirty-year history of the recent Troubles. From his early involvement in the civil rights movement in Derry, to the signing of the Belfast Agreement on Good Friday 1998, he stood consistently, often alone, in the crucible of tribal conflict, preaching reconciliation and agreement. He has served the people of Derry in both the British and European parliaments and in 1997 declined an invitation to run for the presidency of Ireland. In October 1998 he was the joint winner, with David Trimble, leader of the Ulster Unionist Party, of the Nobel Peace Prize. He is married to Pat and they have five children.

John Hume

The time has come for a positive and decisive initiative. It must be taken by both Dublin and London acting together. They should first make it clear that there are no longer any unconditional guarantees for any section of the northern community. There is only a commitment to achieving a situation in which there are guarantees for all.

Second, they should make it clear that there is in fact no pat solution as such, but only a process that will lead to a solution. They should declare themselves committed to such a process, a process designed to lead to an agreed Ireland with positive roles for all. They should invite all parties to participate in this process, the process of building a new Ireland. Some groups will undoubtedly react with an initial refusal, but the process should continue without them, leaving the door always open for their participation at any stage.

Indeed, on embarking on this process we ought to be encouraged by the example of both the United States and the European Community. In the United States, in spite of deep differences of origin and background, they have formed a constitution which is able to harness great differences for the common good. Yet the Italians remain Italian, the blacks are still black, and the Irish still parade on St Patrick's Day. They have created a unity in diversity.

Europe itself has suffered centuries of bloody conflict. In this century alone, the people of Europe have been locked in the savagery of two world wars with a bitterness and slaughter that goes far beyond anything that we have experienced on this island. Yet thirty-four years after the Second World War, as a result of an agreed process, they have been able to create one parliament to represent them, one community – and the Germans are still Germans, the French are still French. They, too, have a unity in diversity.

Is it too much to ask that we on this small island do precisely the same thing? Is it too much to ask that these two responsible governments begin to declare themselves now in favour of such a process? Can we too build a unity in diversity?

Article published in *Foreign Affairs*, Winter 1979/80

ANN MARIE HOURIHANE is a journalist
and broadcaster who lives in Dublin. She
was a writer and performer on a satirical
television programme called *Nighthawks*
and a presenter of the arts programme
Black Box. She writes for *The Sunday Tribune*.

Ann Marie Hourihane

In those days you got to choose who you married. It was a system with serious flaws. The emphasis was on romantic love, and the boredom was extraordinary. You had to live with your sexual partner, and go everywhere with him – even to the cinema. In my grandmother's case this led to a lot of crowded picture houses. You had to dress to keep your man, to show strangers that you were still in the game. She spent a fortune, fruitlessly, on clothes. My grandmother was a heroic smoker – you didn't have to smoke in those days, it was entirely voluntary – and she never worked past sixty, because she had something known as a pension. She spent her old age puffing, and picking spouses for her children. In this regard, as in so many others, she was ahead of her time. An old soldier who saw a change in the war.

FERGUS BOURKE was born in Dublin in 1934. In the 1970s he worked as a photojournalist for *Nusight* and *Magill* magazines and he was the Abbey Theatre's official photographer between 1971 and 1991. He has had more than thirty solo exhibitions. He is a member of Aosdána and lives in Connemara, where he is working on a book of local landscapes.

Fergus Bourke

Covered Wagon in Snow

MÁIRE MHAC AN TSAOI was born in 1922 in Dublin, the daughter of politician and author Seán MacEntee, but spent long periods of her childhood in the Kerry Gaeltacht. While working at the Institute for Advanced Studies, she edited *Dhá Sgéal* *Arturaoíchta* and assisted on Tomás de Bhaldraithe's English–Irish dictionary, before joining the Department of External Affairs. She has published a number of books of Irish poetry, including *An Cion go dtí Seo*, collaborated on a translation of Dante, written numerous critical articles and, with her husband, Conor Cruise O'Brien, produced *A Concise History of Ireland* (1972). In November 1997 she resigned from Aosdána.

Máire Mhac an tSaoi

SEAN–GHRIANGHRAF DE BHEIRT GHEARRCHAILE

An dá aghaidh bheaga, rúnda, gheala ag féachaint aníos orm,

Mar a bheadh samhraicíní faoi chab lice sa tsneachta;

Mé gafa i mistéir lán na pearsantachta;

An deorantaí dhom anois iad, fásta 'na máithreacha áil,

Ná mar 'bhíodar an lá san, nuair 'chonac de'n gcéad uair iad?

AN OLD PHOTOGRAPH OF TWO LITTLE GIRLS

The two little, secret, fair faces looking up at me,

Like primroses under the lip of a stone in the snow;

I am absorbed in the full mystery of personhood;

Are they more foreign to me now, grown into mothers of families,

Than they were that day when I saw them for the first time?

JULIE PARSONS was born in New Zealand
but has lived most of her life in Ireland.
Her first novel, *Mary Mary*, was published
in 1998.

Julie Parsons

The imagination lies quietly. It sighs and stirs. It rolls over and stretches. It listens, and hears. A thought, an idea, a possibility.

A flicker of animation runs through it. It tenses its unused muscles, waiting and wondering. For the opportunity, the chance, the right moment.

Light and colour flood through it. Music, words, noises made by men and beasts seep deep inside. Heat and cold expand and contract the pores of its thin skin. Love, hate, desire, revulsion twist and turn within.

And then it moves. It strikes. It begins its exquisite enterprise. And creates a new world, transforming the elements of the old. Beams of bright yellow light play across the shadowy contours of an unknown land.

Different, every time. Making beginnings and endings. Putting form onto the formless. Creating a place of wonder where none had been before. The imagination, at work.

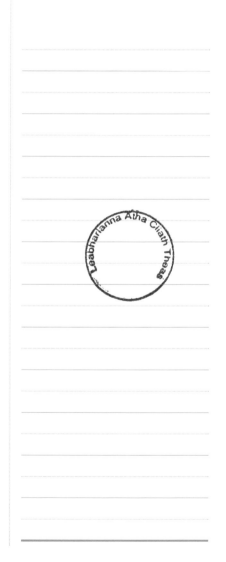

RONAN BROWNE is a master of the uilleann pipes, renowned for his powerful playing, and for expanding the instrument's possibilities. He is the piper on the original hit single of 'Riverdance' and is a founder member of the Afro Celt Sound System for Peter Gabriel's Real World record label. As a member of Cran, whose most recent CD is *Black Black Black*, Ronan plays to Irish traditional music audiences worldwide. He came to prominence with his traditional recording *The South West Wind* (1988) along with Clare fiddler Peadar O'Loughlin.

Ronan Browne

Slow Air
Molto Rubato

Ronan Browne

SEÁN MCSWEENEY, a painter, was born in Dublin in 1935. Since the early 1960s he has exhibited annually in the capital, as well as in various centres around the country. His work has also been shown in England, France, Switzerland, Australia and the United States. During the 1970s he lived in and worked from the Wicklow landscape before moving to Sligo the following decade. Since then, his main inspiration has been the shoreline and bogland beyond Lissadell. He is represented by the Taylor Galleries in Dublin and is a member of Aosdána.

Seán McSweeney

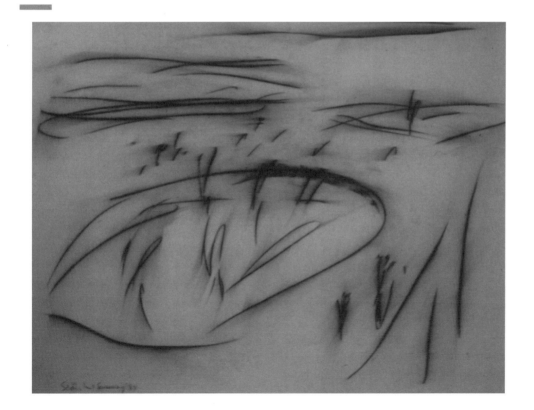

Winter Bogland

PATRICK MCGRATH was born in London, to Irish parents, in 1950 and was educated by the Jesuits at Stonyhurst. He grew up close to Broadmoor Special Hospital, where for many years his father was medical superintendent. He emigrated to Canada in 1971 and lived on an island in the North Pacific, then moved to New York in 1981. He is the author of a story collection, *Blood and Water*, and four novels: *The Grotesque*, *Spider*, *Dr Haggard's Disease* and *Asylum*. He co-edited an anthology of fiction, *The New Gothic*, and wrote the script for the screen adaptation of *The Grotesque*. He is married to the actress Maria Aitken.

Patrick McGrath

So where does it start, then, this vertebrated spine of circumstance and incident and twisted human intention? With Clyte – Clyte! – that whispering principle of negation! – oh, he haunts me still, a dreadful, dreadful man. Thin as a rake, long of jaw and hollow of cheek, dressed in dusty black and no wig on his cropped blue skull, Clyte was the sort who moved always to the shadows, who sought the darkest part of any place he found himself in. He was a man who *slunk*, a man who *stole* away before his person had properly been registered, who was known, in fact, more for his absence than his presence! This had much to do with the line of work he pursued, but also with the very kidney of the creature, for by nature he was more shadow than substance, an instrument of darkness who served a master in constant need of precisely the services Clyte alone could provide. I speak of Lord Francis Drogo...

MEDBH McGUCKIAN was born in Belfast in 1950. She studied English and taught before winning England's National Poetry Competition in 1979, which launched her publishing career. She has produced five collections of poetry, which include *Venus and the Rain* and *Marconi's Cottage*.

Medbh McGuckian

My sister ~~has~~ wears three wedding rings melted into one – my grandmothers', my great-grandmothers', and my greataunts'. The run when I went up to hilltown for the first time recently in thirty cold years to look for my grandmothers' grave I remembered it as being over on the right, in a field down below the road, but I could not trace it with my Polish friend, and had to return to give details to the clerk at the Record office. Even then it was difficult to pinpoint, overshadowed by younger graves. It held the date 1921 the name of my granduncle as having purchased the plot for his young bride who had died in childbirth. There was no indication that the infant was there, ~~though my~~ and no other dates or names, though my grandfather, my grandmother, her brother, my uncle and finally the original owner lately, had all been interred there from the fifties on.

SEAMUS DEANE is a critic, poet and novelist. Born in Derry, educated there, at Belfast and at Cambridge University, he has been Keough Professor of Irish Studies at the University of Notre Dame, USA, since 1993, after a long spell as teacher and professor at University College, Dublin. His works include *Celtic Revivals* (1985), *Selected Poems* (1988), *Strange Country* (1997), ed. The *Field Day Anthology of Irish Writing* (1991), and the novel *Reading in the Dark* (1997).

Seamus Deane

Witchcraft. orgy, cuckoldry, charivari, and massacre, the men of the Old Regime could hear a great deal in the wail of a cat. (Robert Darnton)

The concierge at the hotel in the Rue de la Reine Blanche was a real old bat for whom I had been savouring a series of misfortunes from the moment, only forty-eight hours earlier, when I had first seen her adze-like profile behind the glassed door to her cat-strewn living quarters. When she opened the door to my ring, they all moved and stiffened and slid away to the back regions, carrying their suspicion and fear into a cloud of massed fur, their eyes split with a stable malevolence that I could have admired were it not for the shattering repertoire of snarl and wail they emitted in semi-quavers and demi-semi-quavers, the voices of the mutilated.

JUSTIN QUINN, a poet, was born in Dublin in 1968. He studied English and philosophy at Trinity College, Dublin, where he later completed a doctorate on the American poet Wallace Stevens. His first collection of poems, The 'O'o'a'a' Bird, was published in 1995 and his second, Privacy, in 1999. He is an editor of the poetry magazine Metre. In 1994 he moved to the Czech Republic, where he now lives with his wife and child, lecturing at the Charles University in Prague.

Justin Quinn

orter, meeting, spreadsheets, shopping, breakfast-lunch-o
dinner, test, currency, bridgework, ticket, meeting, t

Someone talking,
Their face,
In twenty-year-old dark.

21.12.2000

December/Nollaig

DAVID KELLY has been on the Dublin stage, as well as playing in all the capitals of Europe, for nearly half a century. He has made four tours of America, where in 1990 he was nominated for the Helen Hayes Award. He was one of the early exponents of Samuel Beckett, and his performance of *Krapp's Last Tape*, which he premiered in Dublin in 1959, was received to great acclaim in recent years in Seville, New York and Melbourne. Television work has made him a famous face and his most recent film, *Waking Ned*, opened at Cannes in 1998. Painting is his hobby.

David Kelly

David Kelly

FRANK MCGUINNESS was born in
Buncrana, County Donegal in 1953.
He is a prolific and constantly developing
playwright, whose works include *The
Factory Girls, Observe the Sons of Ulster
Marching towards the Somme, Innocence,*
Carthaginians, Someone Who'll Watch Over Me
and *The Bird Sanctuary*. He has also adapted
plays by Lorca, Ibsen, Chekhov, Brecht,
Strindberg and Pirandello. He lives in
Booterstown and lectures in University
College, Dublin.

Frank McGuinness

My Lover's Heart Compared to the Golden Gate Bridge

For a start it is not golden
Nor is it a bridge.
                    It is animal,
It is mineral, and the question is,
Does it love itself? It does,
But with discretion.
                    I adore discretion,
For the heart is capable of being ripped
Apart, repaired as if nothing happened,
Repainted, but not golden. It is red,
The heart.

EMMA DONOGHUE was born in Dublin in 1969. She is best known for her fiction, which includes *Stir-Fry* (1994), *Hood* (1995) and *Kissing the Witch* (1997). She has written three historical plays: *I Know My Own Heart*, *Ladies and Gentlemen* and *Trespasses*. As a scholar, she specialises in women's history and lesbian literature. *What Sappho Would Have Said* (1997) is an anthology of love poems, and her first biography is a study of a pair of Victorian poets, *We are Michael Field* (1998). She divides her time between Canada, England and Ireland.

Emma Donoghue

SNOW ANGELS

Whatever happens
tomorrow to our shapes in the snow –
whether rain blots them out entirely,
sun blurs their borders,
wind litters them,
ice takes hold,
or the daily grass
scratches through –

whatever element
finally fills in this pair of outlines,
exultation will seize me ever after,
to think I strayed off the path,
laid me down,
left my mark
on a white corner
of your page.

CIARÁN MAC MATHÚNA was born in 1925 in Limerick, where he attended the Christian Brothers' School before going to University College, Dublin. For the last forty years he has been collecting traditional music and folklore and presenting programmes on the subject on RTÉ radio and television. The best known of these is his Sunday morning programme of twenty-five years, Mo Cheol Thú, which features traditional music, song and poetry. For many years a member of the Cultural Relations Committee of the Irish Department of Foreign Affairs, he has received honorary doctorates for his life's work from University College, Galway and the University of Limerick.

Ciarán Mac Mathúna

DECEMBER/ MÍ NA NOLLAG

A CHRISTMAS FUNERAL 1835

Raftery, the blind Gaelic poet and fiddle player, was born in Killeadan, County Mayo probably in 1779. Different reasons are given for his leaving his native place but leave he did and spent the rest of his life in County Galway as a wandering poet and musician around Athenry, Loughrea, Gort, Oranmore and Craughwell, where he died in 1835. The poet actually died on Christmas Eve and, for reasons not known, was buried in the middle of that night in Killeeneen Churchyard not far away.

In the year 1900 – the beginning of the last millennium – Lady Gregory of Coole Park and her friends erected a headstone over Raftery's grave. My wife, Dolly, comes from that part of the country and her father, Martin Furey, who was full of the traditions of the area, remembered being there in 1900 as a young man and hearing an old man also named Furey relate how he held one of the candles at the graveside on that cold Christmas night in 1835 at Raftery's burial and it is told that none of the candles went out until the grave was filled.

ENYA was born Eithne Ní Bhraonáin in the Gaeltacht area of Gweedore, County Donegal. She studied classical music before joining forces with producer Nicky Ryan and lyricist Roma Ryan. Since then Enya has sold forty million albums worldwide.

Her many awards include the Irish Life Arts Award, two Grammies and being twice voted International Artist of the Year in Japan. All three partners have won the coveted Ivor Novello Award.

Enya

Enya's version of 'Oíche Chiúin' ('Silent Night') is the first recording ever made of the famous carol in the Irish language. Here Enya has penned the music with the words in the old-style Gaelic lettering.

FRANK MCCOURT was born in Limerick in 1932. Brought up in a large family, he left school at thirteen. He worked for many years as a schoolteacher in America. *Angela's Ashes*, his first book, is the graphic and harrowing evocation of his childhood in Limerick. It became an international best-seller, won the Pulitzer Prize in 1996 and was filmed by Alan Parker.

Frank McCourt

In the Forty-Second Street Library in New York you can sit for days reading *The Lives of the Irish Saints* by Father O'Hanlon. Someone at another desk might be compiling a *Lives of the American Saints* – and that would be a welcome volume. But the puzzling thing is that in the American collection you won't find a single Irish–American saint. Not one.

We came to this country and did our bit building everything. We built a great network of Catholic schools and universities. We brought hundreds of priests from Ireland to minister to our souls, to build churches. We brought nuns to build hospitals and heal us.

The first American saint was Mother Cabrini – Italian. Then various Popes canonized people of all shades and nationalities.

Is that sign up again: No Irish Need Apply?

ROBERT ARMSTRONG was born in Gorey, County Wexford in 1953. He has worked as a graphic artist and theatre and film designer, but since the early 1980s he has been a full-time painter. He won a GPA Emerging Artist award in 1984. His work reflects his interest in landscapes as diverse as Wicklow, Papua New Guinea and, more recently, the volcanic terrain of the Aeolian Islands. His painting practice finds analogies in the biological and geological processes in the formation of these various landscapes. He is represented in numerous public and private collections in Ireland and abroad.

Robert Armstrong

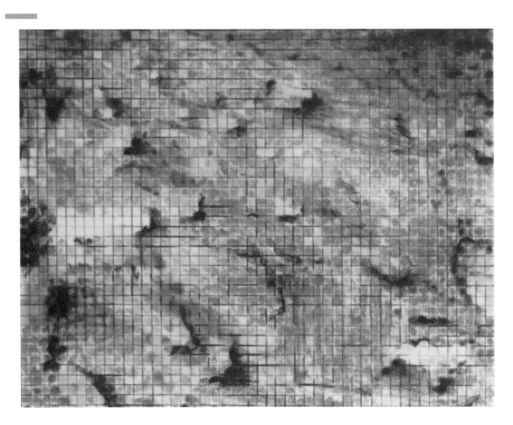

Volcanic Landscape in 2000 Parts

JOE O'CONNOR was born in Dublin in 1963. He has written three best-selling and critically acclaimed novels: *Cowboys & Indians*, *Desperadoes* and *The Salesman*; also a collection of short stories: *True Believers*, four works of non-fiction: *Even the Olives are Bleeding: The Life and Times of Charles Donnelly*, *Sweet Liberty: Travels in Irish America*, *The Secret World of the Irish Male* and *The Irish Male at Home and Abroad*, and two stage plays: *Red Roses and Petrol* and *The Weeping of Angels*. He also wrote the screenplays for the award-winning films *A Stone of the Heart*, *The Long Way Home* and *Ailsa*.

Joe O'Connor

UNUSED TITLES — love stories etc (+ novels?)

The Old One Two — Unconditional Love — My b
Drop Dead Gorgeous — Three card trick — The E
Been There, Done That — Three chord trick : Why!
Cops And Robbers — Satellite Of Love : Who Care
Family Values — Coco the Bastard — No Co
No More Mister Nice Guy — Wife-Swopping so don
You Were Always The Same : I Married A Mo
Yeats Is Dead : Jesus Saves : Th
The Disappointed Columnist : The Princess of Afri
Mercy . Finisterre . Drinking Up Time . Th
The Prince Of Salesmen . Adventures Day Is Over
Elvis Lives . Desolate Shade . Hero

Notebook scrap

MARIANNE FAITHFULL was born in 1946 in England, to Austrian and Welsh parents. Convent–educated, she became a pop star at the age of seventeen. 'Sister Morphine' (1969), co–written with Mick Jagger and Keith Richards, was her creative awakening and she went on to record the astonishing *Broken English* in 1979. She has acted on the stage and on screen and reinterpreted Kurt Weill – *20th Century Blues: An Evening in the Weimar Republic* and Brecht's *The Seven Deadly Sins* – on record and in live performance. She is a Professor of Poetics from the Jack Kerouac School of Disembodied Poets. She lives in Dublin.

Marianne Faithfull

Child wakes up and hears her parents
    talkin' soft and low
Touches the wall behind her head
    and stretches her toes
In another room they are relaxing,
    shining in the dark
And gently talkin' about the state
    of the heart.

Another room, another city and the
    pain's intense
This quarrel has no meaning,
    makes no sense
Across the chasm of their love
    they try to chart
The moment they forgot to check
    the state of the heart.

I sit here waiting for you, hear
    your step out in the street
(again) I look into your eyes, at last
    we meet
For too long, and for nothing we've
    kept ourselves apart
No words to say, we touch and listen
    to the calling of the heart.

KEITH RIDGWAY is the author of numerous
short stories, the novella *Horses* and the
novel *The Long Falling*. He is currently
finishing a second novel. He lives in Dublin.

Keith Ridgway

```
                    Fill This In

What is your name? _____
What age are you?  _____
Are you a drinker □ a lover □ a smoker □ (one only)
What is your favourite food? _____
Are you happy? _____
How old is your milk? _____
What is your favourite secret? _____
What have you done today? _____
Are you in love? _____
Do you think that matters? _____
Do you need more money? _____
What have you stolen? _____
What are you wearing? _____
Are you telling the truth? _____

Finish this sentence : "Twice _____"
Why are you doing this?_____

Cut this out and send it to me. Keith Ridgway, c/o 9
Fitzwilliam Place, Dublin 2, Ireland. Mark your enve-
lope "My day dammit."
```

PETER SHERIDAN was born in Dublin in 1952 and has spent most of his adult life writing, directing and collaborating in the theatre. His plays have been seen in the major theatres in Ireland, London, Montreal, New York and Los Angeles. He was awarded the Rooney Prize for Literature in 1977 and was writer–in–residence at the Abbey Theatre in 1980. He lives on Dublin's north side with his wife, Sheila. They have four children, Rossa, Fiachra, Doireann and Nuala.

Peter Sheridan

Ma and Da decided to throw a New Year's Eve Party in the front room of 44. It was the beginning of a new decade. We'd never say nineteen sixty anything again. It would take getting used to. In a day the sixties would be over. It didn't seem possible. There was the roaring twenties and the hungry thirties. What would people say of the sixties? How would they describe it? What would they remember first, Sgt Pepper's Lonely Hearts Club Band or Belfast burning? At midnight on December 31st, the world would grieve for the passing of the sixties, but it would not be real; real grieving was done alone, it wasn't a public thing and no one could do it for you.

MMI

Hospice / Palliative Care Services

Our Lady's Hospice, Harold's Cross,
Dublin 6.
Tel: (01) 497 8099

St Vincent's Hospital,
Elm Park, Dublin 4.
Tel: (01) 269 4533

St Francis Hospice, Station Road,
Raheny, Dublin 5.
Tel: (01) 832 7535

St Luke's Hospital, Oaklands,
Highfield Road, Rathgar, Dublin 6.
Tel: (01) 497 4552

St James's Hospital, James's Street,
Dublin 8.
Tel: (01) 453 7941

Paediatric Oncology Liaison Nurse
Service, Oncology Unit, Our Lady's
Hospital, Crumlin, Dublin 12.
Tel: (01) 455 8111

St Brigid's Hospice and Home Care
Service, The Drogheda Memorial
Hospital, The Curragh, Co. Kildare.
Tel: (045) 41875/41270

Wicklow Home Care Service,
St Cronan's Health Centre,
Bray, Co. Wicklow.
Tel: (01) 286 6422

Wicklow Home Care Service,
Community Care Offices,
Glenside Road, Wicklow Town.
Tel: (0404) 68400

Laois Home Care Service,
General Hospital, Portlaoise.
Tel: (0502) 60147

Longford Hospice/Home Care,
St Joseph's Hospital, Longford.
Tel: (043) 45851

Offaly Hospice Foundation,
Mount Pleasant, Bluebell, Tullamore.
Tel: (0506) 41904

Westmeath Hospice/Home Care,
County Clinic, Mullingar.
Tel: (044) 40221.
Mobile: 088–626431

District Hospital, Athlone.
Tel: (0902) 75301

Milford Hospice, Plassey Park Road,
Castletroy, Limerick.
Tel: (061) 331505

Palliative Home Care, Community
Care Services, Lisdarn, Cavan.
Tel: (049) 61822

Palliative Home Care Service,
Community Care Centre, Dublin
Road, Dundalk.
Tel: (042) 32287

County Meath Hospice Home Care Service, County Clinic, Navan.
Tel: (046) 27375

Palliative Home Care, Ballybay Health Centre, Ballybay, Co. Monaghan.
Tel: (042) 41157

Donegal Hospice Home Care Service, Letterkenny General Hospital, Letterkenny.
Tel: (074) 25888

Home Care Service, District Hospital, Donegal Town.
Tel: (073) 21019

North West Hospice, Stephen Court, 10–12 Stephen Street, Sligo.
Tel: (071) 43317

Carlow/Kilkenny Home Care Team, St Luke's Hospital, Kilkenny.
Tel: (056) 51133 (ext. 355)

South Tipperary Hospice Movement, County Clinic, Clonmel.
Tel: (052) 22011

Waterford Hospice Movement Ltd, Waterford Regional Hospital, Ardkeen, Waterford.
Tel: (051) 73321 (ext. 2239)

County Wexford Hospice Home Care Team, Wexford General Hospital, Wexford.
Tel: (053) 42233

Marymount Hospice, St Patrick's Hospital, Wellington Road, Cork.
Tel: (021) 501201

Palliative Care Service, Cork University Hospital, Wilton, Cork.
Tel: (021) 546400

Kerry Home Care, Tralee General Hospital, Tralee.
Tel: (066) 27793

Kerry Home Care, District Hospital, Killarney.
Tel: (064) 35026

Galway Hospice Foundation, Renmore, Galway.
Tel: (091) 770868

Mayo/Roscommon Hospice, The Mall, Main Street, Knock.
Tel: (094) 88666

Mayo Home Care Team, Community Care Offices, Western Health Board, Castlebar.
Tel: (094) 22333

Roscommon Home Care Team, Community Care Offices, Western Health Board, Roscommon.
Tel: (0903) 26518

Northern Ireland Hospice, Somerton House, 74 Somerton Road, Belfast BT15 3LH.
Tel: (080 1232) 781836

Beaconfield Marie Curie Centre, Kensington Road, Belfast BT5 6NF.
Tel: (080 1232) 794200

Macmillan Home Care Service, Gilford Health Centre, Gilford, Co. Down.
Tel: (080 1762) 832091

Foyle Hospice, 61 Culmore Road, Derry BT48 8JE.
Tel: (080 1504) 351010

Newry Hospice, St John of God Hospital, Courtney Hill, Newry BT34 2EB.
Tel: (080 1693) 67711

Bereavement Services

Irish Hospice Foundation
Bereavement Service,
Our Lady's Hospice, Harold's Cross,
Dublin 6.
Tel: (01) 497 2101/676 5599

St Francis Hospice,
Station Road, Raheny, Dublin 5.
Tel: (01) 832 7535/676 5599

St John's Ward, Our Lady's Hospital,
Crumlin, Dublin 12.
Tel: (01) 455 8111

Teenage Bereavement Support,
Our Lady's Hospice,
Harold's Cross, Dublin 6.
Tel: (01) 597 2101 (ext. 285)

The Bereavement Counselling Service,
Dublin Street, Baldoyle, Dublin 13.
Tel: (01) 839 1766

The Compassionate Friends,
18 Kilbarrack Avenue, Dublin 5.
Tel: (01) 832 4618

Laois Hospice Bereavement Service.
Tel: (0502) 60984

Longford Bereavement Support
Group, Teallach Íosa,
St Mel's Road, Longford.
Tel: (043) 46827

Rainbow for All God's Children
Family Centre,
St Mel's Road, Longford.
Tel: (043) 46827

Edenderry Support Group,
Blundel Wood, Edenderry.
Tel: (0405) 31255

Tullamore Support Group,
Parochial House, Tullamore.
Tel: (0506) 21587

Milford Hospice,
Plassey Park Road,
Castletroy, Limerick.
Tel: (061) 331505

North Louth Hospice and Home Care
Support Group,
Seafield Lawns, Dundalk.

Meath Hospice Homecare Movement,
14 Oliver Plunkett Road, Kells.
Tel: (046) 41956

The Compassionate Friends,
Ballindrait, Bunbeg, Letterkenny.
Tel: (075) 31493

North West Hospice Bereavement
Service, Stephen Court,
10–12 Stephen Street, Sligo.
Tel: (071) 43317

Bereavement Counselling Service,
Carlow. Tel: (0503) 40977

Kilkenny Bereavement Support
Service, St Luke's Hospital,
Kilkenny.
Tel: (056) 51133

Family Life Service, Bereavement
Care,
St Bridget's Centre,
12 Roches Road, Wexford.
Tel: (053) 23086

The Compassionate Friends,
c/o Invermore, Skehard Road,
Blackrock, Cork.
Tel: (021) 291892/364695

Galway Hospice Bereavement
Support Group,
Renmore, Galway.
Tel: (091) 770868

Mayo Home Care Team,
County Clinic, Castlebar.
Tel: (094) 22333

Roscommon Home Care Team,
Western Health Board, Roscommon.
Tel: (0903) 26518

Northern Ireland Hospice
Bereavement Aftercare,
Somerton House,
74 Somerton Road, Belfast BT15 3LH.
Tel: (080 1232) 781836

Macmillan Home Care Service,
Gilford Health Centre, Gilford,
Co. Down.
Tel: (080 1762) 832091

Foyle Hospital, 61 Culmore Road,
Derry BT48 8JE.
Tel: (080 1504) 351010

The Compassionate Friends,
3 Beddes Avenue, Lurgan, Co. Armagh
BT66 7JH.
Tel: (080 1762) 321508

Newry Hospice, St John of God
Hospital, Courtney Hill,
Newry BT34 2EB.
Tel: (080 1693) 67711

The Compassionate Friends,
'Red Rowans', 5 Tullyhubbert Road,
Moneyreagh, Newtownards BT23 6BY.
Tel: (080 1232) 448618

Notes

Notes

2000	1	2	3	4	5	6	7	8	9	10	11	12
MONDAY					1							
TUESDAY		1			2			1				
WEDNESDAY		2	1		3			2			1	
THURSDAY		3	2		4	1		3			2	
FRIDAY		4	3		5	2		4	1		3	1
SATURDAY	1	5	4	1	6	3	1	5	2		4	2
SUNDAY	2	6	5	2	7	4	2	6	3	1	5	3
MONDAY	3	7	6	3	8	5	3	7	4	2	6	4
TUESDAY	4	8	7	4	9	6	4	8	5	3	7	5
WEDNESDAY	5	9	8	5	10	7	5	9	6	4	8	6
THURSDAY	6	10	9	6	11	8	6	10	7	5	9	7
FRIDAY	7	11	10	7	12	9	7	11	8	6	10	8
SATURDAY	8	12	11	8	13	10	8	12	9	7	11	9
SUNDAY	9	13	12	9	14	11	9	13	10	8	12	10
MONDAY	10	14	13	10	15	12	10	14	11	9	13	11
TUESDAY	11	15	14	11	16	13	11	15	12	10	14	12
WEDNESDAY	12	16	15	12	17	14	12	16	13	11	15	13
THURSDAY	13	17	16	13	18	15	13	17	14	12	16	14
FRIDAY	14	18	17	14	19	16	14	18	15	13	17	15
SATURDAY	15	19	18	15	20	17	15	19	16	14	18	16
SUNDAY	16	20	19	16	21	18	16	20	17	15	19	17
MONDAY	17	21	20	17	22	19	17	21	18	16	20	18
TUESDAY	18	22	21	18	23	20	18	22	19	17	21	19
WEDNESDAY	19	23	22	19	24	21	19	23	20	18	22	20
THURSDAY	20	24	23	20	25	22	20	24	21	19	23	21
FRIDAY	21	25	24	21	26	23	21	25	22	20	24	22
SATURDAY	22	26	25	22	27	24	22	26	23	21	25	23
SUNDAY	23	27	26	23	28	25	23	27	24	22	26	24
MONDAY	24	28	27	24	29	26	24	28	25	23	27	25
TUESDAY	25	29	28	25	30	27	25	29	26	24	28	26
WEDNESDAY	26		29	26	31	28	26	30	27	25	29	27
THURSDAY	27		30	27		29	27	31	28	26	30	28
FRIDAY	28		31	28		30	28		29	27		29
SATURDAY	29			29			29			28		30
SUNDAY	30			30			30			29		31
MONDAY	31						31			30		
TUESDAY										31		

1	2	3	4	5	6	7	8	9	10	11	12	2001
1									1			LUAN
2				1					2			MÁIRT
3				2			1		3			CÉADAOIN
4	1	1		3			2		4	1		DÉARDAOIN
5	2	2		4	1		3		5	2		AOINE
6	3	3		5	2		4	1	6	3	1	SATHARN
7	4	4	1	6	3	1	5	2	7	4	2	DOMHNACH
8	5	5	2	7	4	2	6	3	8	5	3	LUAN
9	6	6	3	8	5	3	7	4	9	6	4	MÁIRT
10	7	7	4	9	6	4	8	5	10	7	5	CÉADAOIN
11	8	8	5	10	7	5	9	6	11	8	6	DÉARDAOIN
12	9	9	6	11	8	6	10	7	12	9	7	AOINE
13	10	10	7	12	9	7	11	8	13	10	8	SATHARN
14	11	11	8	13	10	8	12	9	14	11	9	DOMHNACH
15	12	12	9	14	11	9	13	10	15	12	10	LUAN
16	13	13	10	15	12	10	14	11	16	13	11	MÁIRT
17	14	14	11	16	13	11	15	12	17	14	12	CÉADAOIN
18	15	15	12	17	14	12	16	13	18	15	13	DÉARDAOIN
19	16	16	13	18	15	13	17	14	19	16	14	AOINE
20	17	17	14	19	16	14	18	15	20	17	15	SATHARN
21	18	18	15	20	17	15	19	16	21	18	16	DOMHNACH
22	19	19	16	21	18	16	20	17	22	19	17	LUAN
23	20	20	17	22	19	17	21	18	23	20	18	MÁIRT
24	21	21	18	23	20	18	22	19	24	21	19	CÉADAOIN
25	22	22	19	24	21	19	23	20	25	22	20	DÉARDAOIN
26	23	23	20	25	22	20	24	21	26	23	21	AOINE
27	24	24	21	26	23	21	25	22	27	24	22	SATHARN
28	25	25	22	27	24	22	26	23	28	25	23	DOMHNACH
29	26	26	23	28	25	23	27	24	29	26	24	LUAN
30	27	27	24	29	26	24	28	25	30	27	25	MÁIRT
31	28	28	25	30	27	25	29	26	31	28	26	CÉADAOIN
		29	26	31	28	26	30	27		29	27	DÉARDAOIN
		30	27		29	27	31	28		30	28	AOINE
		31	28		30	28		29			29	SATHARN
			29			29		30			30	DOMHNACH
			30			30					31	LUAN
						31						MÁIRT

ACKNOWLEDGMENTS

EDITOR
Marie Donnelly

PROJECT MANAGER
Eileen Pearson

CONCEPT
John Waters

DESIGN
Ciarán Ó Gaora, *DesignWorks*

ORIGINATION
Paul Doolan, *Keystrokes*
Lesley McColgan, *Keystrokes*

PR & MARKETING
Caroline Kennedy, *Kennedy PR*

PROOFREADERS
Michael Davitt, Kathy Gilfillan,
Angela Rohan, Jonathan Williams

EDITORIAL
Janet Banville, Marion Cody,
Barry Devlin, Robert O'Byrne,
Perry Ogden, Colm Tóibín

DATA INPUT
Rita Byrne

*Special thanks to the American Ireland Fund for
its assistance in marketing abroad, in particular
Loretta Brennan Glucksman, Kingsley Aikins,
Maura McLaughlin and Caitriona Fottrell.*

THANKS TO
An Taoiseach, Mr Bertie Ahern,
Sharon Burrell, Tricia Cahill, Al Costello,
Fiona Crawford, Síle de Valera,
Moya Doherty, Claire Fisher,
Claire Goddard, Donal Hamill,
Paul Kavanagh, Josephine Kelliher,
Paula Kelly, Jean Kennedy Smith,
Ursula Kennedy, Marion Keogh,
Emer Marron, Katherine Moore,
Tom Moran, Ann McCarthy,
Dr James McDaid, David Nea,
Jenny O'Connell, Pádraig Ó hUiginn,
Edel O'Malley, Angela Phelan,
Niamh Sheeran, Susan Towers, Ed Victor

IRELAND

THE WHOSEDAY BOOK
project has been made possible
thanks to the generous support
of AIB Group – the millennium
fundraising partner of the
Irish Hospice Foundation.